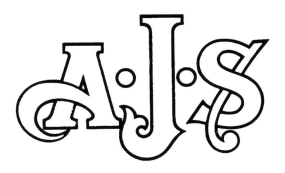

THE COMPLETE STORY

Other Titles in the Crowood MotoClassics Series

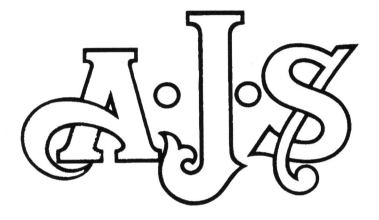

THE COMPLETE STORY

MICK WALKER

THE CROWOOD PRESS

First published in 2005 by
The Crowood Press Ltd
Ramsbury, Marlborough
Wiltshire SN8 2HR

www.crowood.com

British Library Cataloguing-in-Publication Data
A catalogue record for this book is available from the British Library.

ISBN 1 86126 766 5

Mortons Motorcycle Media are market-leading publishers of classic and
vintage titles, and own one of the largest photographic archives of its kind in
the world. It is a treasure trove of millions of motorcycle and motorcycle-related
images, many of which have not seen the light of day since they were filed away
almost 100 years ago. In particular, the collection of glass plate negatives – a
collection weighing almost two tons – is a priceless resource for anyone
interested in the heyday of the motorcycle.

Mick Walker and The Crowood Press are grateful to Mortons Motorcycle
Media for their co-operation in the production of this book and the use
of their archive photographs.

Typeset by Servis Filmsetting Ltd, Manchester

Printed and bound in Great Britain by CPI Bath

Contents

Acknowledgements

AJS (Albert John Stevens) ranks right up there in the league of great British motorcycle marques. The Stevens' brothers of Wolverhampton began to experiment with internal combustion engines at their father's engineering works for several years before, finally, offering their first AJS motorcycle for sale in 1909. Right from the start the company was involved in sport, both trials and racing, the latter in the Isle of Man and at Brooklands.

AJS won its first TT, the 1914 Junior, then after the First World War came three consecutive Junior TT victories in 1920, 1921 and 1922. Also in 1921 Howard Davies, riding a three-fifty ohv AJS, became the first and only rider in TT history to win the Blue Riband Senior event on a Junior machine.

The company introduced its first ohc models in 1927, but like many other companies AJS was badly affected by the worldwide economic depression following the American Wall Street stock market crash in late 1929. By October 1931 the Stevens' empire was on the rocks and the factory door closed. AJS was subsequently acquired by the London-based Collier brothers, owners of the Matchless brand. During the remainder of the 1930s Matchless and AJS, based in the same works in South London, became a major force, and in 1938 AMC (Associated Motor Cycles) was formed.

Following the Second World War, AJS became the first holder of the 500cc World Road Racing Championships in 1949, when Les Graham took the title on the Porcupine twin. Meanwhile AJS singles and twins were in great demand on the export market, meaning that British riders were unable to buy the latest bikes for several years after the end of the war.

The 1950s was a golden era and AJS sales soared. In addition, works-supported riders continued to gain huge success in not only road racing, but trials and scrambles too, plus the ISDT. Then came the 1960s and AMC's fall from grace: in only a few years the group (which included AJS) went from record profits to record losses and eventually went into receivership in 1966.

Dennis Poore saved the AJS name and for a period in the late 1960s and early 1970s the new breed of 2-stroke put AJS back on top, at least in 250cc motocross events. But when success declined, sales also suffered. Development engineer Fluff Brown picked up the pieces to continue limited production for the following two decades.

Many people helped in the preparation of *AJS – The Complete Story*. Just some of those who helped with either information or photographs include: Mortons Media, Pooks Motor Bookshop, George C. Schofield, Tom Mortimer, Brian 'Snowy' Cammock, Colin Dunbar, Alan Shepherd, Tony Teasdale, Peter Williams, Jackie Campbell, Colin Seeley, Richard Thirkell, Mick Hemmings, Eric Kirk, Sammy Miller, John Surtees, Bill Little and Vic Bates.

Mick Walker
October 2004

1 Wolverhampton – The Stevens Brothers

Way back at the very dawn of the combustion engine there were four Stevens brothers, Harry, George, Jack and Joe Junior, who together with their engineer/blacksmith father Joe Senior, lived and worked at Wednesfield, near Wolverhampton, in an area of the West Midlands known as the 'Black Country'.

The Stevens Screw Company

Joe Stevens Senior had built up an excellent reputation in the local area for superior workmanship in his small works, under the trading title of the Stevens Screw Company Ltd (which, incidentally, continued to trade until as late as 1992). He realized during the late 1890s that there were very many potential uses for the small internal combustion engine, including providing motive power for pumps, wood cutting and general machining purposes. However, at that time, there was no such thing as a British-made proprietary engine; instead these pioneer would-be manufacturers of the Victorian era had to make use of imported French De Dion engines and component parts if they intended building their own power plants. Then, in 1897, some American firms began to manufacture engines, and Joe Stevens Senior imported a small single-cylinder Mitchell 4-stroke unit.

It was this engine, together with the introduction of the French Werner motorcycle, that gave the Stevens family the idea of creating their own motorcycle.

A Prototype Motorcycle

Completed later in 1897, the Stevens prototype mirrored the Werner format, with the Mitchell power unit being mounted on the inside of the front down-tube of a conventional pedal cycle frame, with a small capacity fuel tank suspended from the frame's top bar-section. However, unlike the Werner which employed front-wheel drive, the Stevens device drove the rear wheel, with a leather belt passing over an intermediate pulley. And it was this prototype machine (never intended for production) which was to act as the key to the ultimate creation of the AJS brand name.

Engine Manufacturing

During the following ten years, the Stevens Screw Company built up a thriving business

An artist's view of the 1897 Mitchell-powered model; the first complete motorcycle assembled by the Stevens family.

The Stevens brothers with their very first motorcycle; the Mitchell-powered model of 1897.

building engines, not motorcycles, beginning in early 1898 with an improved variant of the Mitchell design. The engine assembly was carried out by the four sons, under the supervision of their father. Soon the Stevens engines had achieved a reputation for excellent build quality and reliability. These early Stevens power units featured automatic valves, trembler ignition and surface carburettors.

In the first years of the twentieth century, the Stevens concern supplied engines to the likes of Wearwell and Wolf. These engines were normally air-cooled single or v-twin units. However, in 1905, Stevens also built a water-cooled parallel twin. Many of the Stevens-made engines were used in cycle-cars rather than motorcycles.

AJS is Born

The eldest son Jack was the visionary who pushed the Stevens into motorcycle sport – as a means of both development and publicity. And in the true pioneer fashion of the period he and his brothers began riding in trials and speed events on their various creations. In 1909 a Stevens-powered Wolf (built by the Wearwell Cycle Company Ltd) was awarded

an ACU certificate for an observed 24-hour non-stop run – quite a feat in those far off days.

This success prompted the Stevens into taking the final step, manufacturing and marketing complete motorcycles. The name 'AJS' was chosen, as they were not happy with the use of the Stevens brand name because it was already associated with the manufacture of proprietary engines for other marques. The initials were chosen because the eldest brother, Albert John (known as Jack), was the only one of the four brothers who had a middle initial.

Production Takes Off in 1911

1911 was an important year in the evolution of the fledgling concern, as not only did AJS contest the Isle of Man TT for the first time, but production took off.

The TT and standard production models were all powered by a particularly neat little side-valve single-cylinder engine. The rear wheel was driven either directly by a belt or with an optional two-stage chain drive punctuated by a 2-speed countershaft gearbox. This latter transmission was proof of the forward-looking approach adopted by the Stevens family in the engineering principles, for at that time multi-speed gearboxes were a rarity. And it was only that year that the daunting Mountain circuit had been adopted for the Isle of Man TT races.

Engine Design

The engine was 298cc (70 × 77.5mm), which was slightly larger in size than the Stevens proprietary unit (292cc – 70 × 76mm). These engine sizes may seem somewhat strange today, however at the time they corresponded to 2½ horsepower of the old rating system then in use.

In the horsepower rating chart, a 500cc displacement was classed as a 3½hp (Stevens had supplied a 3¼, as well as a 2½, to the Wearwall company). The 350cc was 2¾hp, which would eventually become established as the classic AJS size, whilst a 250cc engine was reckoned to be 2¼hp.

The French Influence

However, in France, where AJS was soon to become popular, there was a class for racing motorcycles with the engine displacing ⅓ltr, which did not correspond to anything on the other side of the English Channel, or anywhere else for that matter. French influence upon the Stevens family in Wolverhampton was quite considerable, as shown by an incident in 1912. French riders had been modifying the top frame tubes of their 333cc racing models, sloping them downwards in alignment with the seat stays to the rear hub (to permit a lower seat height) and also at the same time reducing the frontal area. This was to not only become a feature of production AJS models but also a fashion within the motorcycle industry as a whole, both within Great Britain and continental Europe.

Early TT Results

The 1911 TT debut ended with privateer J.D. Corke in fifteenth position and Jack Stevens sixteenth. However, the results don't provide the full story, as Jack had suffered a tumble which saw him delayed having to straighten bent forks, otherwise he would have been in the first half-dozen.

The following year, 1912, the Stevens' were too busy to take an official interest in the TT, but engineering development had seen the old belt-drive system replaced entirely by a more modern and efficient all-chain drive.

The company was back for the 1913 Junior TT, with W.M. Heaton finishing tenth and Cyril Williams being forced to retire.

Bigger and Better for the 1914 TT

With the 1914 TT came an increase in engine limit to 350cc for the Junior event. For this,

The Model D, a side-valve 50 degree v-twin arrived for the 1913 season, rated at 6bhp, it displaced 698cc (74 × 81mm). The 3-speed countershaft gearbox, and single Amac carb and UH magneto were other features.

AJS built a new 349cc engine with 2-speed P&M primary drive, and an additional 2-speed countershaft gearbox, giving four speeds in total. For its time, this was a brilliant bike, and no attention to detail had been spared. For example, in a quest for the ultimate reliability, the cylinder and finning had been machined from a solid billet, whilst the piston too was machined from solid. Compared to the 1911 298cc TT engine which was safe up to 2,500rpm, the 1914 349cc unit could reach what was at that time an incredible 4,000rpm mark.

All this hard work paid off handsomely, as the race proved an AJS benefit. Eric Williams won from Cyril Williams (no relation), whilst the Wolverhampton factory's machinery also took third, fourth and sixth. No less than five of the first six finishers!

The Model D v-twin had both its primary and final drive chain totally enclosed, giving a degree of sophistication not normally found in the early days of motorcycling.

Sales Increase

The 1914 TT blitz resulted in a staggering increase in demand for AJS models. Almost overnight, sales rocketed to such a degree that the old premises could no longer cope and so a move was made to much larger facilities at Graisely House, Penn Road, Wolverhampton. At the same time the company's name was changed to AJ Stevens (1914) Ltd.

As far as production was concerned, by far the most popular machine was the 2¾hp (350cc) single. However, a 6hp (700cc) twin-cylinder bike was also becoming popular, thanks to its use as a sidecar tug. In racing, Cyril Williams dominated the 1914 Brooklands Junior event, on the sole AJS entered at the Surrey speed bowl.

The First World War Intervenes

Then came the outbreak of the First World War. However, it was not until November 1916 that the British government, via its Ministry of Munitions, brought to an end the production of civilian vehicles, including motorcycles. But in any case the Stevens empire was virtually transferred into war production right from the autumn of 1914 through to the armistice in November 1918.

Peace Returns

After the conflict, AJS returned to its peacetime profession of motorcycle design and manufacture, and for 1920, the company returned to the TT.

For its Isle of Man return AJS introduced a new engine of advanced specification.

An early AJS 4-stroke single; probably a 2¾hp Model B, which debuted in 1913 and ran through into the mid-1920s. Seen here at a vintage rally in the 1950s.

Although it shared the 1914 dimensions of 74 × 81mm, the 349cc single had its side valves replaced with a very much improved hemispherical combustion chamber with overhead valves. The transmission was still the pre-war 2-speed 'box combined with 2-speed primary drive, and it was this combination of transmission components that proved to be the bike's weak link. In essence the additional horsepower of the ohv engine was simply too much for the mainshaft. In addition the new engine suffered leakages between the head and cylinder barrel joints.

Of seven AJSs entered for the Junior race only two survived, the others succumbing to mechanical problems or accidents. One of the surviving two examples eventually won the race, but even this was destined to suffer engine failure 4 miles (6.5km) from the finish,

so that its rider, Cyril Williams, had to coast, and push his way home.

Regaining Reliability

During the next 12 months, the Stevens got to work and eliminated the weaknesses which had affected the 1920 TT mounts. So for the 1921 race they were back to their AJS-type reliability. The fragile transmission system was replaced by a newly devised 3-speed gearbox and chain drive, the cylinder joint improved and the valve angle decreased. In addition the frame and many of the cycle parts were uprated.

The result was that AJS monopolized the 1921 Junior TT, with Eric Williams winning and AJS also taking second, third and fourth places. But an even bigger success was achieved during that same 1921 TT, when AJS rider Howard Davies gave AJS its first double TT victory, and in the process became the first – and only man in history – to win the Senior TT on a 350cc machine.

The 'Big Port' Arrives

The next year, 1922, witnessed the arrival of the famous 'Big Port' model, which benefited from improvements such as drum brakes (earlier AJSs featured the inferior stirrup type) and once more the Wolverhampton marque took home the Junior TT trophy. This was to be the last TT victory for several years, even though on many occasions AJS riders were to be on the rostrum. Even so Jimmy Simpson became the first to lap the TT at 60mph (97km/h) in 1924 and 70mph (113km/h) in 1926, the latter on a new 500cc ohv AJS.

Meanwhile the company's racing glory had rubbed off on its series production roadsters, with unparalleled demand for its range, which by now included both sv and ohv singles, plus the then traditional v-twin for sidecar duties. Usually finished in black with gold striping, these machines, even today, are held up as some of the very finest bikes from the vintage period, even being placed above their Wolverhampton rivals Sunbeam – no mean feat!

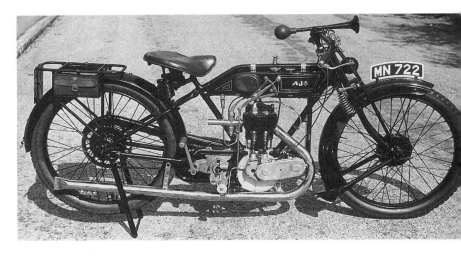

A 1922 Model B, with Isle of Man registration.

Close up of early 1920 Wolverhampton AJS 2¾bhp single showing details including hand-lever for gearchange, forward-mounted magneto, sprung forks, 'John Bull' rubber tankside kneegrip.

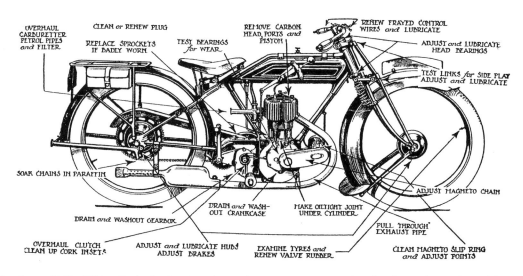

OVERHAUL CARBURETTER PETROL PIPES *and* FILTER

CLEAN *or* RENEW PLUG

REPLACE SPROCKETS IF BADLY WORN

TEST BEARINGS *for* WEAR

REMOVE CARBON HEAD PORTS *and* PISTON

RENEW FRAYED CONTROL WIRES *and* LUBRICATE

ADJUST *and* LUBRICATE HEAD BEARINGS

TEST LINKS *for* SIDE PLAY ADJUST *and* LUBRICATE

SOAK CHAINS IN PARAFFIN

ADJUST MAGNETO CHAIN

DRAIN *and* WASH-OUT CRANKCASE

MAKE OILTIGHT JOINT UNDER CYLINDER

DRAIN *and* WASHOUT GEARBOX

PULL THROUGH EXHAUST PIPE

OVERHAUL CLUTCH CLEAN UP CORK INSETS

ADJUST *and* LUBRICATE HUBS ADJUST BRAKES

EXAMINE TYRES *and* RENEW VALVE RUBBER

CLEAN MAGNETO SLIP RING *and* ADJUST POINTS

Drawing from a 1920s AJS handbook, showing the various maintenance requirements of a side-valve single-cylinder model.

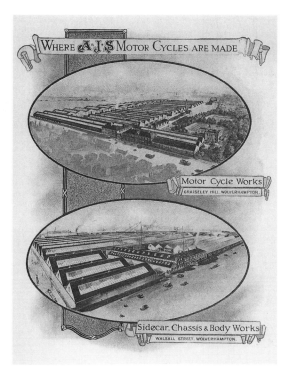

The two AJS production facilities in Wolverhampton, circa 1925. Top: Motorcycle works in Graiseley Hill. Bottom: The sidecar and bodyworks in Walsall Street.

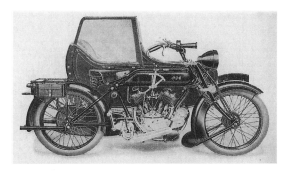

A 1926 7.99hp (799cc) De Luxe Passenger Combination, Model G1. Sidecar outfits were an important section of AJS' sales in the mid-1920s.

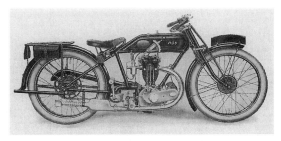

1926 ohv G6 sports single could reach 70mph (113km/h); price £53 – electric lighting an additional £18 10s.

Big Port

Without doubt the most famous of all Wolverhampton-built motorcycles was the 'Big Port'.

The first AJS overhead valve engine was designed by Harry Stevens in 1918, but it was to be a further five years before the company was to offer an ohv for sale. This went on sale for the 1923 season as the 2¾hp Three Speed Overhead Valve TT Model. As outlined in the main text, this coincided with the marque's huge successes during the early 1920s in racing, particularly the Isle of Man TT.

The 'Big Port' name was coined by Joe Stevens Junior, who had been in charge of the racing team at that time. He had used the term to describe the oversize dimensions of the exhaust valve and header pipe as fitted to the 1922 AJS works racing bikes. This nickname stuck and became associated with the roadster versions which followed.

For the 1924 season, the B3 was a 349cc (74 × 81mm) ohv single, with iron head and barrel, coil

valve springs, exposed valve gear, nickel-chrome forged connecting rod (with twin uncaged roller big-end bearings), semi-automatic hand pump lubrication system, chain primary drive, multiple-plate clutch, Amac 2 lever carburettor and 3-speed foot-change gearbox. For fast road or racing use purchasers could specify the limited production B4. This latter model was a super sports mount with a higher compression ratio, but no kickstarter.

A changeover by AJS to a prefix letter code system for the 1925 model year saw the 'Big Port' machines listed as the E6 and E7 (the latter, replacing the B4, being known as the 'Special Sports'). Technically, there was alteration to the cylinder finning on the cylinder barrel and a redesigned cylinder head, featuring a reduced exhaust port size – whilst the inlet port size was increased. The inlet port was also repositioned opposite the exhaust, thus giving a more 'straight through' passage for the fuel and air mixture

Big Port *continued*

A Big Port overhead-valve single, circa *mid-1920s. This photograph was taken by the author at the VMCC Founders Day; Stanford Hall, July 2003.*

gasses both inward and outward. A Binks 2-jet carburettor replaced the earlier Amac 2-lever device. Lubrication was improved by a positive feed to the big-end. At additional cost, there was also the option of mechanical lubrication by way of an AJS Pilgrim pump, this being mounted on the magneto drive cover and driven by the exhaust cam. The more sporting E7 could be ordered to the customer's own requirements, being largely intended for competition use. The specification could also include a straight-through pipe, rather than a silencer as on the E6 model.

For the 1926 season there were in fact no less than three 'Big Port' ohv singles from which prospective customers could choose. There was a standard roadster, the G6; a Sports Special, the G7; and a pure racing model, the GR7. The main difference between the standard road-going G6 and the other two more sporting bikes, was its use of ball and roller bearings for mainshafts and timing gears on the 'hot' models, whereas the stock G6 made do with plain bushes. Another feature of the 1926 model year was that the exhaust port now featured an external stub to secure the exhaust header pipe.

Purchasers of the GR7, designed expressly for high-speed competition work, received two pistons. The

piston for long-distance events (fitted to the machine) had a less pronounced dome; the other was more suited to short-distance speed events (such as sprints and hill climbs) and was intended for alcohol fuels.

It was back to two 'Big Ports' for 1927, the H6 roadster and a racing machine coded H7. Again the engine received work to the cylinder head – which seemed have become an annual ritual for the Wolverhampton works. There were changes to both inlet and exhaust ports, and the exhaust was redesigned, notably the silencer. There were also changes to the bottom half of the engine. Not only was the crankshaft now supported by roller bearings, but the timing case was enlarged for the valve lifter mechanism, with only an external operating arm showing. Lubrication-wise, a Pilgrim sight feed mechanical oil pump was now standard equipment. The gearbox had also been uprated and the frame modified, with the headstock being enlarged.

Mechanically, the H7 racer differed from its roadster brother in much the same way as with the previous years GR7 version, with features such as a specially tuned cylinder head, higher compression ratio, ball-race bearings for the timing gear shafts (whereas the stock model had bushes and no provision for a kickstarter). There were also options as regards components such as handlebars, exhausts and fuel/oil tanks.

The 1928 'Big Port' models were coded K6 and KR6. Even though the new camshaft model had debuted at the 1927 TT, their early teething troubles (which were eventually found to be caused by poor lubrication) meant that for the 1928 season the sports/racing KR6 was offered as a replica of the latest ohv works racer. The 'K' series also saw considerable development expended on them, particularly to the top half of the engine. The main change involved the cylinder head and barrel which were no longer retained by the strap arrangement of earlier years; instead there was now a four stud fixing to attach the barrel to the crankcase, whilst four bolts held the barrel to the head.

In addition, the earlier roller bearing bottom end

was exchanged for a new layout which reverted to plain phosphor bronze bushes housed in a wider crankcase assembly. There were also wider camshaft lobes and two-piece, oil-tight tappets. The frame was also modified to accommodate the new crankcase and gearbox castings.

Although the 'Big Port' moniker was used, as author S.J. Mills states in his excellent book *AJS of Wolverhampton* (S.J. Mills, 1994), to describe loosely all later 350cc overhead valve models produced by the factory (Wolverhampton bikes), 1928 marked what most dyed-in-the-wool AJS enthusiasts would consider to be the last year of the real 'Big Port' models.

It was also the final year of the flat tank styling; during the summer of 1928 the AJS design team took the view that the 'Big Port', as S.J. Mills says, 'had begun to look old fashioned'.

The Camshaft Models Make Their Debut

In 1927 the first camshaft models appeared – and these took a form which was to be retained throughout their long life, which finally ended thirty-five years later when the famous 7R ceased production in the early 1960s. The camshaft lay across the centre of the cylinder head and was driven by a chain with a Weller-type tensioner, the latter being virtually a clock-spring pulled out straight whose natural curvature took up any slack in the drive and at the same time coped with the expansion which took place as the engine got up to working temperature.

The first ohc engines were built for racing in three-fifty (349cc – 74×81mm) and five hundred (498cc – 84×90mm) sizes, but although of advanced design and successful in events both in Britain and continental Europe, TT glory did not come their way. That is, until in 1930 a smaller 250cc version was specially prepared and ridden by the legendary Scot, Jimmy Guthrie, later to win immortality with Joe Craig's Norton team, to victory in the Lightweight TT.

Commercial Expansion

On the commercial front AJS had been expanding at a frantic rate. In 1927, it had begun manufacturing commercial vehicles, then around the same time they entered the radio business and finally, in 1930, the company embarked on a venture to produce a small car. The overhead camshaft engine entered series production for the 1928 season as the K7 and K10, with their engines sharing the same bore and stroke dimensions as the 1927 TT machines. The 1928 AJS range comprised, in total, no less than twelve models, all prefixed K. (The 1927 series was prefixed H, 1926 was given the prefix G and 1925 was given the prefix E.) The K series also included the K1 and K2 (both sidecar combinations powered by a side-valve 749cc (74×93mm) v-twin engine), plus a range of singles of 248, 349 and 498cc with either side-valve overhead valve or overhead camshaft. All of these featured 3-speed gearboxes.

Towards the end of 1928 the 1929 models were announced, coded 'M'. Again sv, ohv and ohc versions were available. 1930 models were coded 'S' and 'R', whilst in 1931 the coding was 'S', 'SA' or 'SB'.

The 1929 AJS works racing team. Left to right: Leo Davenport, Frank Longman, Tommy Spann, Ronnie Parkinson and George Rowley. Wal Handley was also a member, but is not in the picture.

1928 AJS Model K10, a 498cc (84 × 90mm) overhead camshaft single super sports machine.

When you've finished work — get right away from it.

IN other words take to the open road on an A.J.S. Then you can travel far and yet enjoy true relaxation, for riding fatigue and mechanical trouble are conspicuous by their absence in this world-famous machine. *If you haven't a copy of the A.J.S. catalogue — write for one now.*

A·J·S
Motor Cycles.

A. J. STEVENS & CO. (1914) LTD.,
WOLVERHAMPTON

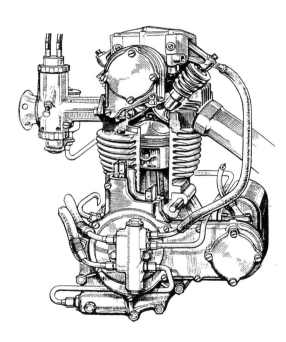

The 1930 AJS cammy engine, with forward-mounted magneto and coil valve springs.

A 1930 AJS advertisement, showing one of the newly released inclined engine models with fishtail exhaust and saddle tank.

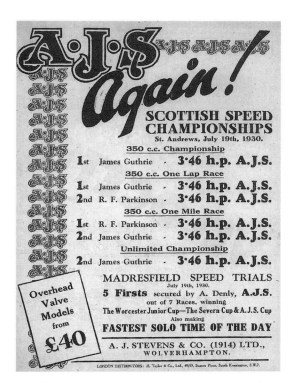

An AJS advertisement proclaiming the marques successes in the Scottish Speed Championships at St Andrews on 19 July 1930. 'James Guthrie' is the legendary rider who was a super-star for Norton until his death in the German GP at Sachsenring in July 1937.

Another AJS period advertisement; this time with a letter from George Himing who ride an R7 three-fifty ohc single in the 1930 Junior TT.

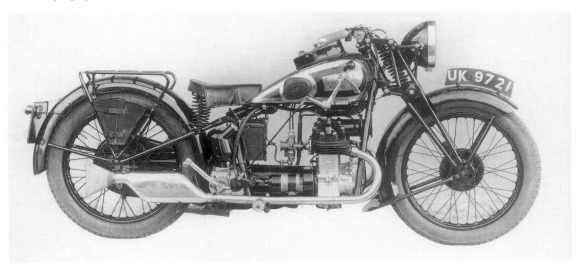

The last throw of the dice for the Wolverhampton AJS brand was the sensational S3, a 498cc (65 × 75mm) transverse twin, first details of which were released in April 1931.

The S3 was a side-valve V-twin with its cylinders disposed at 50 degrees and a single Amal carburettor fed both cylinders; detachable aluminium cylinder heads were another feature of the design.

Financial Problems Followed by Takeover

Unfortunately for AJS the Great Depression, fired by the Wall Street stock market crash of October 1929, lay ahead. In Great Britain the slump really arrived in 1931 and with it came the end of an era – and the end of AJ Stevens Ltd, if not AJS itself, in October 1931.

Although AJS went into liquidation none of its creditors lost out as, gentlemen that they were, the Stevens family paid up in full. But this left the family in dire straits and even though they did eventually manage to set up in business, the AJS motorcycle division was not to be part of this restart.

One of the companies that attempted to take over the remains of AJS and its name was BSA, but in the end AJS went to the Matchless company, which was controlled by the Collier brothers. They moved AJS production lock, stock and barrel to their Plumstead works in London, south of the Thames. The full details of this marque can be found in *Matchless: The Complete Story* (The Crowood Press, 2004).

The Aftermath

Although the Stevens brothers lost much of their personal wealth following the collapse of

The AJS Car Project

Besides motorcycles, the Stevens brothers also produced radio sets (from 1924) and a range of commercial buses (from 1929), whilst in 1930 a 9hp light car made its debut. But in fact during summer 1927 AJS had secured a contract to manufacture car bodies for one of their neighbours, the Clyno Engineering Co, via their subsidiary company, Hayward Motor Bodies.

The Clyno car, the Nine, designed by Arthur G. Booth, was introduced in September 1927 and followed Clyno convention by having a liquid-cooled side-valve 4-cylinder engine, 3-speed gearbox and single Cox-Atmos carburettor. But unlike previous Clyno cars, the Nine was equipped with a modern, single-plate clutch, rather than the earlier cone-type. Unfortunately, instead of aiming to produce a high quality vehicle, Clyno chose to compete with the likes of Austin, Morris and Ford. This meant not only a cheap price, but cost-cutting which led to poor quality. The result was inevitable and in February 1929 a receiver was appointed and the company wound up. Unfortunately this had a bad effect on AJS, as it lost money from non-payment on the Clyno account, just as it was launching its first commercial vehicles.

So, in an attempt to recoup some of the money it had lost on the Clyno exercise, AJS decided to build its own light car. The design was placed in the hands of none other than A.G. Booth who had created the Clyno Nine. The result was the AJS Nine, although it must be stressed the two cars had little in common apart from basics such as a 4-cylinder inline engine and 3-speed gearbox.

The AJS car was powered by a bought-in Coventry Climax side-valve engine displacing 1,018cc (60 × 90mm). Actually, the AJS four-wheeler was an advanced design in several ways, including a full-pressure lubrication system, featuring a gear-pump; a cast-iron detachable cylinder head; 12-volt Lucas coil ignition and a power output of 25bhp at 3,000rpm. Expanding shoe drum brakes were on each of the four wheels.

First announced in late 1929, and introduced after a thorough test programme in August 1930, the AJS Nine was offered in three versions: open two-seater at £210; fabric saloon £230; or coach-built saloon £240.

Its high quality, hide-leather seats, light accurate steering and an engine so flexible that it was possible to run down to a mere 5mph (8km/h) in top gear, made the AJS Nine popular with the press and public alike. Only the high purchase prices stunted sales. As marque specialist S.J. Mills says in *AJS of Wolverhampton* (S.J. Mills, 1994):

> Compared to many other rival makes in the class, the AJS was simply too expensive. As a result in February 1932, the Company reduced prices by £11 0s 0d on all models and introduced a new four door, utility, fabric bodied saloon, christened the 'Richmond' at £197 0s 0d.

In a bid to slash production costs and use up spare capacity, AJS decided to build its own engine. But Coventry Climax was none too pleased; particularly when it discovered the AJS unit was as S.J. Mills says, 'a carbon copy of the Coventry Climax, with nothing to distinguish between them.'

However, as is revealed elsewhere, AJS was in trouble, and in October 1931, the firm was in voluntary liquidation, due to losses in both the motorcycle and commercial vehicle divisions. Still, when one considers that in the height of the worst economic depression in history, and the very high purchase price, that some 3,000 cars were sold in eighteen months, it was quite some achievement.

After the financial collapse of AJS, although the buses were dropped entirely, manufacture of the car was taken over by Willys-Overland-Crossley Ltd of Southport, Lancashire. This latter organization built another 300 units, all coach-built saloons. They also tried launching a larger 1.5ltr car, but this got no further than the 1932 Olympia Show and Willys-Overland-Crossley went into liquidation itself some twelve months later.

AJS, they were still able to retain the ownership of the Regent Street works, which had been used by their father as an extra working facility for the surviving Stevens Screw Co. Eventually, in May 1932 they were able to form a new company, Stevens Brothers (Wolverhampton) Ltd.

At first this produced (with hand-picked staff) a three-wheel light commercial van, powered by a single cylinder water-cooled 588cc side-valve engine. Then in March 1934 they re-entered the motorcycle field with a new 249cc ohv single which, like the three-wheeler, was marketed under the Stevens brand name. For 1935 the 349cc model was added, which was joined in April 1935 by a 495cc (79 × 101mm) fitted with a 4-speed hand-change Burman gearbox. During a period of just over four years, some 1,000 bikes were built. But even though the new machines were of excellent quality they were never big sellers; so with war looming the Stevens brothers ended motorcycle production in the summer of 1938 and returned to general engineering. After undertaking defence contracts during the conflict, Stevens returned to civilian work post-war. Jack Stevens (whose initials AJS had used) died in 1956.

For the AJS marque, there was to be a new and exciting future, although unfortunately this was not to include the Stevens family, and a new home in South London, at Plumstead.

2   Moving to Plumstead

As already mentioned in Chapter 1, after the Wolverhampton-based Stevens-controlled AJS marque went into liquidation during October 1931, there were several companies interested in acquiring the AJS brand name. But it was the Collier brothers with their Matchless works in Plumstead, south-east London, who were finally successful in purchasing not only the name, but also the designs and tooling of the stricken marque, from the liquidators.

The Marriage

And so AJS were 'married', its new partner being one of the oldest names in the industry, Matchless, a winner of three TTs before AJS had even travelled to the Isle of Man.

The founder of the London-based firm, Henry Collier, had originally registered the Matchless trademark in 1891 for use on a new pedal cycle design he intended to market with a partner, John Watson. But this partnership lasted only a few months and Watson left to concentrate on his original laundry business. The cycle business, with Collier now as its sole owner, manufactured pedal cycles in reasonable numbers, and also carried out general engineering work, including subcontract work to the Royal Arsenal. By 1898 the company was not only profitable but had expanded considerably.

The First Matchless Motorcycle

In 1899 Henry Collier and his sons, Harry and Charlie, entered the motorcycle world,

constructing their own engine and mounting this over the front wheel of one of the Matchless pedal cycles. But, as with other pioneer efforts, including the French Werner concern, it was soon realized that this was not an ideal location. They then set out, via a series of experiments, to find a better location for the engine, which proved to be the centre, bottom of the frame.

Charlie Collier was already an established cycle racer, having taken part in events staged on banked circuits, so when motorcycle racing began to be held at these same venues it was perhaps natural that he should take part too. The Colliers constructed their first production model in 1902 and the Matchless name was established as a motorcycle brand name. In 1907, Charlie Collier put himself and Matchless in the history books by winning the first ever Isle of Man TT (Single Cylinder class). Both Charlie and brother Harry were victorious (Harry in 1909; Charlie in 1910). The brothers also won many other races and set several world speed records in the years leading up to the First World War.

Into the 1920s, Matchless and AJS became great rivals – at least as regards sales of production road-going machines. However, Matchless did not continue its racing programme, leaving this to the likes of Norton, Sunbeam and AJS.

Thus, by the time the Colliers took over AJS, Matchless was firmly established as not only a top brand name, but one which was making profits on a yearly basis. Besides its range of single cylinder and v-twin models, it had just introduced the Silver Hawk. Powered by a 600cc narrow-angle V4 engine with overhead camshafts, this was the talk of the industry.

The 1931 AJS Range

In the months leading up to the Matchless takeover, the AJS range comprised not only their traditional sv and ohv singles (now with some models featuring sloping cylinders and twin-port heads), but the sporting and racing ohc singles and the latest version of their 996cc side-valve v-twin — and most sensationally a totally new transverse twin. This featured a 498cc (55 × 75mm) side-valve engine with the cylinders at 50 degrees (mounted akin to a modern Moto Guzzi). The detachable cylinder heads were of light alloy, each being secured to the crankcase by seven bolts. The valves were operated via separate camshafts, placed inside the Vee, inclined towards the centre axis. Both exhaust ports faced forward. There was a short driveshaft, featuring Hardy-Spicer flexible couplings, taking the power to the 3-speed gearbox and thereafter by chain (fully-enclosed) to the rear wheel. The engine of the AJS transverse twin was mounted in a particularly neat frame, with duplex tubes for both the front and rear sections, but a single top tube.

The machine was coded S3, and included a single Amal carburettor to feed both cylinders. No cam followers were employed, instead the tappets had wide curved bases which operated directly onto the cams. The rear of the nearside (left) camshaft was used to drive a coil ignition distributor. It also had three-ring domed aluminium pistons, single-row caged roller big-ends, and ball-race main bearings. Lubrication was by an adjustable, double-acting Pilgrim pump.

Complete with electric lighting, tank-mounted instruments and chrome-plated fuel tank, the S3 was priced at £65 0s 0d in April 1931.

Together with the S3 described above, the 1931 AJS range which the Colliers inherited comprised no less than sixteen models ranging from the ohv 248cc S12 and SA12 singles to the S2 with a 996cc side-valve v-twin engine.

Production Resumes

After a brief period of production, the transverse twin and ohc models continued to be offered by the new owners. However, these machines were soon axed from the AJS (Plumstead) lists. The new owners also chose not to exhibit AJS at the London Olympia Show in late 1937. Quite simply it would not have been practical as not only was there all the stock of machines, spares and tooling to be moved south, but obviously with new management and personnel the situation was somewhat fluid and the first priority was to get the newly acquired brand rehoused in the new home.

Testing the Product

In its 12 May 1932 issue, *The Motor Cycle* was able to test one of the first machines to emanate from the new home of AJS at Plumstead (1932 models were coded T). This bike was the 498cc (84 × 90mm) Model TB8 'Big Port' ohv single, with single exhaust port, Lucas magdyno, sloping cylinder, dry sump lubrication, Amal carburettor and 3-speed hand-change gearbox. It cost £47, plus an additional £5 10s with the Lucas magdyno lighting.

An AJS advert of the period described the TB8 in the following manner:

The AJS Big Port 500 provides a genuine speed capability of 80mph plus stupendous acceleration and amazing flexibility. Outstanding features include Inclined engine . . . Semi-cradle Frame with Duplex Chain Stays . . . patent Quick-detachable Rear Wheel . . . Hinged Mudguard . . . 26″ × 3.25″ tyres . . . Steering Damper . . . and Oil Bath to Front

Chain Case. There is no motorcycle more reliable or consistently capable of high speed performance . . . it is the one machine that predominates in Trial and Test.

1933 Models

In July 1932 AJS launched a revised version of their big sv v-twin – the first of the 1933 models to be released by any British manufacturer! The machine still featured a 50-degree Vee configuration, but the old 84 × 90mm 998cc dimensions and engine displacement had been revised to 85.5 × 85.5mm – 982cc.

It was to be marketed in two guises: either Standard with footrests, semi-sports handlebars, right-hand gearchange and hand clutch, or Export with footboards, long touring handlebars, left-hand gearchange and a foot-operated clutch. Other details included a 7-stud fixing for the detachable cylinder heads, the barrels had a 3-stud fixing, the third of these being hidden inside the valve-spring chest. The valves were completely enclosed, as was the primary drive, which ran a simplex chain in an oil bath casing.

The price of either model, coded '2', was £65; a Lucas electric lighting set adding an additional £5 17s 6d to the price. Amongst the other options were an electric horn (15s), a gearbox-driven speedometer (£2) and eight-day clock for the tank-mounted instrument panel (£1 10s).

The Return of Camshaft Models

But undoubtedly the highlights of the 1933 AJS programme, when the remainder of the range was announced in October 1932, were new 350 and 500cc overhead camshaft 'Trophy' singles, the 33/7 350 or 33/10 500. The Trophy tag was in recognition of George Rowley's performance in the ISDT and Brooklands (*see* Chapter 3).

K.R. Bott with one of the recently re-introduced overhead-cam singles – thanks to George Rowley's unauthorized ISDT success on such a model in 1932.

The full 1933 AJS range was as follows:

33/12	248cc ohv	'Big Port'	4-speed	£41 10s
33/5	350cc sv		3-speed	£40 0s
33/B6	350cc ohv	'Big Port'	4-speed	£42 5s
33/B8	500cc ohv	'Big Port' de luxe	4-speed	£55 0s
33/9	500cc sv		3-speed	£49 10s
33/7	350cc ohc	Trophy		£65 0s
33/10	500cc ohc	Trophy		£70 0s
33/2	982cc sv	v-twin (Standard or Export)		£65 0s
T/5	350cc sv	(30s tax)		£39 10s
TB/6	350cc ohv	'Big Port' (30s tax)		£41 0s

There were also three sidecars; models A, B and C.

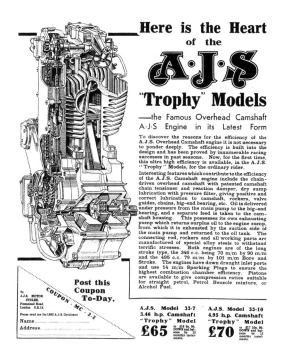

Here is the Heart
of the
A·J·S
"Trophy" Models
—the Famous Overhead Camshaft
A·J·S Engine in its Latest Form

To discover the reasons for the efficiency of the A.J.S. Overhead Camshaft engine it is not necessary to ponder deeply. The efficiency is built into the design and has been proved by innumerable racing successes in past seasons. Now, for the first time, this ultra high efficiency is available, in the A.J.S. "Trophy" Models, for the ordinary rider.

Interesting features which contribute to the efficiency of the A.J.S. Camshaft engine include the chain-driven overhead camshaft with patented camshaft chain tensioner and reaction damper, dry sump lubrication with pressure filter, giving positive and correct lubrication to camshaft, rockers, valve guides, chains, big-end bearing, etc. Oil is delivered under pressure from the main pump to the big-end bearing, and a separate feed is taken to the camshaft housing. This possesses its own exhausting pump which returns surplus oil to the engine sump, from which it is exhausted by the suction side of the main pump and returned to the oil tank. The connecting rod, rockers and all working parts are manufactured of special alloy steels to withstand terrific stresses. Both engines are of the long stroke type, the 346 c.c. being 70 m/m by 90 m/m and the 495 c.c. 79 m/m by 101 m/m Bore and Stroke. The engines have down draught inlet ports and use 14 m/m Sparking Plugs to ensure the highest combustion chamber efficiency. Pistons are available to give compression ratios suitable for straight petrol, Petrol Benzole mixture, or Alcohol Fuel.

Post this Coupon To-Day.

COUPON MC 2.2

To
A.J.S. MOTOR
CYCLES,
Plumstead Road,
London S.E.18

Please send me the 1933 A.J.S. Catalogue

Name ....
Address ....

A.J.S. Model 33-7	A.J.S. Model 33-10
3.46 h.p. Camshaft "Trophy" Model	4.95 h.p. Camshaft "Trophy" Model
£65 or £18 5s. 0d. DOWN and balance by 12 monthly installments.	**£70** or £17 10s. 0d. DOWN and balance by 12 monthly installments.

A 1933 AJS advert for the Plumstead-built overhead cam Trophy models, built in 346 and 495cc guises.

Three New Models

From then until three new models were announced at the end of September 1934, there was little change to the AJS model line-up of 246, 347 and 498cc. These 'new' bikes were the first AJS models to have a close affinity to their Matchless brothers, and were all ohv singles with vertical cylinders.

The first machine, the Model 35/12, used a 246cc (62.5 × 80mm) engine mounted in a duplex cradle frame with a single front down-tube. Dry sump lubrication was employed, and the price including dynamo lighting, coil ignition and horn, was £39 18s.

The second newcomer was the 347cc (69 × 93mm) Model 35/16, which was of a similar design to the two-fifty and replaced the B6 Big Port; price including coil ignition and lighting was £42.

Again with a vertical cylinder, but this time a side-valve of 498cc (84 × 90mm), the third machine was the 35/4. With dynamo lighting and coil ignition, the price was £49 10s. An unusual feature of the new five-hundred side-valve single was its use of a down-draught carburettor.

Together with the three newcomers, there were twelve models in the 1935 programme, including the two ohc singles (mainly intended for competition work or racing) and the 982cc side-valve v-twin. The latter was mainly intended for sidecar duties, and for 1935 AJS offered five sidecars with prices ranging from £17 15s to £25.

Sports and Touring

When the 1936 AJS programme was announced, *The Motor Cycle* (12 September 1935 issue) said 'Steady improvement seems to be the motto of the AJS design department. There are no revolutionary changes in the

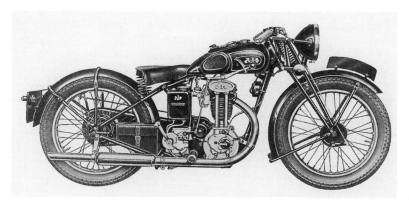

The 1935 Model 12, a 246cc (62.5 × 80mm) single port ohv machine, with a 4-speed gearbox. Hand-change was standard, but foot-change could be ordered for an additional twelve shillings and six pence.

A side-valve workhorse for either solo or sidecar use, the 35/9 498cc (84 × 90mm) single port, De Luxe model.

programme for 1936, but a number of modifications.'

However, a few weeks later at the end of November 1935 came a major shock, with the launch of a breathtaking 495cc (50 × 63mm) overhead camshaft V4! This appeared a little more than a few hours before the opening of that year's London Olympia Show. Known as the Model 20, it created a huge amount of interest, but although listed it was never put into series production. However, from the concept came racing versions which are described in Chapter 3.

So it was the singles and the big v-twin to which potential customers turned their attention. The three-fifty and five-hundred ohv models now all featured vertically set engines and were offered in both single and twin port guises. Larger and deeper fuel tanks held 3gal (13.6ltr) of petrol. The two-fifty had improved brakes. All models now came with a 4-speed (hand-change) Burman gearbox. There were no fewer than three side-valve 498cc singles.

Totally Enclosed Valve Gear

Several important alterations had been carried out for the 1937 AJS range when it was

announced at the end of September 1936. One model with a 498cc ohv single port engine had been totally redesigned. Many of the alterations were common to all models. The valve gear on both ohv and sv engines was now totally enclosed and positively lubricated. On the overhead-valve models extensions of the rocker box casting enclosed the rockers and valve springs. These extensions were divided in the centre and the detachable portions were held to the main casting by two set screws.

On the pushrod side of the rocker box was a large detachable plate, which was neatly ribbed in the case of the 250cc and 350cc engines. Removal of this plate exposed the tappet adjustment, and the tappet chest was large enough to allow plenty of room for maintenance work.

The redesigned ohv five-hundred model had a single port engine with the new valve-gear enclosure. Some machines had coil ignition, but the more sporting (and expensive machines) featured Lucas magdyno.

Silver Streak

For the 1938 season a super-sport version of each ohv single was introduced in each engine

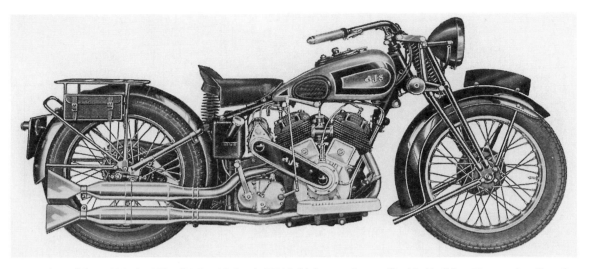

During the mid/late 1930s the 982cc (85.5 × 85.5mm) AJS Model 2 sv v-twin was offered in English or Export guises. One of the latter is shown here and it differs from the English version by way of footboards and American-style handlebars.

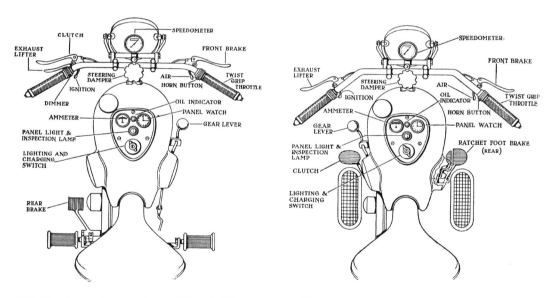

The 1935 side-valve v-twin control layout: UK to the left, export to the right.

size (250, 350 and 500cc). These were fitted with specially tuned engines and given an exciting finish – with lots of bright chrome plate – mudguards, chaincase, chainguard, oil tank, toolbox, wheel rims and headlamp. The fuel tanks were also plated with black panels

and blue and silver lining. The Silver Streak was often referred to in abbreviated form as 'SS'.

For 1939, all ohv models were fitted with a new design of cylinder head and rocker box. But then came the outbreak of the Second

For many years, both at Wolverhampton and then Plumstead, AJS offered its own range of sidecars; this is the new-for-1935 Model D Sports-Tourist chair. It was finished in mottled aluminium and all fittings were chrome-plated; cost £23.

The Model 18, a 498cc ohv single could be ordered with either a high-level (shown) or low-level exhaust. This is the 1935 bike.

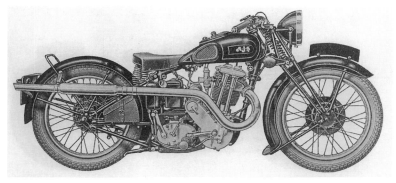

A page from the 1935 AJS brochure showing examples of detail features throughout the range.

EXAMPLES OF A.J.S. "PERFECTION IN DETAIL"

This sketch shows the design of the overhead rocker gear on 35/6, 35/18 and 35/8 Models. The rockers are duralumin forgings, attached by splines to the hollow alloy steel rocker spindles. Observe the ample diameter of the bronze bushes for the spindles and the neat manner in which the ball-ended duralumin push rods are enclosed.

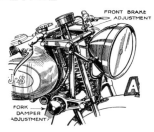

A well-known feature of "A.J.S." Motor Cycles is the exceptionally sturdy front fork assembly shown above. Note the accessible finger adjustment for the front brake, the convenient shock absorber adjusting knob, and the stiff headlamp mounting.

On the Big Twin Models the magdyno is protected by the efficient shield shown above, which ensures reliable ignition even in tropical downpours.

This view shows the simple adjustment for the oil pump provided on Models 35/5, 35/6, 35/8, 35/18 and 35/9.

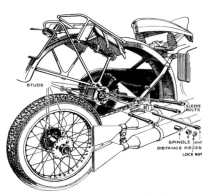

The arrangement of the "A.J.S." quickly detachable wheel is clearly shown above, the wheel being removable without disturbing the chain or brake. This design is used for front and rear wheels of the Big Twin Models, the wheels being interchangeable, and for the rear wheel only of Models 35/6, 35/7, 35/B8, 35/8, 35/9 and 35/10.

This cutaway view of the highly efficient front brake used on all Models except 35/12, 35/5, 35/16 and 35/4, shows the alloy drum with its cooling fins, which serve also to stiffen the drum to prevent distortion, the aluminium alloy brake shoes, and the neat manner in which the operating cable is concealed by passing through the front fork tube, whence it emerges at the finger adjuster shown in the top illustration.

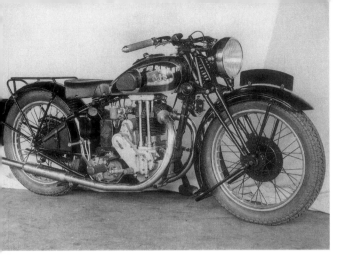

The 1936 Model 8 ohv twin port single, displaced 498cc and came with a vertical rather than sloping cylinder which had been a feature of the 1935 model. Footchange 4-speed gearbox, but still exposed valve gear. An identical 349cc version was also available (known as the Model 6).

World War on 1 September that year, and it was very much Matchless, rather than AJS, which was given the War Department contracts. These resulted in the famous G3/L three-fifty ohv single, from which post-war was to come the Heavyweight singles with both Matchless and AJS versions (*see* Chapter 4), as part of AMC (Associated Motor Cycles).

AMC – the Corporate Body

After acquiring AJS in 1931, at the height of the Great Depression, the Collier brothers had gone on to take over Sunbeam (also, like AJS, originally from Wolverhampton). The Colliers took over from ICI, who had themselves taken over Sunbeam earlier in the decade, in August 1937. This meant that the Colliers now owned three quite different marques, which were all famous brand names in their own right. The directors of the Matchless company decided that a more suitable name was needed to encompass all three and so on 12 October 1937 the company was re-registered as Associated Motor Cycles Ltd (AMC).

As the 1930s came to a close, AMC enjoyed a level of financial stability which was the envy of the remainder of the industry, achieved

September 1937 advertisement, featuring the new Silver Streak models for the 1938 season; these were offered in 246, 347 and 498cc engine sizes – and with ohv and enclosed valve gear.

through good management, a good range of products and excellent quality control.

In 1940 AMC sold the rights to Sunbeam to the BSA group. The war years dealt the double blow of the loss of two of the three Collier brothers, with the death of Bert Collier in 1941 followed by Harry A. Collier in 1944. Thus when the war ended in Europe on 8 May 1945, only Charlie Collier remained. This was a much more serious blow than anyone outside the immediate close circle could have envisaged, since young Bert Collier was just beginning to show all the hallmarks of being a brilliant designer, whilst at the time of his death the older brother, Harry A. Collier, was AMC Chairman.

3 Inter-War Racing

The story of the racing history of the AJS marque immediately following the First World War, whilst under the ownership of the Stevens brothers in Wolverhampton, is covered in Chapter 1 and charts the successes and failures of the ohv and ohc singles up to 1931. The story contained here relates to the period from late 1931 until the outbreak of the Second World War, and also what transpired in the late 1940s when Jock West briefly revived the pre-war V4 before the FIM banned superchargers in 1947.

Rowley Intervenes

When the Collier brothers bought the ailing AJS concern in late 1931, its racing pedigree does not seem to have been one of the reasons for the purchase. Oddly, although former TT winners themselves, Harry and Charlie Collier left the AJS works racers to rot until the famous AJS rider George Rowley prepared one of the three-fifty camshaft singles for the 1932 International Six Days Trial and went on to win a gold medal. Even after Rowley's gold medal success, the Matchless directors remained unconcerned about the whole affair and when the bike arrived back in England after being 'lost' in Italy, the Colliers refused to pay the £10 owing on the freight bill!

But Rowley, unknown to the Colliers, went ahead and paid the outstanding money, retrieved the machine, and converted it back into a racing model and entered it for the 350 and 500cc Grand Prix at Brooklands. This infuriated the Matchless regime, for Rowley's name, linked again with AJS, prompted press speculation that his private entry was a prelude to an official works return. This was not so, claimed the Plumstead concern, but it was nonetheless significant that they did not actually stop Rowley from racing the AJS, which they could have done as it was their property which Rowley had redeemed, prepared and entered without the firm's knowledge.

But, after excellent placings of fifth (350cc) and seventh (500cc) against clearly superior opposition, the Collier brothers were so delighted that instead of sacking him, their congratulations were followed by the re-establishment of the camshaft model's production status and furthermore authorization of an official AJS works racing squad. So, in effect, everything which went afterwards, including the post-war 7R (*see* Chapter 9), owes a big 'thank you' to George Rowley's efforts.

And from that time until 7R production eventually ended in the early 1960s, the Plumstead factory continued a policy set up by the Colliers in 1933 that it would 'produce and sell sufficient competition machines to finance subsequent development and maintain a racing department'. When it entered production the Collier-backed AJS sohc racer, based on the Stevens ohc unit, was coded the R7. The final bikes in 1938 and 1939 displaced 346cc (70 × 90mm) and put out 27bhp, giving a top speed of 102mph (165km/h).

Early type ohc single produced at Plumstead, as used in 1932–33 by George Rowley and others. The magneto was now placed at the rear of the cylinder (the Wolverhampton-built bikes had it at the front).

1938/1939 R7 Specifications	
Engine	Single overhead camshaft with chain-driven cam and Weller-type tensioner. Aluminium cylinder head and barrel, the latter with a cast iron liner
Displacement	346cc
Bore & Stroke	70 × 90mm
Compression ratios	8.8:1 (or 11:1 with special high compression piston)
Tappet clearance	Inlet 0.018in; exhaust 0.025in
Oil regulating screw	Open to 1½ turns
Valve spring type	Hairpin
Valve spring pressure	130lb valve on seat
Valve timing	Inlet opens 54° BTDC Inlet closes 60° ATDC Exhaust opens 67° BBDC Exhaust closes 45° ATDC
Ignition timing	42 degrees fully advanced
Recommended spark plugs	KLG 731 and 689 Lodge RL49 and RL51
Megaphone size	15½in long; 4⅜in mouth
Engine sprocket	21 teeth
Gear ratios	5.3, 6.15, 7.69 and 9.65
Tyre sizes	Front 27 × 3.00 Rear 27 × 3.25
Maximum power	27bhp at 7,200rpm
Maximum speed	102–104mph (164–167km/h)

NB: All the AJS ohc models up to the end of 1937 used Sturmey-Archer type gearboxes. From the 1938 model onwards a BAP Burman-type box was employed. The footchange arrangement of the Sturmey-Archer gearbox was manufactured by AMC, but suffered an unusually long pedal travel. The Burman gearbox with its positive stop design was a considerable improvement.

The V4 Takes its Bow

But these single cylinder efforts were to be somewhat overshadowed in late 1935 when, at London's Olympia Show, AJS introduced a magnificent V4 roadster prototype designed by Bert Collier. Offered only for the 1936 season, the Model 20 displaced 495cc (50 × 63mm), but it certainly created a lot of publicity for the marque. Not only this, but it was the factory's stated aim to race the bike as a works entry in addition to selling it to the public. The engine was air-cooled, with the two sets of cylinders set apart at 50 degrees. The single overhead cams were driven, in the traditional AJS manner, by chain. There was a quartet of exhaust pipes and two carburettors, whilst the ignition was taken care of by a pair of magnetos, bevel driven and mounted on the

offside of the crankcase. As for the cycle parts, these were very much standard issue components similar to those used on other AJS models at the time.

Two of the 495cc V4s were raced in the 1936 Senior TT, but both retired. One of these was piloted by Harold Daniell and the

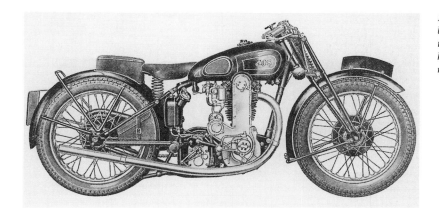

By the mid-1930s the engine had been redesigned, as shown here from the 1935 catalogue of the five-hundred camshaft over-the-counter racer.

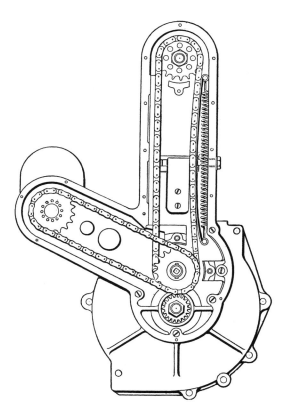

Drawing showing AJS camshaft drive which incorporated a tensioning device and re-action damper.

other by George Rowley. It is worth noting that Daniell rode for AJS from 1934, but after the V4 debacle he switched to Nortons, gaining three Senior TT victories (1938, 1947 and 1949) before retiring at the end of 1950 to concentrate on his London (Norton) dealer-ship.

The V4 project was put to one side for some 18 months before being passed to Matt Wright who carried out something of a redesign for 1938. The 1938 V4 had been altered in several ways since the machine made its debut in the 1936 Senior TT. Matt Wright had made the camshaft gear and rocker boxes to more closely resemble those of the single cylinder ohc

Tom Arter pictured at the 1938 Manx Grand Prix with his R7; he finished thirteenth.

models. Improvements had also been made to the 'plumbing' of the exhaust and inlet pipes. Another feature was that it now ran on a petroil mixture! This was not because the V4 had become a 2-stroke, instead it was an ingenious idea to overcome the necessity of a special oil pump to lubricate the Zoller supercharger which had been added to the bike's specification. To achieve this end a small quantity of oil (actually 2 per cent) was mixed with the petrol. As soon as the engine was running the oil became separated from the petrol vapour by the centrifugal action of the supercharger on the same principle as petroil lubrication on a conventional two-stroke engine. On the AJS V4, a single Amal carburettor supplied the mixture to the supercharger which, in turn, passed it to the cylinders at a pressure of between 5–6lb/sq.in.

To improve the handling and roadholding of the V4, Matt Wright set the engine assembly further back in the frame. This in turn, called for the removal of the oil tank. This alteration had the advantage of curing another problem: on the original bike the oil tank tended to mask the pair of rear cylinders. On the 1938 machine the oil tank was relocated to a new home inside the large fuel tank. This change considerably improved both the cooling and the steering. Another change was the adoption of a spring frame, featuring plunger-type rear suspension, together with a link action from a front-mounted pivot.

But unfortunately all this was to no avail as the sole AJS starter in the 1938 Senior TT, Bob Foster, retired on lap 2 with 'engine problems', after lying eighth at the end of lap 1. The other AJS V4 rider, E.R. Thomas, didn't even make

AJS depot at the TT races in June 1934. Left to right: Bert Collier, Reg Barber, Freddie Neill, Tyrell Smith, George Rowley and Harold Daniell.

A later 1930s R7 engine showing oil pump, rev-counter drive and gearbox.

onto the drive-side of the crank case. The impeller mechanism was outside the engine and supercharger drive sprockets and was connected directly to the mainshaft. Its first outing was the North West 200 in Northern Ireland during May 1939, but rider Walter Rusk was forced to retire with a blown head gasket.

Between the North West and the TT several alterations were made to the cooling system, whilst the radiator was increased in size. One result of the switch from air to water for the cooling was that the exhaust ports for the rear cylinders faced to the rear and thus enabled the use of 'straight' exhaust pipes. In the 7-lap race, Walter Rusk was eleventh and Bob Foster thirteenth in a race dominated by the supercharged BMW twins of Georg Meier and Jock West.

it to the start line, after suffering engine problems in practice. Foster retired in the Junior when he skidded and his rear brake pedal was so damaged that he could not continue.

Further Development of the V4

During the winter there was more development on the V4. The biggest change was a switch to water-cooling, the circulation of which was by an impeller that was housed in a casting bolted

The V4's Finest Hour

Not only was the Ulster Grand Prix the last such race prior to the outbreak of war some two weeks later, it was also the AJS V4's finest hour. As although Darino Serafina won the 500cc race, averaging 97.85mph (157.5km/h), the Irishman Walter Rusk and the AJS multi became the first to lap the famous Clady circuit at 100mph (161km/h) – for which they were awarded the MCUI (Motor Cycle Union of Ireland) Medallion. Practice speeds

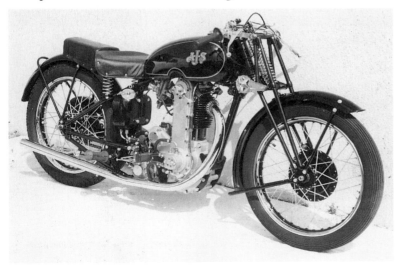

Nicely restored late 1930s cammy Ajay with some non-standard items, such as mudguards.

The AJS V4 project. This air-cooled, supercharged engine came between the fully equipped roadster prototype shown at the 1935 London Olympia Show (which never entered production) and the ultimate liquid-cooled Grand Prix bike of the late 1930s.

were high with Rusk and the AJS, now sporting megaphone rather than simply straight pipes, setting the best speed of 98.14mph (158km/h). Race day came, cloudy but dry. There were in fact two AJS V4s, the other ridden by Bob Foster. Both AJSs fired instantly and Rusk and Foster made the most of their initial lead. Behind them came Maurice Cann on a works Moto Guzzi v-twin, L.J. Archer (Velocette) and Serafina on the Gilera four. At Aldergrove on the first lap Serafina led from Freddie Frith (Norton) with Bob Foster third. Then came the long Clady straight and Rusk had blitzed the opposition on speed to take up the running. At the end of the lap it was Rusk, Frith and Serafini. *The Motor Cycle*'s race report commented: 'How the crowd gasped, for the sight was breathtaking to say the least', going on to say:

> In a matter of seconds these three flashed past the stands, all doing well over 100mph. As lap 2 began the retirement, started including Foster, who coasted into his pit with an engine that was burning too much oil. But there was no stopping the other Ajay in the hands of Rusk. He proceeded to pull away from both Frith and Serafina and dispatched the second lap with a speed of 99.73mph (a new lap record). And as Rusk went through at the end of his third circuit his lead over Frith was even greater and everyone waited

with baited breath for his time. And yes, news came through that Rusk had circulated at exactly 100mph! The crowd went wild with excitement. Unfortunately this state of affairs didn't last for long as, on the 4th lap Rusk was forced into retirement when the offside lower fork link fractured, thus putting the dampers on an otherwise magnificent performance for the AJS squad.

Racing Halted During the War

Then came the war and for six long years motorcycle racing was to be placed on the back burner throughout a Europe darkened by Nazi tyranny. The sight and sound of the AJS supercharged V4 was something never to be forgotten and it is sad to realize that when at last Matt Wright and his team appeared to possess a formula which could have beaten the German and Italian bikes, Hitler put a giant spoke in the AJS wheel of fortune.

Liquid-cooled engine of the 1938–39 period. It was tremendously powerful, being the first to lap at over 100mph (160km/h) in the 1939 Ulster GP, before rider Walter Rusk was forced to retire.

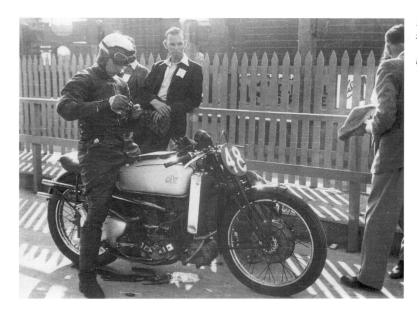

Bob Foster, with one of the two supercharged AJS V4s raced in the 1939 Senior TT. Foster finished thirteenth averaging 79.57mph for the 7-lap, 246.11 mile race; team-mate Walter Rusk was eleventh.

A New 3-Cylinder Engine

During what was known as the 'Phoney War' (September 1939–May 1940), Harry Collier and his draughtsmen developed an entirely new 3-cylinder engine. This sported chain drive to the three overhead camshafts; it was also created for forced induction; the intention being to lay the engine with its parallel cylinders, horizontally in the frame, with blower and induction system located beneath the fuel tank. Much controversy surrounds the fate of this project. Suffice to say that when the factory returned to post-war production it had disappeared, its place taken with an entirely new design, which was to eventually become the famous Porcupine parallel twin (*see* Chapter 5).

The Last Outings for the V4

As for the pre-war V4, this made two final appearances after the war had ended in 1946 and before superchargers were banned by the FIM the following year. The former wartime fighter airfield of North Weald in Essex was used by Jock West to test various new components such as plugs and tyres. Then came an outing at Chimay in Belgium, and later at Albi in France. In the latter event a big-end bearing seized and this particular machine was put into storage – the only liquid-cooled AJS V4 to survive. It was finally restored by Sammy Miller in 1980 for his well-known museum project.

But even though AJS went on to achieve considerable post-war success with designs such as the 7R, Porcupine and 3-valve, it never quite regained the glamour which surrounded those last four months of peace in 1939, when the water-cooled V4 howled its way around the circuits of Europe. If only that engine had had an equally competitive set of cycle parts to match the undoubted speed of the engine, AJS could well have become European (the forerunner to the world series) champions in 1940. But of course that year will be remembered for the exploits of British airmen in the Battle of Britain and not for racing.

4   Heavyweight Singles

There is little doubt that of all the post-war British single-cylinder roadsters in the 350/500cc categories the AJS (and their Matchless brothers) were amongst the very best in terms of quality finish, reliability and longevity. Both the three-fifty Model 16 and five-hundred Model 18 ran from 1945 right through to AMC's final demise in 1966.

Back into Production

When *The Motor Cycle* in its 28 June 1945 issue carried a story proclaiming 'Two AJSs Enter Production', every 'Ajay' enthusiast was, at long last, after some six long years of war, given motorcycling news about which he could get excited. Clearly based around the 348cc WD (War Department) Matchless G3/L, perhaps the most striking feature of the new machines (the 350 Model 16 and 500 Model 18) was that, as *The Motor Cycle* commented, they did not give 'the slightest impression of being "Army". Even the three-gallon tanks with their black and gold finish, look deeper.'

The first machines were scheduled for delivery 'some seven or eight weeks hence' said the report. The official AMC position was that 'the company are continuing the manufacture of motorcycles for the Army, three-quarters of the factory production capacity being devoted to the supply of WD motorcycles and spares, the machines for the civilian market have to be based on their Army model'. *The Motor Cycle* described these new civilian versions in the following terms: 'They are, however, thrillingly civilian in their finish,

and have their acid-dipped crankcases, polished magneto chain covers, scintillating levers and even rubber for footrests and kneegrips, though not at the moment for the foot-change lever.' Of course the reader has to remember that wartime shortages meant the WD models used by the British forces had to make do without rubber components such as those described above, and steel instead of alloy engine outer covers – and certainly no chrome plate or polished alloy!

Technical Details

Whereas the military model was only built as a three-fifty, the new civilian bikes were to be produced in 350 and 500cc guises.

The 1945/46 Model 16 three-fifty was clearly based around the successful War Department Matchless G3/L military motorcycle, and had a rigid frame and AMC Teledraulic front forks.

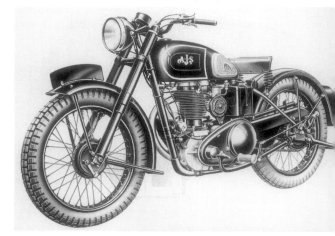

The bikes benefited from lessons learned on the battlefield, with features such as a full-cradle frame and the by now famous hydraulically damped Teledraulic front forks. The latter provided a total possible movement of 7⅛in (181mm), divided approximately into 3in upward and 4in (75/100mm) on the rebound. Four-speed, foot-change Burman gearboxes were a standard fitment and gave the 'Civvy Street' models the following ratios: 5.8, 7.5, 10.3 and 15.4:1 on the 350cc machine (compared to 5.8, 7.5, 12.2 and 18.5:1 on the WD version). On the 500cc model, the ratios became 5.25, 6.8, 9.3 and 13.9:1.

As before, the AJS singles had a shielded magneto at the front of the engine (compared to the Matchless, which carried the magneto at the rear of the cylinder and employed a different magneto chaincase). The compression ratio of the 350cc model was also different from the WD mount, as there was no compression plate,

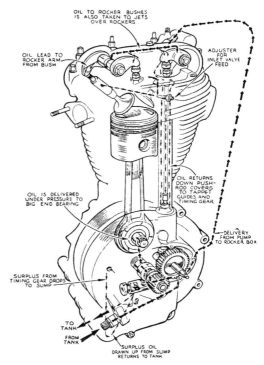

AMC Heavyweight single-cylinder lubrication system.

which meant the ratio was 6.3:1 instead of 6:1. The compression ratio of the five-hundred was 5.9:1; Lo-Ex (Low Expansion) aluminium pistons were used on both engine sizes.

The 497cc (82.5mm × 93mm) engine was of the single-port type similar to the unit marketed in late 1939, with the latter's heavier flywheels and a new inlet-valve timing. A 1⅛in (28.6mm) Amal two-lever carburettor was fitted. A cylinder head steady running from the rear nearside rocker-box bolt to the top tube of the frame was fitted in the case of this model. On the 348cc (69 × 93mm) engine there was a 1in (25.4mm) bore carburettor, as against a ⅞in (22.3mm) instrument on the WD machine. Like the latter, the 350 AJS had its exhaust header pipe above the offside (right) footrest; the 500, which had a 1¾in (44.5mm) pipe, had this set below.

Other features of the machines were 3.25 × 19 Dunlop tyres, internally illuminated speedo

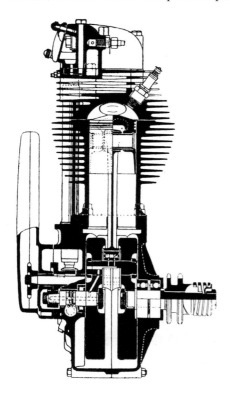

Factory technical drawing of the AJS single-cylinder engine.

The AMC Teledraulic Front Fork

The story behind the development of the AMC Teledraulic front fork is not one simply of design and manufacture, but of competitors, contracts and ultimately tragedy.

Back in the 1930s the Isleworth, Middlesex, company AFN Ltd held the British import rights for the German range of BMW cars and motorcycles. And in 1935 BMW had introduced the world's first production oil-damped telescopic front forks to the motorcycle world. First seen on the R7 prototype, these forks entered series production with the R12 and R17 models. In addition, the German marque also used developments of these forks on its racing and record-breaking machines.

Also in 1935, Jock West, who was later to join AMC, had begun work at AFN. As a result of his riding ability (he had successfully raced Ariel, Triumph and AJS machines) Jock was subsequently invited to become a member of the official BMW works racing team, and he went on to win the Ulster Grand Prix on more than one occasion on one of the German machines – and more famously finished runner-up behind BMW team-mate Georg Meier in the 1939 Senior TT.

However, before this, in 1937 Jock West had been instrumental in organizing for AMC to purchase a set of BMW telescopic front forks via AFN. This all came about because he was on such good terms with the Collier brothers who then owned AMC. Having taken delivery of the forks, AMC set about making their own version of the telescopic forks, under the Teledraulic trade name. Like BMW forks, the Teledraulics operated on the action of compression of an extended coil spring in each fork leg by means of an aluminium slider. The alloy moving slider members

of the Teledraulic fork assembly supported the front wheel, mudguard and brake anchorage and, most importantly of all, housed the hydraulic damping mechanism. The operation of this mechanism depended upon the motion of small, disc-like damper valves with a limited range of movement. These disc-type valves were designed to obstruct progressively the transfer of oil, employed as the damping medium, between damper compartments whilst the slider was moving. This served to slow down at the moments of both impact and rebound, whilst coil springs took up the inertia of the moving parts of the fork as it attempted to bottom out.

The majority of the development work in transferring the technology to actual production was carried out by the youngest of the Collier brothers, Bert, who was then manager of the AMC works at Plumstead. However, on 31 October 1941, whilst carrying out further tests on the public highway near Sevenoaks, Kent, Bert Collier was involved in a serious accident and was taken to hospital with a fractured skull, from which he died. He was only thirty-four years of age at the time of his death.

This incident came only weeks after the Teledraulic front forks had made their debut on the new 348cc Matchless W41/G3L military model. It should also be noted that these forks were the first British-made examples of the telescopic front fork to feature hydraulic damping on a production motorcycle.

As is related elsewhere, although the principle of the Teledraulics remained, the actual fork design underwent continual development over many years of service during the 1940s and 1950s, to improve both its operation and serviceability.

heads, the latter mounted on top of the cross-member of the Teledraulic forks, a built-in type rear number plate, an AMC-made prop stand, a spring-up rear stand, a tubular front stand-cum-mudguard stay, a 4pt (2ltr) oil tank with separate oil filter, a 7in (178mm) headlamp, and hand adjusters for the front and rear brakes and the clutch.

Road Impressions

In the 28 June 1945 issue of *The Motor Cycle*, 'Torrens' wrote about the 1945 model.

What about taking it away with you? Said Mr Manufacturer. I was decked out in pin-strip city suiting – a very wartime, much worn suiting – and had no goggles, no gauntlets and not even a mackintosh. Everything had pointed to a day in the office. Then there was this bolt from the blue: the AJS programme for next week's issue. The day was hot and seemed likely to remain fine. I need not ask you what you would have done in my case, for, like me you would have jumped at the opportunity of riding 'something' 1945. What model AJS? The overhead-valve, five-

The 1946 16M	
Engine	Air-cooled ohv single with vertical cylinder; iron head and barrel; vertically split aluminium crankcases; fully enclosed valve gear, coil valve springs; built-up crankshaft; roller bearing big-end; gear-driven cams
Bore	69mm
Stroke	93mm
Displacement	348cc
Compression ratio	6.3:1
Lubrication	Dry sump
Ignition	Magdyno, Lucas, 6-volt
Carburettor	Amal Type 76 1in
Primary drive	Chain
Final drive	Chain
Gearbox	4-speed, foot-change, Burman
Frame	Diamond-type with single front down-tube
Front suspension	AMC Teledraulic forks
Rear suspension	Rigid
Front brake	5.5in, SLS drum, single-sided
Rear brake	5.5in, SLS drum, single-sided
Tyres	3.25 × 19 front and rear
Wheelbase	54in (1,372mm)
Ground clearance	5.5in (140mm)
Seat height	30in (762mm)
Fuel tank capacity	3gal (14ltr)
Dry weight	344lb (156kg)
Maximum power	16bhp @ 5,600rpm
Top speed	71mph (114km/h)

The 1946 18	
Engine	Air-cooled ohv single with vertical cylinder; iron head and barrel; vertically split aluminium crankcases; fully enclosed valve gear; coil valve springs; built-up crankshaft; roller bearing big-end; gear-driven cams
Bore	82.5mm
Stroke	93mm
Displacement	497cc
Compression ratio	5.9:1
Lubrication	Dry sump
Ignition	Magdyno, Lucas, 6-volt
Carburettor	Amal type 89 1⅜in
Primary drive	Chain
Final drive	Chain
Gearbox	4-speed, foot-change, Burman CP
Frame	Diamond-type with single front down-tube
Front suspension	AMC Teledraulic forks
Rear suspension	Rigid
Front brake	5.5in, SLS drum, single-sided
Rear brake	5.5in, SLS drum, single-sided
Tyres	3.25 × 19 front and rear
Wheelbase	54in (1,372mm)
Ground clearance	5.5in (140mm)
Seat height	30in (762mm)
Fuel tank capacity	3gal (14ltr)
Dry weight	353lb (160kg)
Maximum power	23bhp @ 5,400rpm
Top speed	81mph (130km/h)

hundred. I particularly wanted to ride this machine.

Torrens was already familiar with the three-fifty, 'having ridden dozens of Army ones during the course of the war.'

This, the first of the new models, came as a surprise to me. I was expecting 'just a G/3L with a bit more urge', and found one of the nicest, liveliest 500cc singles I have ridden for a long time . . . The engine is flexible. One can trickle along at 18mph in the top gear of

5.25 to 1 and then, if one retards the ignition a trifle, accelerate away quite happily . . .

But, he continued:

It was the 'urge' that surprised me most. At 55 to 60mph one is moving along on quite a small throttle opening without the engine appearing to be 'at work'. 'Umph!' you say to yourself. 'The rest of the throttle opening won't mean much,' and you are wrong – utterly wrong. Tweak the twistgrip open with the machine doing sixty and things happen. I will not say that it whooshes forward, but the acceleration from a mile a minute is very useful indeed. There is a liveliness about the machine that makes it a real joy, and it is something which I do not recall with the previous five-hundreds . . . And what I also liked about the machine was that it feels such a quality job. Riding it one has the sensation of handling a mount that has been built and not merely assembled.

And so the Model 16 and Model 18 began their long careers.

The 1947 Model Year

When AMC announced details of its 1947 AJS (and Matchless) motorcycles at the beginning of November 1946, there were a considerable number of improvements. Some of these had come via a 'suggestions book' which sales supremo Jack West had compiled; this showed his 'hands on' approach and was something unique in the British motorcycle industry at the time.

One of those points 'needing rectification' that West had placed in his book concerned the oil-bath primary chaincase. This now featured a longer screw in the securing band which held the two halves together, because it had been found that the rubber sealing washer was liable to expand after use, and as a result, an owner might experience problems refitting the band. Simple as this particular alteration might have appeared, it was nonetheless a good illustration of the attention to detail that was being made by AMC at the time.

Changes had also been carried out to the AMC-made Teledraulic front forks. These now featured new springs that had been wound in such a way as to provide three different rates: the coils were set at different distances apart, and the springs, claimed AMC, now afforded 'a soft, easy movement at initial deflection of the forks, and increasing resistance with increased fork travel.' Buffer springs had been added to reduce the fall of the wheel,

and this had meant that the front brake cable could be shortened 3¼in (83mm), therefore providing a neater arrangement of the cable, which now featured a guide on the nearside fork blade.

Another important change was that the gudgeon-pin bosses were now set ½in (13mm) lower in the Lo-Ex split-skirt piston, and the connecting-rod had been reduced in length by an equal amount. The intention was to reduce piston slap, which had become a feature of the latest AJS (and Matchless) motorcycles, thanks to rather large piston/bore clearances, thus greatly reducing the likelihood of a piston seizure during the running-in period. At the same time, the oil circulation had been doubled. The oil pump speed had been increased by the introduction of a two-start worm on the timing-side engine shaft, and a larger feed pipe, measuring ⁷⁄₁₆in (11mm), from the oil tank, and larger ducts in the engine to suit.

In the case of the 350cc engine, the lubricating oil operated at an appreciably lower temperature owing to a change in the exhaust-pipe design. Previously the pipe had been fitted in as close as possible to the crankcase and timing chest, above the rider's footrest. Now it was arranged beneath the footrest which, in addition to improving the appearance of the motorcycle, resulted in a greater range of adjustment for the footrest and, as already stated, cooler running. The pipe was still well tucked away, thus providing sufficient ground clearance.

Another, more minor change was the new front number plate and its fixings, described by *The Motor Cycle* as 'altogether neater'. The development team had placed rubber between the mudguard and the channelled member which now formed the mounting of the front plate.

Chromium-plated wheel rims and handlebars had now been standardized: the rims featured black centres lined in gold (silver on Matchless models), with all wheel spokes cadmium plated. The AJS badge, in gold, adorned the fuel-tank sides. A pillion seat and carrier were now available, the cost for the pair being an additional £2 11s 11d. A lifting handle on all models was now integral with the rear mudguard stays, making for a much neater arrangement. AMC made much of its factory finish, saying:

> the durability of enamel is proportional to the stoving temperature, and no stove enamel allows the employment of so high a baking temperature as does black. What is especially pleasing about the latest production is the exceptionally high quality of the finish. All enameled parts have three coats of Pinchin Johnson's best black enamel on a rustproof Bonderized base.

The 1948 Model Range

The 1948 AMC programmes for AJS and Matchless were announced to the public during mid-October 1947, with *The Motor Cycle* reporting 'a number of interesting and important changes'. Whilst there were no new models, as regards the single cylinder roadsters the improvements were many and significant. Thus essentially there were four AJS (and four Matchless) models, a three-fifty and five-hundred in each marque, and each of these available in roadster and competition guises (the latter covered in Chapters 7 and 12).

1948 AJS Model 18 five-hundred with iron head and barrel, Burman 4-speed foot-change gearbox, tubular headlamp brackets and Amal Type 89 1⅛in carb.

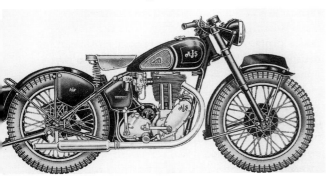

All engines were of the single port, ohv single-cylinder type, mounted in cradle frames. The main differences between the Matchless and AJS models were that the former had engines with the magneto to the rear of the cylinder barrel and a silver-and-black finish, whilst the latter had the magneto positioned between the front of the cylinder and the front downtube and with a black-and-gold paint job. No changes had been made to the engines except for the oil pump and its housing. The pump spindle, its cam screw and pin had been strengthened, with the object of increasing the factor of safety; this coming after changes to considerable increase the flow rate the previous year. AMC recommended a period of 5,000 miles (8,000km) between oil changes.

There were major alterations to both the steering and the braking; sales boss Jock West making the following statement:

> Associated Motor Cycles maintain that perfect high-speed steering is not enough; the rider should also have absolute confidence at low speeds – be complete master of his machine – and this is so, right from the slowest of traffic crawls.

To this end the company had carried out an extensive test programme regarding steering layout.

For 1948, there was a new steering-head angle, together with a revised rake and trail of the front forks. The aim was to provide a motorcycle which could be ridden feet-up almost to a standstill, was really light to handle at low speeds, yet would maintain perfect stability at high speeds. *The Motor Cycle* reported 'A short run on one of the new models showed that the steering is exceptionally good, and under traffic conditions close to remarkable.'

One also has to remember that both AJS and Matchless roadsters benefited greatly from AMC's support and participation in trials and scrambling at the highest level. Furthermore, in Hugh Viney it also had probably the finest rider of the era at its disposal to provide vital feedback which could be incorporated into the series-production models.

Important modifications had also been made to the Teledraulic front forks. For the 1948 season the hydraulic damping had been considerably simplified, yet was as effective as before. Immediately above the piston, which was fitted at the lower end of each 1⅛in (28mm) chrome-moly fork stanchion, there was a light alloy shuttle of slightly smaller external diameter than the piston, with an internal diameter fractionally larger than the stanchion. When the front wheel encountered a poor road surface (a pothole, for example), the slider moved upwards, compressing air in the upper section of the fork tube; this forced oil through four ¼in (6mm) holes in the tube, raising the shuttle off its seat on the piston and automatically centring the shuttle relative to the main tube and the slider, thus cushioning the fork action. Should the shock be particularly violent, one of the patented taper plugs would come into action, providing an increasingly rapid cut-off and, at extremes, almost complete cut-off, thus acting as a hydraulic buffer.

On rebound the shuttle was forced downward, sealing itself on the piston, and thus sealing the lateral passage through which the oil passed, causing the oil to return to the fork tube via the predetermined passages between the bore of the shuttle and the fork tube. The arrangement was continued whereby the main fork springs, one per leg, were wound so as to provide a progressive action, but thanks to the elimination of the previously fitted distance piece, the springs were now 1½in (38mm) longer than before. With this new set-up the amount of oil per leg was 'critical' (AMC), the factory's official recommendation being 6oz of Mobiloil 'Artic' per leg, against 6½oz previously.

Another important feature of the 1948 range was that new, larger brakes were specified for all models: 7in diameter, with ⅞in-wide linings. The drums were cast in Chromidium, and quite apart from the excellent construction of the hubs themselves, they were fitted with (*Motor Cycling*) 'some of the most rigid, deep section aluminium-alloy brake shoes that have ever been fitted to production models.' When tested by *The Motor Cycle*, their verdict was that the result was 'a pair of brakes which are free from lost motion and from sponginess, and while extremely light in operation and thoroughly progressive, are outstandingly effective.'

There were also a series of more minor changes. These included a larger (3.50) section rear tyre on the Model 18, improved saddle-spring mountings, giving modified comfort on both the 350 and 500, revised fuel piping (providing easier access to the carburettor for maintenance), a revised exhaust-pipe bend (on the 500 only), a neater, chromium-plated battery strap, chromium-plated rings part-way down the front fork cover tubes, and neater toolbox fixings.

The AJS Single-Cylinders for 1949

When the AJS range for 1949 was announced at the beginning of October 1948 they were all single-cylinders. The new parallel twin (*see* Chapter 8) was not unveiled until a few weeks later, on the eve of the London Show. There were over a dozen modifications: some of major significance (such as the redesigned frame and cylinder heads), others far less so.

As in the past, the frame (still without rear suspension) remained of the cradle type, but the seat tube was now positioned further to the rear, giving additional clearance at the carburettor. This enabled a flat, cylindrical Vokes air filter to be fitted (as a cost option). In addition, the new frame allowed a larger oil tank, with a capacity of ½gal (2ltr) to be fitted. Another feature was a sidecar connection point provided at each rear fork and lug.

Another change as a result of the redesigned frame was that the chain line had been widened by ³⁄₁₆in (4mm) so that a 4in (100mm) section rear tyre could be accommodated if required. The engine was also ⁷⁄₁₆in (11mm) lower, which improved accessibility and also

lowered the centre of gravity. AMC also claimed 'improved roadholding'. However, the frame was still rigid, with no form of rear suspension.

Both the cylinder head and rocker box had been redesigned, mainly because a switch had been made from coil to hairpin valve springs. The AMC development team considered that the latter type would give better service at very high engine revolutions. In addition, the valve-stem caps had been dispensed with, and instead, the valve-stem ends were now hardened.

A new aluminium-alloy rocker box which also enclosed the valve springs was retained by a total of nine bolts. A boss in the rocker box housed the exhaust-valve lifter; this took the form of a simple cam which, when brought into operation, pressed down on the exhaust rocker arm. This cam, its shaft and the external lever were a one-piece stamping. A torsion spring round the shaft returned the cam out of contact with the rocker when the handlebar lever was released. With the exhaust-valve lifter mechanism now being in the rocker box in place of the timing gear, the crankcase exterior had been cleaned up considerably. A deeper cover plate was fitted to the new rocker box, providing improved access for rocker adjustment.

The cylinder-head finning had been revised to prevent 'fin ringing', whilst the top of the cylinder bore now featured a spigot for locating into the cylinder head; but the joint between the cylinder and head was still made by means of a gasket at the faces.

The dynamo armature speed had been

upped. The sprocket on the engine mainshaft was now larger, resulting in the armature being driven at 1½ times engine speed, thus improving the charging rate when travelling slowly. Another electrical change was a right-angle extension of the battery platform to provide a new mounting for the lighting voltage-regulator.

Other changes included new handlebars, new headlamp shell and rectangular rear lamp (with modified number plate), and the saddle was now adjustable for height at the nose as well as at the springs. New saddle springs reduced lateral sway. There were also synthetic rubber seals for the wheel bearings, and a square-section footrest bar that was integral with the nearside (left) hanger; this latter assembly was secured by a single nut against the boss of the hanger on the other side.

When the new AJS Spring Twin (and Matchless G9) five-hundred vertical twins were announced in mid-November 1948, AMC also stated that the new spring frame was to be made available for the single-cylinder models for an additional £20 6s 4d. Many customers opted to pay the extra charge for this conversion to the swinging-arm frame in order to take advantage of the improvement in comfort and handling and to give their bikes a more modern appearance. The rear suspension units were of AMC's own manufacture and were referred to as being of the 'candlestick' type – much narrower both top and bottom than the famous 'Jampot' type which was to replace them.

The 1949 18S	
Engine	Air-cooled ohv single with vertical cylinder; iron head and barrel; vertically split aluminium crankcases; fully enclosed valve gear; hairpin valve springs; built-up crankshaft; roller-bearing big-end; gear-driven cams
Bore	82.5mm
Stroke	93mm
Displacement	497cc
Compression ratio	5.9:1
Lubrication	Dry sump
Ignition	Magdyno, Lucas, 6-volt
Carburettor	Amal Type 89 1⅜in
Primary drive	Chain
Final drive	Chain
Gearbox	4-speed, foot-change, Burman CP
Frame	Two-part with single front down-tube
Front suspension	AMC Teledraulic forks
Rear suspension	Swinging arm with twin AMC 'candlestick' shock absorbers
Front brake	7in, SLS drum, single-sided
Rear brake	7in, SLS drum, single-sided
Tyres	3.25 × 19 front, 3.50 × 19 rear
Wheelbase	55.2in (1,402mm)
Ground clearance	5.5in (140mm)
Seat height	31in (787mm)
Fuel tank capacity	3gal (14ltr)
Dry weight	390lb (177kg)
Maximum power	23bhp @ 5,400rpm
Top speed	80mph (129km/h)

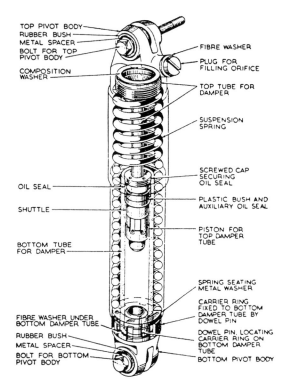

The first rear suspension units offered by AMC were known as the 'Candlestick'.

More Changes for 1950

Yet more updates came with the launch of the 1950 AJS models for the 1950 model year – summed up by these comments printed in *The Motor Cycle*, dated 13 October 1949:

Further refinements of standard and competition machines are announced by Associated Motor Cycles for the 1950 AJS and Matchless ranges. As widely known, these two

marques have much in common; the most obvious difference, other than the finish, is that on the single-cylinder engines the AJS has the magneto mounted on the front of the cylinder, and on the Matchless the magneto is behind the cylinder.

A minor change, already introduced in production but which could well be described as a modification for 1950, was the steering-crown lug with a steel stamping, with the fork leg clamps pinned and brazed in position. This steel stamping incorporated the steering stops, and was both stronger and lighter than the previously used malleable casting.

The brakes remained unchanged, except that for the 1950 machines the rear pedal was of a slightly different shape – more 'directional', as one journalist described it at the time. All models, including the singles, now sported a long shoe-plate torque arm for the front brake. This, it was claimed, provided smoother braking under hard application than the previous set-up, where the shoe-plate was retained by two bolts passing through a lug on the fork slider.

Both the front and rear mudguards had been redesigned; these were now of a deeper section, with a circumferential rib to provide greater stiffness. The front mudguard stay was of tubular one-piece construction, flattened and curved where it ran under the mudguard blade (previously, the stay had been of the pressed-steel variety). The rear mudguard, also supported by tubular stays, had been given a detachable tail section to help wheel removal.

A centre stand was provided for models featuring the new swinging arm frame, whereas the rigid frame retained the almost vintage rear-wheel type. A toolbox was located between the chain stays of the rigid models.

The silencers of the single-cylinder models had been redesigned, and were now described as being 'offset'; this was done to avoid grounding. The footrests had also been modified considerably, so that each combined footrest and hanger was fitted inside the frame tubes, and the hanger boss had twelve internal splines to fit on a square-section clamping rod. The rear hubs were now wider and as a result, the taper roller bearings were placed slightly further out from the centre, providing more support. These bearings were now separate races, which could be detached complete from the hollow spindle. The diameter of the solid spindle had been increased to ½in (13mm), whilst the Amal carburettor now came with a longer body, making the previous intake distance piece unnecessary. The prop stand was modified, allowing the pivot bolt to pass through the frame tube and thus provide greater support. There were also new-type tank bolts with hexagonal heads, and distance pieces which allowed the bolts to be fully tightened, yet ensured the rubber buffers were correctly compressed.

All the above changes, other than the rear mudguard, applied to the spring frame.

Finally, a five-spring clutch had been adopted on the 500 single – and the new twin – but not on the 350.

Significant Improvements for the 1951 Singles

In mid-September 1950 significant improvements for the 1951 singles were announced. New die-cast DTD 424 light-alloy cylinder heads and alloy pushrods were now specified. The advantages, the factory claimed, were 'cooler running, the possibility of employing slightly higher compression ratios, increased fuel economy and, of course, lighter weight.' The new heads featured cast-in austinetic valve inserts, and they also provided a slightly different angle for the exhaust port and for the exhaust header pipe. The compression ratio for the Model 14 was 6.35:1, and for the Model 16, 6:1. By removing a compression plate on the 500cc engine, 7.24:1 was available, suitable for better quality fuels available in countries such as the USA.

There was also a new clutch (shared by the twins and the competition models), based on racing experience gleaned with the 7R. This clutch featured a steel-drum housing for the plates, whilst the guides for the driven plates were formed inside the drum by means of slats spot-welded in position.

The primary chaincase sealing had also received attention, and the long-established V-section rubber band ditched in favour of what AMC called a 'mushroom' section sealing band. This formed a gasket between each half of the chaincase, also fitting into the light-alloy retaining strap.

Developed as a result of their participation in dirt bike racing, AMC introduced their now-famous 'Jampot' rear shock absorbers for all touring models as well as the pure competition/racing bikes for the 1951 season. These units had a much fatter appearance than the outgoing 'Candlestick' shocks they replaced. It

1951 AJS Model 18S ('S' for Spring-Frame) with optional dual seat fitted. This was the first year of both the new AMC 'jampot' rear shocks and the alloy cylinder head.

was claimed that the new assemblies would provide slightly less fork-arm movement than had been the case before, but would 'definitely avoid all tendency towards "bottoming" when used either over really rough country (in competition) or poor surfaces when touring.'

The front suspension was entirely redesigned for 1951 (again benefiting from the works competition department) and would, it was claimed, provide 'complete freedom from oil leaks', the loading on the hydraulic seals of the forks having been considerably reduced. The fork drain plugs had also been redesigned.

All 1951 models benefited from an improved type of Lucas 6-volt dynamo. This instrument provided a sturdy ball-type bearing at the commuter end, and provided good access to the brushes for maintenance purposes. All models were also fitted with a new, flexible horn-mounting, since the older, rigid type had proved prone to breakage.

The 1952 Model Year

For 1952 all the single-cylinder models were given a new type of timing-side main bearing. This incorporated a large flange, permitting an extremely fine clearance to be employed without the risk of seizure. The compression

Teledraulic front forks went through several changes. These date from 1951, the first year to feature polished alloy sliders.

This beautifully restored early post-war, rigid-frame model is mainly to the original specification except for the later silencer. It was photographed in the mid-1980s with its owner, Terry Organ.

plate for the 500cc roadster engine was no longer fitted: instead, alteration to the compression ratio could be achieved by fitting a higher compression piston, now listed by the works.

A modification to the cylinder head was that the cast-iron pedestal which formerly retained the open ends of the duplex hairpin valve springs had been abandoned in favour of a steel channel in which the springs lay and automatically aligned themselves. Another advantage of the change was that the assembly was much easier to install. It was possible to do the installation by hand, though a small factory workshop tool had been made available.

A new, improved Burman gearbox, coded B52, superseded the CP unit fitted previously. In all its major details this new gearbox was similar to that developed for the 7R racing model. It was lighter and narrower, the shafts were more rigid, and sturdier engagement dogs were employed; it was also claimed

BURMAN & SONS LTD   WYCHALL LANE   BIRMINGHAM 30

The Birmingham-based Burman concern supplied AMC, and thus AJS, with gearboxes and clutches until superseded with AMC components from 1957 onwards.

that gear-change quality was improved. The sequence of foot-lever movements remained unchanged. The clutch-cable adjusting screw on the new gearbox was located on the top of the cover and faced forward and upward, improving adjustment considerably. Another transmission advance concerned the primary chaincase: an inspection plate was installed which provided access to the clutch thrust-rod adjustment and also to the clutch-spring adjusters, without having to remove the case itself.

To comply with British government restrictions on the use of plating (caused through shortages of materials), changes had to be made to the appearance of AJS (and Matchless) machines for 1952. Even so, chromium plating was retained for the exhaust system, handlebars, handlebar controls, gear levers and filler caps. Wheel rims were no longer chromium plated, but instead employed a matt anuminized finish developed by AMC and known as 'Argenizing'. Wheel rims were first Bonderized and then sprayed with the Argenizing solution. After baking for 1½ hours, a finish resembling smooth matt aluminium was produced. This finish was very thin, but also very hard – essential for withstanding tyre changing and the like.

Another change to the finish was that the light alloy fork slider bottom cover was now left unenamelled; instead it was buffed and polished. The steel front brake plate had been superseded by a light alloy component, which was also polished. Pushrod cover tubes, steering-crown dome nuts, fork nuts and the like were bright cadmium-plated.

A freshly designed handlebar headlug clamp (top yoke) permitted a much neater speedometer mounting. The handlebar clamp was retained by a trio of recessed Allen screws, for which a key was provided in the toolkit. This kit itself had been revised, and now included a box spanner for use when adjusting the clutch via the primary chaincase clutch inspection cover plate mentioned previously.

The wiring had also been tidied up,

1953 Model 16MS three-fifty with Burman B52 gearbox; this featured a smaller end cover than the CP box it replaced.

The 1953 Model Year

When the 1953 AJS models were announced in mid-September 1952, there were once again a number of changes, many involving the single-cylinder touring machines. The most notable of these was the fitting of dual seats as standard equipment (pioneered on the twin-cylinder bikes), and a new front brake of increased power.

Although a dual seat had been a standard fitment on the Model 20 Spring Twin from its launch in late 1948, the singles had had to make do with the traditional AMC sprung single saddle and a separate pillion pad. But now, a new dual seat was standardized on both the twins and the singles for the 1953 model year. This new seat was of the same length, but it was narrower and was equipped with blue piping (red on the Matchless). It was undoubtedly practical, and also endowed the single-cylinder family with a much more modern appearance. Certainly it was an improvement as regards comfort – at least for the pillion passenger!

The front brake had been redesigned, although there was in fact very little that was different in the appearance of the new brake as compared to the one it replaced. The changes and improvements came very much in the detail. To start with, the brake shoe plate had been moved anticlockwise through a number of degrees, whilst the cam lever had been turned relative to the camshaft, so that the lever projected forwards instead of backwards. The cable stop had been moved to match, and was now at the front of the fork leg. AMC claimed that the new position of the cam lever provided 'maximum mechanical efficiency on the leading shoe instead of the trailing shoe, and hence better stopping power.'

There was also a chromium-plated top piston ring – AMC's contention being that extensive testing (of various Model 18 engines) had shown that using the chromium-plated ring reduced bore wear by no less than a third. Other changes were a new primary chaincase sealing band, a new type Lucas rear

coloured cables being provided throughout, making for easier identification. The new wiring also included a positive-earth system. And to make life easier for the automatic voltage control regulator, this unit was now flexibly mounted on the rearward side of the battery carrier. There was a new Lucas headlamp too, featuring a square-pattern lens designed to provide a more powerful main beam, and an even spread of light when the dip filament was employed. Finally, the external appearance was altered by the introduction of an underslung 'Gondola'-type pilot lamp.

Roadster prices (including UK taxes) for the 1952 AJS single-cylinder range as at 13 September 1951 were as follows:

16M	348cc	rigid	£172 10s 0d
16MS	348cc	spring-frame	£194 4s 6d
18	497cc	rigid	£190 7s 10d
18S	497cc	spring-frame	£212 2s 3d

light, revised petrol piping, and modified front-fork top covers (these could now be re-positioned packing purposes when the head-lamp assembly was removed).

On the AJS (and Matchless) singles, the magneto weathershield had been shortened, and was now mounted to the magneto base-plate bolts. There was also an improved sweep for the high-tension lead from the magneto pick-up, a 90-degree type of pick-up having been achieved. The rear mudguard was a bolted up two-piece affair, rather than being hinged as one assembly, which made the task of painting at the Plumstead factory easier.

There were improvements to both the centre stand and rear lifting handle on the spring-frame models. The finish of all machines was in black stove enamel. Wheel rims were Argenized on bikes for the home market, but for 1953 the rims on export machines were once again to be chromium-plated, and plated fuel tanks were available at an additional cost.

The 1954 Range

When the 1954 AJS range was launched in September 1953, the most noticeable change was the full-width, light-alloy front hub. A new design of fuel tank had been standardized on all 500cc-class machines (both singles and

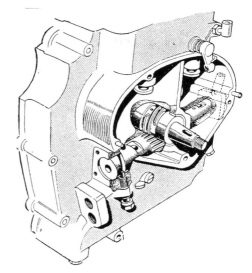

The AMC single gear-type oil pump; this ran from the mid-1940s up to 1963.

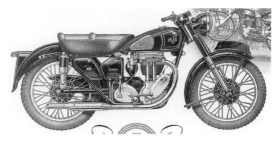

Brochure illustration for the 1953 Model 18S, with by now standard fitment dual seat for swinging-arm models.

Separate oil tank and toolbox assemblies were used until the end of 1955.

Nearside view of a 1953 Model 16MS showing leak-prone AMC pressed-steel chaincase, 'Jampot' rear shocks and single-sided brakes.

AJS advert from May 1953 showing first usage of the small circular tank badge. Fuel economy was impressive; the 16MS was capable of reaching 90mpg (3.14ltr/100km) under touring conditions.

twins), whilst the singles of that engine size now featured automatic ignition advance and rotating magnet magnetos. In addition, internal modifications had been carried out to all the single-cylinder engines to improve power output, durability and mechanical quietness.

Shortly before the 1954 range was officially announced, Phillip Walker, AMC's chief designer, was interviewed regarding these engine improvements. He was asked why the flywheel weight of the 1954 single-cylinder engines had been reduced by 3–4lb (about 1.5kg) a pair, since many people, including the interviewer Alan Baker, the technical editor of *The Motor Cycle*, considered this to be a 'retrograde step'? Phillip Walker's response was as follows:

> It is true that some loss in low-speed torque is an inevitable result of lightening the flywheels. But the modern single is extremely docile. My feeling is that, bearing in mind the rapid changes in speed of modern traffic, the need is for increased responsiveness. Engines have to be lively if they are to give the utmost rider-satisfaction.

And this, I feel, is more important than low-speed slogging. It is no secret, of course, that really heavy flywheels are desirable for trials engines where low-compression ratios, retarded ignition and ultra-low speeds are de rigueur.

A notable engine modification on the singles was a stiffened-up crankshaft assembly to cope with the increase in power output. The timing-side mainshaft diameter had been increased from $\frac{7}{8}$in (22mm) to $1\frac{1}{8}$in (28mm). In addition, the shaft was now a keyed parallel fit in the flywheel instead of a taper fit. This new layout provided a more rigid setup, and was also easier to manufacture.

As mentioned previously, the crank flywheels had been reduced in weight and thereby engine liveliness had been enhanced, without any serious impairment to low-speed smoothness. New cams and a larger inlet port and carb size were responsible for the considerably improved power output of both the 350 and 500cc engines. The 1954 carburettor sizes (1953 figures in brackets) were $1\frac{1}{16}$in (1in) for the 16M and 16MS and $1\frac{3}{32}$in ($1\frac{3}{32}$in) for the 18 and 18S.

The cams provided a slightly higher lift than the 1953 type, and the timing was also altered slightly. It was notable that the different characteristics of the two sizes of engine had required an appreciably different exhaust-valve timing, although identical exhaust cam profiles were employed on both. The increase in carburettor and inlet port sizes had not, as one might have expected, resulted in a loss of low-speed torque in favour of an increase of top-end power. If anything, both low- and high-speed figures had improved.

The five-hundred single-cylinder engine had proved rather sensitive to ignition advance. Therefore, in view of the reluctance or laziness of many owners to use a manual control to the best advantage, centrifugal automatic control had been adopted for the Model 18 series. Its incorporation had necessitated a bulge on the magneto drive cover, so there was now an easy means of identifying the engine size. Also, in light of racing experience, Phillip Walker and his development team had equipped the five-hundred single with a rotating-magnet magneto, a Lucas SR1 unit.

The search for mechanical quietness had been the driving force behind the provision of a positive oil feed to the valve-stem ends on both capacities of the AMC single. A longitudinal groove was machined in the rocker arm, and the oil, after lubricating the rocker spindle, emerged and ran along the groove, under centrifugal force, to the pad which bore on the valve stem.

On all models the bottom front engine-mounting bolt, which also connected the cradle to the front down-tube, had to be increased in size from 5⁄16in (8mm) to 3⁄8in (9mm) to improve rigidity.

The new AMC full-width alloy front hub certainly gave the 1954 AJS and Matchless singles and twins a 'neat, handsome and modern appearance' as one journalist of the era described the new assembly, as compared to the outgoing, single-sided brake. The new hub shell was a strong, ribbed, light-alloy die-casting that was easy on the eye and easy to clean. Straight spokes were a distinctive feature, and had the advantage of being stronger than the usual curved type; because of this a slight reduction in gauge size had proved possible. A flanged, 7in (178mm), cast-iron brake drum was shrunk into the hub shell and bolted through the flange. AMC also claimed that this brake was waterproof, the conical face on the outside of the spoke flange acting as a water-flinger device.

Also new was the cast-alloy shoe plate, of slightly domed exterior and equipped with a grease nipple for the cam spindle. The shoe's operating mechanism and anchorage were virtually identical to the 1953 components. A light-alloy circular plate closed the offside (right) of the hub shell. With the relaxation of nickel restrictions, chromium plating made a return for components such as wheel rims, the latter having enamelled wells with gold lining for AJS models (silver for Matchless).

There were several more minor changes for 1954. A domed clutch cover with eight screws replaced the previous small inspection cover, twin pilot lights were provided, along with flared mudguards, a new side-stand spring, flexible fuel lines, and cable lubricators. The voltage regulator was repositioned under-seat and a larger fuel tank (same as twins) was provided on the Model 18 series, the same as on the Model 20 twin.

Prices as at 10 September 1953 (including UK purchase tax) were:

348cc	16M	£166 16s 0d
348cc	16MS	£191 8s 0d
497cc	18	£184 4s 0d
497cc	18S	£208 16s 0d

1955 Range

According to *The Motor Cycle*, modifications to the 1955 range of AJS (and Matchless) bikes could be called 'evolutionary development'. It went on to say:

Numerous refinements are incorporated in the range of AJS and Matchless machines for 1955. As is widely known, the two makes have much in common and are famous for the mechanical quietness of their engines and excellence of machine finish. There are no new models, and the changes to existing models are with a view to increased component life, improved accessibility, enhanced appearance and better protection for the machine and rider from water flung up by the front wheel.

Automatic advance and retard, fitted a year earlier to the 500cc singles, was standardized on the 350cc range.

On all single-cylinder engines, two notable bottom-end changes had been made and it was claimed that these gave longer life and more silent running of the crankshaft main bearings. The flange of the timing-side bronze bush had been beefed up, whilst the diameter of the inboard drive-side ball-race bearing had been increased.

One or two cases of noisy operation of the automatic advance mechanism at low engine speeds had been reported. This problem was addressed by fitting plastic sleeves over the retard limit stops to cushion the return of the operating fingers.

There were several modifications that were common to all engines. Previously, air filters (an optional extra) had been of differing types on the singles and twins – one type had not been standardized throughout the range. The lubrication system had been tidied up on all models by repositioning the main feed and return pipes below the oil tank. Also, when viewed from the offside (right) of the motorcycle, on earlier models the pipes lay side by side; in the revised layout, one pipe was behind the other.

The full-width, light alloy front hub with straight spokes had been one of the outstanding innovations of the British motorcycle industry in 1954, and for the 1955 season the hub had been improved, giving it a more rounded appearance. This had been achieved by making the centre cooling fins deeper than the outer. And now the same type of hub was used on both wheels, the wheel being quickly detachable on rear-sprung machines (the rigid-frame 16M and 18 were still being offered).

Yet another important innovation for 1955 was the introduction of the brand new Amal Monobloc carburettor. Developed over a two-year period, the new instrument had three main priorities: improved performance; economic manufacture; and easier to tune and maintain. In retrospect, it has to be said that it achieved all three aims.

The most striking external difference between the Monobloc and the old-type Amal carburettor it replaced was that the float chamber was no longer a separate unit; a single, very neat die-casting in Mazak zinc-based alloy provided both mixing and float chambers. The throttle slide featured a full skirt, and a separate, detachable pilot jet was

utilized. The float needle, operated by hinged float, was a nylon moulding. The Monobloc carburettor also featured two-way compensation to provide a richer mixture for accelerating and a weaker cruising setting. This compensation was achieved by the simple means of a bleed hole near the base of the needle jet. There were three basic Monobloc types: 375, 376 and 389.

A year earlier (as already recorded) a 3¾gal (19ltr) fuel tank was standardized on 500cc roadsters (twins and singles); for the 1955 model year this tank was also fitted on the 350cc models. A combined mounting for the oil tank and battery carrier had been designed which was both tidier and stronger than the 1954 type. The frame seat tube had also been modified and provided with a malleable casting, so a hole could be provided to take the air filter hose.

Other changes for 1955 singles included larger diameter front forks, modified 'Jampot' rear shock absorbers, pressed steel lugs for

For 1955 the roadster singles were offered with full-width alloy brake hubs front and rear – after having introduced a full-width alloy front hub (of different design) for the 1954 season. 1955 also marked the end of the line for the rigid frame (shown here); this was phased out at the end of that year's production.

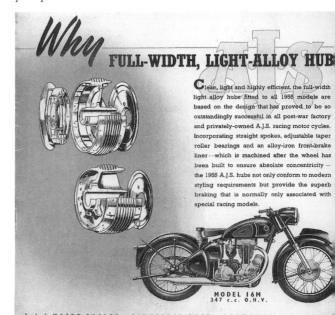

Why **FULL-WIDTH, LIGHT-ALLOY HUB**

Clean, light and highly efficient, the full-width light alloy hubs fitted to all 1955 models are based on the design that has proved to be so outstandingly successful in all post-war factory and privately-owned A.J.S. racing motor cycles. Incorporating straight spokes, adjustable taper roller bearings and an alloy-iron front-brake liner—which is machined after the wheel has been built to ensure absolute concentricity— the 1955 A.J.S. hubs not only conform to modern styling requirements but provide the superb braking that is normally only associated with special racing models.

MODEL 16M
347 c.c. O.H.V.

A·J·S MOTOR CYCLES · PLUMSTEAD ROAD · LONDON, S.E.18 · ENG

pillion passengers, a deeper headlamp shell carrying the speedometer, a deeper chain-guard, a rear reflector, a new front mudguard without front stay; while rigid-frame models now had barrel saddle springs.

A New Frame for 1956

There was a new frame for all the touring models, both singles and twins, for the 1956 model year. In this design the seat tube, instead of running diagonally from under the seat to the engine and gearbox plates, now ran vertically at the rear of the gearbox. Lateral rigidity had been improved compared to the earlier spring frames by housing the swinging-arm pivot in a substantial, malleable-iron lug clamped between the cradle tubes and brazed to the lower end of the seat tube. Conventional brazed and bolt-up construction was employed, and considerable attention had been applied to make the frame more suitable for sidecar work.

At the same time the end of the line had arrived for the old rigid frame, single-cylinder models. *The Motor Cycle*, dated 8 September 1955, commented:

> That no solid-frame machines are to be produced by the Plumstead concern in the coming year is hardly surprising in view of current trends. Rear springing is gaining popularity in trials just as quickly as it did for sidecar work. And, of course, production and servicing efficiency can be improved as the number of different models in a given range are decreased.

For 1956, the touring singles were given higher compression ratios. That of the 16MS three-fifty went up from 6.5 to 7.5:1, whilst the 18S was increased from 6.3 to 7.3:1. To prevent the possibility of the exhaust valve guide on the singles moving when hot, circlip location had been increased earlier in 1955. Another change was the inclusion of a magnetic sump oil filter, shared with the twins.

The introduction of the new frame for both the single and twin roadsters brought with it the integration of the oil-tank and toolbox assemblies. These now filled much of the area to the rear of the carburettor to the front of the rear shock absorbers, on both sides of the motorcycle. At the same time the capacity of the oil tanks had risen from 4 to 5½pt (1½ to 2½ltr). The two assemblies were bridged at the front by a detachable steel pressing. If the optional air filter was fitted it was concealed behind this cover. The 'toolbox' housed the 6-volt battery at its forward end. The battery was secured by a quick-release rubber strap, instead of the conventional British-style metal strap. At the upper right of the toolbox was the automatic voltage control unit, mounted in sponge rubber.

Other changes for 1956 were a combined horn and dipswitch, and a revised, longer dual seat, with the horn under the seat. In addition, the front brake cam lever was located above the wheel spindle, and a cover was provided over the gearbox with the primary chain adjuster underneath. Also new were a rear brake adjuster at the front end of the brake rod, an aluminium rear-brake backplate, and the cables group routed via the fork crown.

Details of the 1956 AJS prices for the touring singles (including UK purchase tax), published on 15 September 1955 were as follows:

| 348cc | 16MS | £211 8s 5d |
| 497cc | 18S | £223 16s 5d |

Changes for 1957

Two notable changes occurred for the 1957 season, and were announced in late September 1956. These were the introduction of the newly released AMC-made gearbox (*see* Chapter 8), and the replacement of the company's own 'Jampot' rear shock absorbers by ones of Girling manufacture. It was the first time since rear springing had been introduced in the 1949 programme that

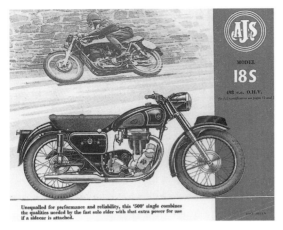

Unequalled for performance and reliability, this '500' single combines the qualities needed by the fast solo rider with that extra power for use if a sidecar is attached.

1957 Model 18S factory brochure. The singles now sported a deeper headlamp shell incorporating speedo (1955), larger oil tank and toolbox assemblies (1955), new front mudguard (1955), auto advance with bulge in timing cover (1955), new frame (1956), horn under seat (1956), increased compression ratio (1956), AMC gearbox (1957) and Girling rear shocks (1957).

was a smaller dome in the primary chaincase outer cover.

A new inlet cam was given to the singles, in a quest for more speed and acceleration; otherwise the engines of both the three-fifty and five-hundred single remained unchanged. The only other components to be altered were the oil tank and toolbox lid, which both received a series of three small ribs either side of the AJS logo in the centre of each, plus push-on oil pipe lines. In addition, there were some minor cosmetic alterations, mainly aimed at tidying things up, and improving the five-pin drive of the quickly detachable rear wheel on the touring models.

Finally, a mid-season alteration to the Teledraulic front-fork damping was continued for 1957. On both shock and recoil movements the hydraulic action was more progressive in action, resulting in a decrease in front-end pitching.

Prices had again risen, and on 27 September 1956 were as follows (including UK purchase tax):

348cc	16MS	£211 8s 5d
497cc	18S	£223 16s 5d

proprietary shocks were employed in place of AMC-manufactured assemblies. The AMC gearbox also saw the adoption of a Norton-type clutch with shock absorber, so there was no engine shock absorber. Another change

AJS 1957 price list for the eight-model range including roadster singles and twins, off-road bikes and the 7R racer, issued in October 1956.

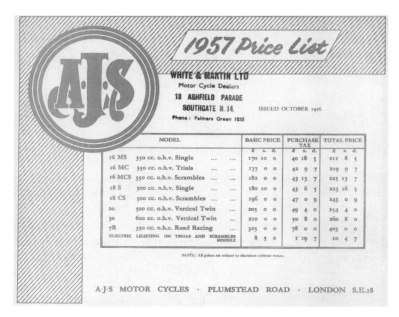

1957 Price List

WHITE & MARTIN LTD
Motor Cycle Dealers
18 ASHFIELD PARADE
SOUTHGATE N. 14.   ISSUED OCTOBER 1956
Phone : Palmers Green 1035

MODEL				BASIC PRICE			PURCHASE TAX			TOTAL PRICE		
				£	s.	d.	£	s.	d.	£	s.	d.
16 MS	350 cc. o.h.v. Single	...	...	170	10	0	40	18	5	211	8	5
16 MC	350 cc. o.h.v. Trials	...	...	177	0	0	42	9	7	219	9	7
16 MCS	350 cc. o.h.v. Scrambles	...	...	182	0	0	43	13	7	225	13	7
18 S	500 cc. o.h.v. Single	...	...	180	10	0	43	6	5	223	16	5
18 CS	500 cc. o.h.v. Scrambles	...	...	196	0	0	47	0	9	243	0	9
20	500 cc. o.h.v. Vertical Twin	...	...	205	0	0	49	4	0	254	4	0
30	600 cc. o.h.v. Vertical Twin	...	...	210	0	0	50	8	0	260	8	0
7R	350 cc. o.h.c. Road Racing	...	...	325	0	0	78	0	0	403	0	0
ELECTRIC LIGHTING ON TRIALS AND SCRAMBLES MODELS				8	5	0	1	19	7	10	4	7

NOTE: All prices are subject to alteration without notice.

A·J·S MOTOR CYCLES · PLUMSTEAD ROAD · LONDON S.E.18

From Magneto to Coil for 1958

The external appearance of the AJS (and Matchless) heavyweight single-cylinder engines was radically changed for the 1958 season, by the adoption of AC generator and coil ignition in place of the long-running dynamo and magneto set-up. Not only this, but the familiar pressed steel (and leak-prone!) primary chaincase had at last been axed in favour of a brand new, cast-aluminium assembly; this was also employed to provide a rigid mounting for the stator of the crankshaft-driven alternator. Because there was no longer a magneto or dynamo, both sides of the engine had a considerably different look.

Located on an extension of the offside (left) end of the crankshaft, the alternator used on the roadster singles was the Lucas RM15. This was similar to the already well-known RM13 model in featuring a rotor of 2¾in (70mm) diameter, but it was approximately ¼in (6mm) wider. Three ¼in BSF studs and nuts held the stator in place in the dome of the chaincase outer half. Since the running clearance between rotor and stator was only 0.015in (½mm), clearance was needed to ensure co-axiality of the two components. Firstly, a spigot formed on the rear of the chaincase inner section registered in a hole bored in the crankcase nearside (left) co-axial with the main bearing housing. Secondly, two dowels

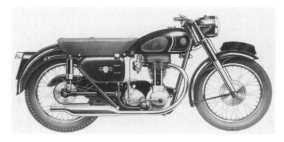

1958 16MS three-fifty single had the new-for-year AC generator, coil ignition and much improved aluminium primary chaincase. The much criticized small headlamp-mounted pilot lights were deleted.

in the chaincase inner section ensured accurate location of the outer half. Both halves of the chaincase were clamped to the crankcase by a stud screwed into a boss just behind the main bearing housing. One of these dowels (⅜in/9mm diameter) was hollow and fitted over the stud; the other dowel (5⁄16in/8mm) diameter) was pressed into the nearmost portion of the joint face.

The new aluminium primary chaincase was highly polished, the two halves held together by fourteen screws. Two flush-fitting aluminium plugs in the outer half of the case incorporated milled slots to help removal and replacement. One of the plugs was for checking primary chain tension, and filling the case with oil to the correct level; the other provided access to the clutch adjustment screw in the centre of the pressure plate.

In place of the outgoing timing cover (which embodied the inner portion of the magneto chaincase) there was a deep, circular, light-alloy casting which contained the automatic advance and retard, plus the contact breaker assembly. This housing was secured to the crankcase by five screws, and the unit was driven by an extension of the inlet camshaft which was tapered and threaded to suit. Access to the contact breaker for adjustment involved removal of only two screws and an aluminium cover. The single circular ignition coil was mounted under the top frame tube, just aft of the steering head.

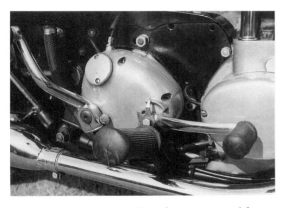

Introduced for 1957, the AMC gearbox was improved for 1958 with a lighter, more positive change.

The cylinder finning of the 350cc (Model 14MS) cylinder barrel had been increased, and in addition, on both engine sizes, the space previously occupied between the front engine plates by the magneto had been superseded by a channel-section member. In absence of a dynamo the rear engine plates were now solid and were bridged by a modified clip-on cover which concealed the gearbox draw-bolt.

The electrical cables from the stator passed through a synthetic rubber grommet situated in the inner half of the chaincase, and were led over the gearbox (where they were hidden by the engine-plate cover) and up behind the bulkhead that bridged the front of the oil tank (on the offside) and the toolbox (on the near-side). A four-way snap fastener at the point meant that the cables could be disconnected as required.

The rectifier was placed beneath the seat nose, just aft of the battery and inboard of the tool compartment. It was attached by a single bolt only, making replacement simple. The

procedure was, first, to take off the dual seat by removing its two rear securing bolts and loosening the nuts holding the forked ears to the front. Then the leads were disconnected from the rectifier, a nut was undone inside the toolbox, and the rectifier lifted away. There was also more room in the toolbox itself, as the voltage control unit was no longer needed.

As with all Lucas AC sets at the time, an emergency-start facility was provided whereby the majority of the generator output was directed to the ignition coil. This meant that the engine could be kickstarted even if the battery had gone flat. The generator output balanced the full lamp load at an engine speed of 1,400rpm, this being equivalent to 22mph (35km/h) in top gear on the 500cc Model 18S and 18mph (29km/h) on the 350cc Model 16MS. A lighting modification common to all the touring models (both singles and twins) was a change from two separate pilot lights to the more conventional arrangement of one small bulb in the reflector.

Various other changes were made to the AJS models that year: for instance, the 350's frame design was brought into line with that of the 500 by unification of the attachment lugs for the subframe and the rear of the fuel tank. Also the gearchange of the AMC gearbox, introduced the previous year, was lightened by means of a lower-rate selector spring; this modification also applied to the twin-cylinder road bikes and competition machines. The Girling rear shocks were short-ened on both the singles and the twins, a change which made the seat height lower; another alteration was that chromium plating was now used for the entire wheel rims (the middles were now chromed as well as the sides).

Once again prices had risen. The new price list, published on 12 September 1957, was as follows:

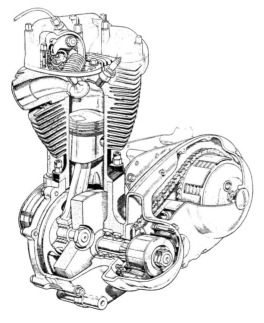

The 1958 and onwards AJS Heavyweight single cylinder engine with alternator electrics and coil ignition, plus alloy chaincase.

348cc	16MS	£233 18s 2d
497cc	18S	£247 12s 7d

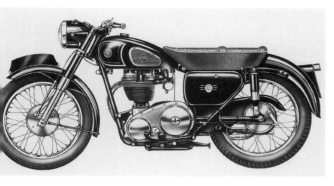

Nearside of the 1958 Model 16MS (the five-hundred 18S was identical except engine capacity). This view shows the new primary chaincase.

Modified Girling rear shocks gave a lower ride height and conventional bottom fixing in place of the previous clevis fitment.

The 1958 16MS	
Engine	Air-cooled ohv single with vertical cylinder; alloy head and iron barrel; vertically split aluminium crankcases; fully enclosed valve gear; hairpin valve springs; built-up crankshaft; roller bearing big-end; gear-driven cams
Bore	69mm
Stroke	93mm
Displacement	348cc
Compression ratio	7.5:1
Lubrication	Dry sump
Ignition	Battery/coil 6 volt; alternator
Carburettor	Amal Monobloc 376 1¹⁄₁₆in
Primary drive	Chain
Final drive	Chain
Gearbox	4-speed, foot-change, AMC
Frame	Two-part with single front down-tube
Front suspension	AMC Teledraulic forks
Rear suspension	Swinging arm with twin Girling shock absorbers
Front brake	7in, SLS, full-width
Rear brake	7in, SLS, full-width
Tyres	3.25 × 19 front, 3.50 × 19 rear
Wheelbase	55.2in (1,402mm)
Ground clearance	5.5in (140mm)
Seat height	31in (787mm)
Fuel tank capacity	3.76gal (17.1ltr)
Dry weight	380lb (172kg)
Maximum power	19bhp @ 5,750rpm
Top speed	74mph (119km/h)

A Recess in Development

Very little development took place on the Heavyweight roadster singles for some two years between the end of 1957 and the end of 1959. The only change was that deeper section mudguards were introduced (from the 1959 season). Why was this? Well, the answer comes from other models in the AJS (and Matchless) ranges; the dirt bikes, the twin-cylinder series, the new G50 road racer and most of all the new 'Lightweight' family of two-fifty and three-fifty singles. These latter bikes are fully described in Chapter 11. AMC believed that these new lightweights would eventually replace the traditional heavy-weights. However, this never really happened, and in fact the new three-fifty was destined to have a relatively short career, and the Model 16MS outlived it by several years!

There is no doubt whatsoever that the

parent company AMC firmly believed its heavyweight singles were on the way out. For example at the London Earls Court Show in November 1958 hardly a mention was made of any of the Heavyweight singles, the AJS (and Matchless) stands being dominated by other models in their respective ranges.

Another view of 1959 Model 16MS showing the aluminium primary chaincase to advantage.

1959 AJS Model 16MS with virtually no change from previous year except new, deeper section mudguards.

Back in Favour for 1960

However, when the 1960 model range was launched in autumn 1959, the heavyweight bikes appeared to be back in favour, for there were several changes, the most major being a brand new frame for both the Heavyweight singles and the twin-cylinder AJS and Matchless machines.

Of full cradle layout, this featured duplex front down-tubes which ran back underneath the engine and gearbox. A single 1½in (38mm) diameter, 12-gauge top tube and a vertical seat tube completed the main frame, which was manufactured on the time-honoured AJS principle of malleable-iron lugs brazed in position; *The Motor Cycle* described as 'massive indeed' the cast lugs which formed the steering-head and swinging-arm pivot housing. The rear subframe was bolted to lugs just below the rear of the gearbox and the very front of the dual seat. AMC sources said that the new frames increased rigidity, and an increase in the front fork trail provided improved steering and handling abilities. Another change was that the three-point fuel-tank mounting, previously a feature of the two-fifty Model 14, was now a feature of the new frame, with two mountings at the front and a single one at the rear.

Another change for the 1960 model year was that the gearbox internal ratios had been

The last of the single downtube 18S models, circa 1959, with cost-option chrome tank panels.

A 1960 Model 18S five-hundred on test with Motor Cycling *that year. This photograph comes from the Morton's archives.*

A duplex frame arrived for 1960, together with new dual seat and closer gearbox ratios; the oil pump was strengthened in 1961, together with minor cosmetic changes. For 1962 there was a new 350 (shown). Still coded 16, this featured a shorter stroke engine (74 × 81mm) and pushrod tunnels integral with the cylinder barrel. Additionally it was given the name Sceptre.

revised to provide a more even spacing, reducing the gap between third and top. Therefore bottom was now slightly higher at 2.56:1 (previously 2.67), second remained unchanged at 1.77, and third was increased from 1.33:1 to 1.22:1.

The cylinder head of the 500 single had been redesigned. The combustion chamber shape was now hemispherical, with a new flat-top piston, the latter featuring small recesses for the valves; the compression ratio remained unchanged at 7.3:1. The inlet tract, now best described as an arc between the inlet valve and the carburettor, had been designed to promote the swirl of gases – another bonus being that the valve stem and protruding portion of the valve guide were now at one side of the tract, where AMC claimed 'they offer less restriction to gas flow'. In parallel with the new combustion chamber shape and inlet port was a valve-included angle reduced to 39 degrees. The felt oil filter fitted previously had been replaced by one featuring wire gauze of two different mesh sizes.

Other changes included a new Lucas 12-amp hour battery of more compact design, a smaller headlamp shell, still housing the speedometer, and a two-level dual seat.

A More Conservative Approach for 1961

With such major alterations the previous year (duplex frames and new cylinder heads) the 1961 changes were far more conservative, with the emphasis on detail improvements throughout the range. All single-cylinder models received a modification intended to strengthen the drive to the rotary reciprocating oil pump. Both the crankshaft worm and the oil-pump pinion featured a redesigned tooth form, thus improving their engagement.

With the introduction of the Lightweight Model 8 three-fifty, AMC bosses had expected that sales of the old Heavyweight Model 16 would decrease, and that it could be

'pensioned off'. But they were to receive a nasty shock, because in truth the newcomer proved hard to sell. Far from sales falling off, demand for the Model 16 (and its Matchless brother the G3LS) actually increased during 1960, which meant that production had to be raised for 1961.

The detail changes included an external circlip at the upper end of the valve guide for the 497cc Model 18 engine, to ensure positive guide location when the engine was really warm and working hard. Cosmetically, there were colour changes to the mudguards, tank badges and colours. The deeply valanced front and rear mudguards had been shortened, and tyre clearance at the leading edge of the front assembly had also been increased. AMC had seen fit to introduce some fresh colour schemes. For the AJS models birch grey replaced blue as the predominant colour for two-tone finishes; where chromium-plated fuel-tank panels were fitted, the tank was grey with blue panel beading. In practice the traditional black finish was often chosen, the chrome tank panels brightening this up considerably.

As for prices, at 25 August 1960 (when the 1961 range was announced) the Model 16MS was listed at £236 8s 6d and the Model 18S at £249 13s 10d, both including UK taxes. Chromium-plated fuel-tank panels cost an additional £2 8s 10d.

In retrospect the last few months of 1960 were to be a period which AMC were not to encounter again. The previous year (1959), sales to British customers had peaked. There were over 400 dealers throughout the British Isles selling AJS motorcycles, which meant representation in virtually every major city or town. And of course, the Japanese had not yet invaded Europe, except on the GP race circuit. Much the same could be said of the export market, where British bikes, including AJS, were still in demand. Unfortunately all this was about to change – and change drastically. Many of these same dealers who were selling AJS in 1959/1960, were over the next few years to jump ship, and very soon be stocking their showrooms with Hondas, Suzukis and Yamahas. In fact AMC, before its fall from grace in 1966, had become the British importer for Suzuki! And so in little more than half a decade, AMC was to lose its position as a market leader, and descend into financial meltdown. Of course it was much the same for the rest of the once great British motorcycle industry; a sad picture indeed.

Just two weeks prior to the launch of the 1962 model range, sales director Jock West resigned (*see* Chapter 8) at the end of August 1961.

A Short-Stroke 350 for 1962

The big news regarding the Heavyweight singles when the 1962 AJS and Matchless ranges were announced in mid-September 1961 was a short-stroke 350 engine. *The Motor Cycle* described its arrival by saying:

> You want a big, lively roadster with relatively low insurance rates of a three-fifty? Then for you AMC have extensively redesigned the single-cylinder engine of the Matchless G3 and AJS 16. As a result, maximum power is boosted from some 19 to 23bhp at 6,200rpm without sacrifice of tractability, and the engine is said to give pleasant top-gear surge when the twistgrip is tweaked at around 55 to 60mph [88 to 96km/h]. And since the engine is now a shade shorter, with the pushrod tunnels cast in the cylinder barrel and head, it has a cobby appearance, giving the models a more up-to-the-minute air.

Both the bore and stroke had been revised and were now 74×81mm instead of the former 69×93mm, and advantage had been taken of the increased bore size to provide bigger valve sizes. The choke diameter of the Amal Monobloc carburettor had also been stepped up, from $1\frac{1}{16}$in (26mm) to $1\frac{1}{8}$in (28 mm), whilst the exhaust pipe diameter had been increased by $\frac{1}{8}$in to $1\frac{5}{8}$in (40mm). The light alloy head had been modified by slightly reducing its included valve angle, compression ratio having been increased from 7.5 to 8.5:1.

From now on, with the exception of the road racers (AJS 7R and Matchless G50), every model in the two ranges was given a name as well as a catalogue code number. The AJS Model 16 and Matchless G3 became, respectively, the Sceptre and Mercury. In addition, there was now a 'hot' version of each, the Sceptre Sports (Model 16S) and Mercury Sports (G3S), the two latter machines featuring dropped handlebars and bright chromium finish to the mudguards and final-drive chainguard. But it should be noted that the Sports versions did not have any increase in performance . . . and as history now records, the names never became popular and were rarely referred to by owners.

The Five-Hundred Single

The 497cc single (in which the bore and stroke remained unchanged) became the AJS Model 18 Statesman and Matchless G80 Major. But unlike their smaller-engined brothers, there were no sporting variants of the large-engined bikes. There was, however, a whole list of what are best described as minor modifications. These included a revised oil-tank breather tower, a roll-on centre stand, and a stronger kickstart spring. The battery reverted to former dimensions, with enclosure box enlarged to suit and a new horn (smaller, lighter and louder) was provided. An ignition key took the place of the knob switch. A larger fuel tank, larger tank badges of chrome-plated zinc-alloy, and new soft-rubber tank mountings, including a sponge rubber pad at the rear were also featured.

Testing the Model 18 Statesman

A comprehensive three-page road test of the Model 18 Statesman was published in *The Motor Cycle* dated 1 March 1962.

Discretion, dignity and an ability to cope with hard work without showing signs of stress – these are some of the essential attributes of a Statesman . . . A robust, good-looking roadster single with an ancestry reaching back to well before the last war, it can claim in the motorcycle sense, to embody all these qualities. The main source of the Statesman's appeal is that it offers a pleasing compromise between the modern and traditional in matters of styling.

Tester Peter Fraser seemed impressed:

Riding the AJS the first few miles reminded one, at a time when vertical twins are fashionable, of the particular charm of the lusty, tractable single. With a maximum in the eighties, the Model 18 is certainly no sluggard. In fact the machine was capable of sustaining 70–75mph [113–121km/h] indefinitely. In that range the engine was working well within its limits. Hills or headwinds on main roads could be tackled comfortably, the engine pulling hard in top gear. If the occasion demanded that the speed be maintained, a quick change into third was the drill. This ratio (6.13 to 1) proved invaluable when a high average was required, especially on hilly, winding roads. Speedy overtaking could be achieved in third – which provided good acceleration between 30 and 70mph [48 to 113km/h]. At the lower end of the scale the engine would slog like a side-valve. The combination of good flywheel effect, a moderate (7.3 to 1) compression ratio and an efficient auto–advance control made a major contribution to this impression.

As for handling and roadholding abilities, Peter Fraser described the Statesman's road manner as follows:

Handling inspired confidence at all times. The machine could be ridden to a standstill in heavy traffic, feet-up without undue effort. Steering lock was felt to be rather limited for a model of this nature. The lack of it made man-handling in and out of limited garaging space, a twice-daily task for ride-to-work enthusiasts, more awkward than was thought desirable. Centre and prop stands are provided. Both were easily operated and gave safe support. On the open road the Statesman could be ridden to the limit of its performance without betraying any tendency to deviate from the chosen line. Zestful cornering was encouraged by the way in which the model could, with little effort, be banked from side to side through bends . . . As the miles on a journey mount up so the suitability or otherwise, of the riding position makes itself known. In this respect the Statesman earned high marks. If any criticism is due, it is that the footrests could with benefit be positioned an inch or so further to the rear, to relieve the rider's arms from some strain when cruising for long periods in the seventies. Controls fell readily to hand, or foot, as the case was. The dual seat proved very comfortable and generous enough dimensionally to accommodate a passenger without cramping.

As the test was carried out in the winter, Fraser commented:

Starting a big single when overnight temperatures are around freezing point calls for a certain amount of technique. On the Model 18 the drill was to flood the carburettor slightly, close the handlebar-mounted air lever and, with the exhaust-valve lifter in operation, give a long, swinging kick, releasing the lifter when the kick-starter pedal was at the bottom of its travel. In practice the method advised by the makers of easing the engine over compression, releasing the valve lifter and then kicking did not spin the engine sufficiently to start in severe conditions. It was quite effective enough, though, as soon as the engine was warm.

The transmission was described as follows:

> Clutch operation was progressive, but on the heavy side. Hard usage during the test caused no loss of adjustment. Gear changes in both directions were both positive and silent. Bottom-gear engagement with the engine idling caused, at worst, no more than a slight click (personal experience has shown me that the clutch needs freeing when starting from cold to avoid making somewhat louder noises than a 'click'), neutral could be selected without difficulty.

During the March 1962 test a maximum speed of 87mph (140km/h) was achieved; however, it should be noted that these figures were obtained with a 'strong following wind'. Minimum non-snatch speed in top gear was 20mph (32km/h). Peter Fraser concluded:

> The Statesman is finished in black relieved by touches of chromium plating. The absence of the familiar AJS gold lining on the fuel tank will be regretted by many enthusiasts. But for those who prefer colour, the model is available in blue with white mudguards. To sum up, then, the Statesman is a good-looking, well-mannered mount, equally suitable for the daily round or for long week-end runs.

The 1963 AJS Range

Yet more development work had been carried out by the AMC engineering team during the spring and summer of 1962, so that when the 1963 AJS range made its bow that autumn, there were more changes. In addition, the poor-selling 'sports' three-fifty had been axed only months after its introduction, although its chrome-plated mudguards remained an option.

One of the alterations for 1963 was a new front brake hub with fewer (five) fins and wider brake shoes. Another change was a new subframe and swinging arm; there were now stock Girling units without the traditional AMC clevis pins, a restyled and more rounded oil tank and matching toolbox. The wheels had become narrower, with 18in wheels replacing the former 19in assemblies. In adition, there were a narrower dual seat, D–section mudguards, direct-action stop-light switch, a new cigar-shaped silencer without the usual AMC tail-pipe, and a revised fuel tank with knee grips in the recesses. Yet another modification was a switch from taper roller to ball races for the wheel bearings. The seat height was also reduced, thanks in the main to the reduction in wheel size.

The 'Norton Influence'

At the very end of 1962, AMC closed the Norton factory at Bracebridge Street, Birmingham and moved everything south to Plumstead; so now AJS, Matchless and Norton were to be built under one roof, so to speak. By the latter part of the following year the first sign emerged of what was to be labelled the 'Norton influence' with AJS and Matchless models being equipped with Norton Roadholder forks and full–width alloy hubs, 8in (203mm) at the front, and AMC duplex frame modified to suit.

Another major change for the 1964 model year saw the remaining touring singles (plus the trials three-fifty) receive engines based around the dirt-racing scrambles power unit. So in both the three-fifty and the five-hundred assemblies the stroke was set at 85.5mm, bore sized being 72 and 86mm respectively. On the smaller engine the compression ratio was 9:1; on the five-hundred, 7.3:1. Pushrod tunnels were integral with the cylinder, and all engines featured head sleeve nuts screwed to extended crankcase studs.

Internally there was a substantial steel connecting-rod, single row, aluminium-caged roller big-end (similar in design to the G50 road racer), steel flywheels, and a timing-side roller plus plain bronze bush to replace the old flanged main bearing.

Another Norton component, the gear-oil

pump, replaced the long-running AMC reciprocating plunger type; this was driven in typical Norton fashion by a worm nut which also held the timing pinion in place. The AJS lubricating system was modified with a direct feed into the end of the crankshaft to the sides of the big-end rollers, whilst the rocker lubrication was now taken from the scavenge line and so was less intrusive.

The 1964 Model 16	
Engine	Air-cooled ohv single with vertical cylinder; alloy head; iron barrel; vertically split aluminium crankcases; fully enclosed valve gear; hairpin valve springs; built-up crankshaft; roller-bearing big-end; gear-driven cams; integral pushrod tunnels in barrel
Bore	72mm
Stroke	85.5mm
Displacement	348cc
Compression ratio	9:1
Lubrication	Dry sump; Norton gear-oil pump
Ignition	Battery/coil 6-volt; alternator
Carburettor	Amal Monobloc 389 1⅛in
Primary drive	Chain
Final drive	Chain
Gearbox	4-speed, AMC, foot-change
Frame	Duplex, full-cradle
Front suspension	Norton Roadholder forks
Rear suspension	Swinging arm with twin Girling shock absorbers
Front brake	8in, SLS, Norton full-width
Rear brake	7in, SLS, Norton full-width
Tyres	3.25 × 18 front and rear
Wheelbase	55in (1,397mm)
Ground clearance	6in (152mm)
Seat height	30in (762mm)
Fuel tank capacity	4gal (18ltr)
Dry weight	382lb (173kg)
Maximum power	18bhp @ 5,750rpm
Top speed	78mph (125km/h)

The 1964 Model 18	
Engine	Air-cooled ohv single with vertical cylinder; alloy head; iron barrel; vertically split aluminium crankcases; fully enclosed valve gear; hairpin valve springs; built-up crankshaft; roller-bearing big-end; gear-driven cams; integral pushrod tunnels in barrel
Bore	86mm
Stroke	85.5mm
Displacement	497cc
Compression ratio	7.3:1
Lubrication	Dry sump; Norton gear-oil pump
Ignition	Battery/coil 6-volt; alternator
Carburettor	Amal Monobloc 389 1⅛in
Primary drive	Chain
Final drive	Chain
Gearbox	4-speed, AMC, foot-change
Frame	Duplex, full cradle
Front suspension	Norton Roadholder forks
Rear suspension	Swinging arm with twin Girling shock absorbers
Front brake	8in, SLS, Norton full-width
Rear brake	7in, SLS Norton full-width
Tyres	3.50 × 18 front and rear
Wheelbase	55in (1,397mm)
Ground clearance	6in (152mm)
Seat height	30in (762mm)
Fuel tank capacity	4gal (18ltr)
Dry weight	394lb (179kg)
Maximum power	28bhp @ 5,600rpm
Top speed	84mph (135km/h)

Last in the Line

From then on, development of the AMC Heavyweight single-cylinder line effectively came to an end, even though production was to continue for another three years or so. Why? Well, by now the factory's management were firmly locked into a downward spiral of what, in today's commercial world, would be described as 'downsizing', but unfortunately this only created more problems than it solved, since lower production meant fewer sales and, of course, less revenue. And in contrast to this situation, from what had been a highly profitable organization at the end of the 1950s, by the end of 1963 AMC was running at a loss.

From then on, things simply got worse as each year unfolded. This caused the management to seek ever more intensive ways of cost-cutting, and also some truly feeble and unpopular ways of attempting to market their bikes. Typical was the move to offer the AJS 16 and 18 models with Norton badges screwed to their tank sides! This was not well received, in fact it alienated all three sets of enthusiasts, whether AJS, Matchless or Norton owners, and acts as proof of just how out of touch and desperate the decision makers at Plumstead became.

These attempts at standardization had, unfortunately, robbed the big singles of their identity, and AJS owners, although they had for many years accepted badge-engineering of their brand and Matchless, had still viewed an AJS as just that. But with Norton forks, wheel hubs, the 'cigar'-shaped silencer and other unloved introductions, the bikes had finally lost their appeal to the very customers who had continued to buy the Heavyweight singles down through the years.

During 1966, Associated Motor Cycles' financial position worsened (*see* Chapter 8), and production of the touring singles came to an end. The Official Receiver was called in, and eventually, in September 1966, Manganese Bronze took over the remains of the AMC empire, registering the new concern as Norton-Matchless. The new range of bikes comprised the twin-cylinder models and only one single, the Matchless G85CS scrambler. As for AJS, this was eventually to be reborn as the Stormer motocrosser and Inchley-inspired road racer (*see* Chapters 13 and 14). However, even then these new machines were powered by two-stroke, rather than four-stroke engines. So as far as the traditional Heavyweight AJS singles were concerned, 1966 marked the end of the road.

But for many, the author included, the Model 16 and Model 18 (and their Matchless equivalents, the G3 and G80) were classical examples of British single cylinder motorcycles at their very best, offering a robustness and simplicity that few others could match, combined with economy, safe handling and braking, plus a level of quality which not only gave them long life, but endeared them to generations of riders down through the years.

5   Porcupine

It's a strange fact that AJS's most glamorous post-Second World War racing motorcycle was originally the brainchild of the man largely responsible for the development of the works Norton singles, Joe Craig.

Joe Craig

Just prior to the outbreak of war, Ulsterman Craig had quit the famous Bracebridge Street, Norton marque, first going to BSA (also in Birmingham) and thence to AMC in Plumstead, south-east London. And so it was that Joe Craig spent the war years with AJS and Matchless. The reason behind Craig's move? Well, he had become extremely annoyed with Norton's policy during 1939, of building bikes for the military, rather than continuing to go racing. It must be said that managing director Gilbert Smith's decision was sound financially, even though it allowed the likes of BMW, Gilera and AJS to steal Norton's thunder on the race circuits of Europe during that final fateful summer before the conflict arrived.

So as a protest Craig upped and left. When he finally arrived at AMC, the company had already developed the extremely fast but somewhat fragile water-cooled V4, on which Walter Rusk had become the first man to lap the Clady circuit, the scene of the Ulster Grand Prix, at over 100mph in August 1939, before being forced to retire with of all things, a broken girder fork leg. Craig then convinced the Collier brothers (owners of AMC) to abandon the V4 in favour of an all-new parallel twin, code-named E90. But because Craig was not a designer in the real sense of the word, but a development engineer, this meant that the detailed drawings and design work were in fact carried out by Phil Irving and Vic Webb.

A Supercharged Design

Unfortunately, in light of a post-war ban on supercharging, the E90 got off to a less-than-perfect birth. Without the benefit of hindsight, Craig, Irving and Webb sought to beat the two main problems which arise when supercharging is envisaged, accommodating the engine assembly in the frame and cooling the cylinder heads. AJS of course had considerable experience thanks to its pre-war supercharged V4. It was at the time considered that an across-the-frame Gilera-style four would have placed restrictions on items such as valve gear, cylinder head hemispheres and cylinder bore size. And so the design team chose a parallel twin as the best compromise. Unfortunately, throughout its life, the machine which became known as the Porcupine was a Compromise with a capital 'C'. As Jock West was later to remark, in 1949:

> So we chose the twin. And almost the best way of air-cooling the cylinder heads is to face them forward; another good point is that the weight is kept well down in the frame and centre of gravity of the machine is thus very low, which is half the battle of good handling.

For compactness sake, unit construction of the engine and gearbox was employed – rare on a

British bike at that time, but not unique. In several other ways the design was far in advance of anything else conceived in Great Britain during the 1940s, but sadly its full potential was never to be realized because it was built for supercharging, only to be 'rehashed', as one AMC source said, to comply with the new rules when the FIM banned blowers in 1947. Thus, from then on the E90, soon to be nicknamed 'Porcupine' due to its spiky cylinder head finning, was at a major disadvantage compared to purpose-built machinery conceived after the supercharger ban was put in force.

The first the general public heard of the newcomer was in the spring of 1947, when AMC invited the world's press to its Plumstead headquarters for the official launch. Details subsequently appeared in the specialist press, in the 29 May issues of both *Motor Cycling* and *The Motor Cycle*.

With a displacement of 499cc, the bore and stroke of 68×68.5mm dimensions were almost square. The engine's twin overhead camshafts were driven by a train of spur gears which also operated the oil pump and magneto. The side-by-side cylinders lay 15 degrees above the horizontal, with the widely spaced camboxes, which also housed the overlapping hairpin-type valve springs, forming a large catchment for the cooling arm (an important feature in the original design brief for its supercharged role). However, this was to lead to a problem in itself; that of getting enough cool air for the cylinder barrels, which were hidden by the heads and camboxes.

All the main engine castings other than the heads and barrels were manufactured in magnesium alloy and, unlike contemporary parallel twins, the crankshaft, machined from a single steel forging, supported three bearings, the centre one being a plain journal to which lubricant was fed and from which the lined split plain big-ends in the light-alloy connecting rods were lubricated.

The primary drive was by straight-cut gears (again unusual in a British design at that time),

and the engine running backwards; the clutch which ran at 80 per cent of engine speed, was located outside the drive casing and so liberally drilled for air-cooling that *Motor Cycling* said it 'closely resembles a crumpet'! The 4-speed close ratio gearbox was of conventional design, except that it had a 'crossover' drive with the rear chain on the offside, whilst the clutch withdrawal mechanism was housed outside the final drive sprocket.

One of the Porcupine's star features was its excellent and powerful lubrication system. One pump supplied oil to the mains and big-ends whilst another, housed in the same body and located above the crankcase, supplied jets which were applied directly on to each cam face. Oil from the crankcase was returned by another pump located in the sump. This positioning of pumps was intended to avoid the possibility of heat interchange between outgoing and ingoing oil, which is bound to occur where pressure and scavenge pumps are formed in the same body in the conventional manner. In its original form (without of course the deleted supercharger) the Porcupine gave 40bhp at 7,600rpm.

A full duplex cradle frame, with swinging-arm rear, had the AMC-designed Teledraulic front forks, which were based around those pioneered on the famous WD (War Department) Matchless G3L three-fifty ohv single, used extensively during the war by the British armed forces. The rear shock absorbers were of the oil and air variety.

Racing the Porcupine

The racing debut of the Porcupine came in no lesser event than the Isle of Man Senior TT, where Les Graham and the veteran Jock West, now AMC sales manager, both completed the course. During practice for the 1947 TT, the two riders soon discovered the machine's poor starting (and I mean poor!) caused through oil drag of the plain engine bearings, the lack of a flywheel effect and the tendency for the engine to stall coming out of a slow corner (a direct result of the engine's change from super-charging to normal aspiration). Starting from cold was so bad, in fact, that quite often the bikes had to be towed before they would eventually fire into life. The curse of poor cold starting was eventually improved by pre-heating the oil.

In the race Graham finished ninth, whilst West was fourteenth. However, it is fair to point out that West's performance was hampered by being dramatically slowed on the first lap by clutch gremlins, with his fastest lap (the fourth) being only a mere 3 seconds slower than the quickest of the race.

In the Dutch TT at Assen, West was forced to retire with unspecified engine problems, whilst in the Ulster Grand Prix the same rider finished an excellent third, with new signing Ted Frend fifth. The E90 Porcupine's first victory came at the first post-war Bemsee (BMCRC – British Motor Cycle Racing Club) Hutchinson 100 meeting, when Frend won the 100-mile Grand Prix at an average speed of 87.17mph (140.3km/h) from George Brown (Vincent HRD) and Jack Brett (Norton).

During the 1948 Senior TT, Frend, West and Graham were all retirements, whilst in the Dutch TT West came home third behind Artie Bell (Norton) and Nello Pagani (Gilera four). The following weekend Jock West improved upon this with a second in Belgium. The Ulster GP that year was given the title 'Grand Prix of Europe', Les Graham was the top placed AJS rider in third spot. And as recorded in Chapter 6, during November that year, a Porcupine (Frend's TT bike) took a total of eighteen World Records at Montlhéry, with backing from the Mobil Oil Company.

For the 1949 season, the sport's governing body, the FIM, instituted the first series of Grand Prix-type events counting towards the newly-introduced World Championships, both for riders and constructors.

There were a total of six races counting towards the 500cc title. And it was AJS who had the honour of winning that first year, thanks to victories by Les Graham in Switzerland and Ulster. Graham also had the disappointment of leading the 7-lap Senior TT for virtually the entire race, only to suffer a last-lap breakdown due to a sheared magneto armature shaft. Even so he managed to push-in to finish tenth. And when you consider that in the Junior TT, Bill Doran was eliminated on the final lap whilst in the lead on his 7R (due to the failure of his Burman gearbox) the gods did not smile on the AJS equipe at that year's TT races.

After the TT came victory by Doran in the

Les Graham in full flight during his 1949 500cc World Championship-winning year aboard the E90 Porcupine twin.

A 1947 advertisement for Lodge plugs, following Ted Frend's victory at Dunholme, in the BMCRC 100 Miles Grand Prix that year on his works AJS Porcupine.

Bill Doran was another of the AJS works Porcupine team, seen here giving a rather rude gesture to the photographer.

The 1949 E90 Porcupine on display in the Sammy Miller Museum; circa 2002.

E90 Porcupine engine showing original finning – the reason it got its name – and widely spaced front down-tubes.

Belgian 500cc Grand Prix, to add to Graham's two wins in Switzerland and Ulster. Graham was also runner-up in the Dutch round. This not only meant that Les Graham won the 1949 title, but new team member Bill Doran finished an excellent fourth. The other championship table positions were Nello Pagani and Arturo Artesiani (Gilera fours) second and third respectively and Artie Bell (Norton) fifth.

So into 1950 and the AJS twin was modified by the fitment of a new larger 6-gallon (27ltr) fuel tank (for longer races), a redesigned oil tank, revised handlebar layout and a streamlined tail with bucket seat. There were technical changes too, including a variation in the carburettor mounting. But a serious blow to the team

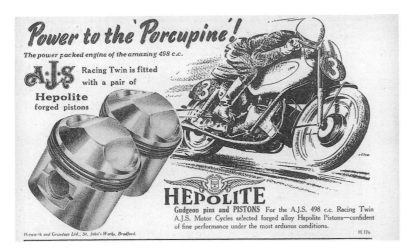

September 1950 Hepolite advertisement 'Power to the Porcupine!' It goes on to say 'The power packed engine of the amazing 498cc AJS Racing Twin is fitted with a pair of Hepolite forged pistons.'

came early in the season when Bill Doran broke his leg in a TT practice crash. During the race Les Graham finished fourth, but was generally outpaced by the newly-introduced Featherbed-framed dohc Norton singles of Geoff Duke, Artie Bell and Johnny Lockett, who took the first three leaderboard placings.

Another aspect of the 1950 Porcupine was a variation between individual machines as regards carburettor mounting. With the float chamber mounted on brackets attached to the duplex front down tubes, the carbs projected outwards at more than one angle.

Besides the emergence of the new, much-improved Nortons, 1950 was also the year of the infamous Dunlop tyre problems. For example, the entire British works entry was forced out of the Dutch TT that year through this particular problem (which centred around losing lumps of tread!) Although Graham won in Switzerland and finished runner up in Ulster, his hopes of retaining the title had evaporated. As a sign of his frustration with lack of results came the news that he was leaving to join the emerging Italian MV Agusta factory.

Further Modifications

Realizing that something was needed, the AMC Porcupine development team, now

Les Graham's double victory in the 1950 Swiss Grand Prix on a Porcupine in the 500cc race and a 7R in the 350cc event.

headed by Matt Wright, carried out a number of modifications that winter. These included sump lubrication, separate cylinder heads (with less finning), smaller wheels (down from 20 to 19in) and lower weight. There was also a shorter wheelbase, shorter Teledraulic forks and a new shape for the fuel tank (similar to the 7R), together with a much smaller and lighter seat.

Most noticeable was the absence of an oil tank. Instead, lubricant was carried in a long sump bolted underneath the crankcase and extending rearward under the gearbox. A magnesium casting, the sump held approximately 1 gallon (4.5ltr). The base of the crankcase was open to the sump and oil drained into it by gravity. External oil pipes had been eliminated with the exception of the feed and return pipes to and from the cylinder head camboxes. The former gear-type return pump was now the delivery pump, whilst the original delivery pump had been eliminated. The oil was circulated at approximately 30 gallons (136ltr) an hour at 7,500rpm.

Separate cylinder heads had been introduced to aid experimentation. A notable feature was that the spark plug was positioned centrally in each head.

Much modified, the Amal carbs were now of the monobloc type, with two mixing chambers (one for each cylinder), a single centrally located float chamber and horizontal jets. This last feature was of vital importance, since it allowed a much shallower assembly, thus providing more latitude with induction pipe layout. Previously the shape of the carburettors had meant overlong induction piping.

The 1951 squad consisted of Bill Doran, now recovered from his Isle of Man crash of the previous year, and the up-and-coming Irishman, Reg Armstrong. Athough they did not win any of the World Championship rounds, (it was Geoff Duke's famous Norton double year), the AJS teamsters put up a far more effective challenge, gaining a trio of second places, with Doran finishing the year fourth in the 500cc table (with the same rider third in the 350cc contest).

The E95

The following year saw the introduction of the E95 version of the Porcupine. Designed by P.A. (Phil) Walker, this combined new with old in what was the Porcupine's first really major update.

By swinging the cylinders up from their hitherto near horizontal position to an inclination of 45 degrees, Walker improved the cooling facilities (particularly of the cylinder barrels) and the line of the inlet tracts, but against this created a higher centre of gravity. The redesigned engine, new non-loop frame and a shorter wheelbase gave the revised Porcupine a different appearance (which, to the author's eye at least, was not as attractive as the original E90 model). *The Motor Cycle* referred to it as 'cobby'.

Because of the new engine position, Walker removed all vestiges of the 'spike' finning which had led to the Porcupine's name. Instead, finning of the cylinders, the lower area of the heads and cambox housings was now of conventional appearance.

Another change was that there was now chain drive to the magneto (instead of gear). There was also a new rear brake, revised gearchange mechanism and new reverse-cone megaphones, the latter in an attempt to broaden the power band. The twin Amal carburettors were inclined 25 degrees to horizontal and a light-alloy scoop below the tank deflected cold air onto these instruments.

The 1952 and 1953 Seasons

The 1952 championship season could not have started better, because at the very first round, the Swiss Grand Prix in Berne, AJS machines finished first, second and fifth in the 500cc race. This truly magnificent result was garnered by Jack Brett, Bill Doran and the New Zealander, Rod Coleman. Unfortunately, this run of success couldn't be repeated, however, even though the talented Bill Lomas joined the team in time for the Isle of Man TT. Robin Sherry also rode a 1951-type Porcupine at selected

Robin Sherry winning at Boreham, Essex on Saturday 26 July 1952 on a 1951-type Porcupine.

British short circuit events and at the Italian GP; Sherry was also in the factory squad when the 1953 line-up was announced the following January, together with Doran and Coleman.

Technically there were few changes to the Porcupine that year, with the major alteration being a new full-loop frame. Like Norton (now owned by AMC), AJS found the going ever tougher as the Italian multis in the shape of Gilera, MV Agusta and Moto Guzzi began to not only possess great speed, but also inherit the British handling prowess; the latter in no small part thanks to the input of their newly signed British riders, including Geoff Duke and Reg Armstrong.

Updates for the Final Season

In a final attempt to remain competitive, the Porcupine was updated yet again for the 1954 season, with a new lower frame, streamlined fuel tank and rehashed carburation system. However, the improvements which would really have made a difference were not incorporated, even though they were tested. Notably these were fuel injection, 5-speed (instead of 4-speed) gearboxes and comprehensive streamlining. Adding these three features would no doubt have moved AJS much nearer their Italian rivals. Unfortunately, factory policy (read politics) vetoed their inclusion.

As for riders, with Doran in retirement,

New Zealander Rod Coleman joined AJS in the early 1950s and was to prove their most successful rider after Les Graham had quit to join Italian rivals, MV Agusta.

1951 and Bill Doran (see here at Silverstone), together with Jack Brett, Rod Coleman and Bill Lomas, rode for AJS as official factory entries.

A youthful Tom Mortimer sits astride the revised 1954 Porcupine, just after it has been wheeled out of the race shop at the Plumstead works for the first time.

1953 Mark 2 Porcupine, the E95, which had debuted in the middle of the previous year. This featured quite a major redesign, with the cylinders sitting at 45 degrees in an attempt to reduce megaphonitis and improve carburation.

Bob McIntyre with the works Porcupine the Scot rode in the 1954 Senior TT. He finished fourteenth in atrocious weather conditions, which caused the race to be halted earlier than expected.

McIntyre at the foot of Bray Hill, during the 1954 Senior TT.

Coleman was joined by Bob McIntyre and Derek Farrant. The Porcupine's best place that year was a second in the Ulster GP, thanks to the efforts of Rod Coleman. But in reality the performance of the Italian multis was simply too great to make any real challenge that year. So together with Norton, AJS withdrew from specialized works racing at the end of the 1954 season.

The Epilogue

However this was not to be the end of the Porcupine saga. First the Glaswegian entrant/tuner Joe Potts obtained an E95 engine on loan in 1957. This was one of the last to be constructed and by then put out 56bhp at 7,400rpm. But Bob McIntyre's Gilera contract that year meant that the engine remained unused by the Potts equipe and eventually returned to Plumstead.

In 1964 Kent AMC specialist Tom Arter borrowed a 1954 Porcupine (which was eventually to become his property), together with a spare engine. This led to the Canadian rider Mike Duff testing the machine, but again plans to race it were shelved after Duff signed for the Japanese Yamaha concern.

Much, much later, in the spring of 2000, this bike, spare engine and various components were auctioned off at The Classic Motor Cycle Show at Stafford Showground. The bidding, which included bids from George Beale and Rob Iannucci, was fierce, the results being a whopping £157,700 (original estimate £80,000) for the bike, £78,500 for the engine and perhaps, even more amazing, around £20,000 for a box of various small component parts. The Porcupine was obviously deemed a vital piece of British racing heritage – as these prices go to prove! It is generally agreed that a total of eight complete bikes were built, four of the original E90s and four of the later E95s.

Later during the 1960s one of the 1954 Porcupines was raced by Canadian Mike Duff for the Canterbury dealer/entrant Tom Arter.

Porcupine engine auctioned by Bonhams at the Stafford Classic Motor Cycle Show, spring 2000, for over £70,000.

6   Three–Valve

A single, which at first glance gave every indication of being a twin, is today one of the least known of all post-war British racing motorcycles. This design, the three-fifty, triple overhead camshaft, 3-valve, AJS 7R3 is also one of the most technically interesting.

By 1951 AMC was beginning to get somewhat frustrated with its Grand Prix racing efforts. This might seem strange given Les Graham's inaugural 1949 500cc World Championship title, the Porcupine (*see* Chapter 5) thereafter seeming incapable of delivering a consistent performance. So, the Plumstead factory's chief racing engineer, H.J. 'Ike' Hatch was given the task of rescuing AJS's pride, a task not made easier by strict financial control imposed by the AMC group's board.

A New 3-Valve Layout

For a start Hatch was forced, through the limited budget described above, to use the existing 7R production racer as a basis. However, this did not stop Ike Hatch showing innovation by employing an ingenious 3-valve layout employing a separate camshaft for each valve. One of his priorities was to achieve lower exhaust valve temperatures and thus, theoretically, increase volumetric efficiency by reducing heat transfer to the incoming charge.

As much of the heat picked up by an exhaust valve is dissipated through its seat when the valve is closed, Hatch reasoned that by employing two smaller valves instead of a single, large component, this would mean a lower temperature, whilst providing an

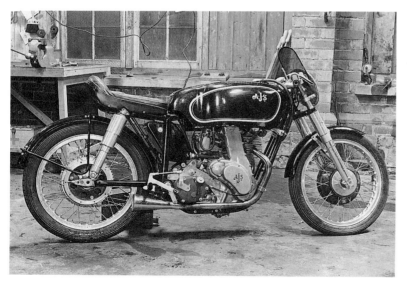

The first version of the 3-valve (7R3A), with experimental Porcupine-type chassis. Note the tiny megaphones for exhaust.

A 3-valve works AJS single-cylinder engine, viewed from the camshaft driveside.

material. The engine was mounted in a stock 7R chassis, with promise of a purpose-built assembly at a later date. The twin-port cylinder head used short, small diameter exhaust header pipes with equally tiny megaphones, whilst the rev-counter drive was taken from the offside exhaust camshaft.

New Bore and Stroke Dimensions

Compared to the 7R, the 3-valve engine featured new bore and stroke dimensions of 75.5 × 78mm, providing a considerably shorter stroke than previously. AMC never officially released a power output figure, but speaking to a former race shop member the author has been told the output in 1952 was in the region of 36bhp at 7,200rpm. It is also interesting to relate former AMC race mechanic (and a fine racer in his own right) Ted Iffland's recollection:

> It was a horrible bike to work on. Setting up the valve timing was a real nightmare because there were two vernier adjustments in the cam box and the two exhaust valves were on plain tapers. Getting the timing right, for both valves was like a big game of roulette.

Iffland also claimed that rather than saving money, the 7R3

> cost AMC a small fortune, and not only because of the complex make-up of the cam box. There were in fact, no less than ten different types of cylinder head, with varying port and valve angles. Another problem centred on, as with the Porcupine twin, that of carburation. This glitch – which meant the engine gave no power below 5,500rpm – saw a bench-tested version of the 7R3 constructed with fuel injection, which cured the megaphonitis, but was still not adopted.

More Technical Details

On the original design, the camshafts were driven by chain (as on the production 7R).

equivalent valve-opening area. In addition the splitting of the exhaust track would allow a superior airflow round the ports with a consequent improvement in cylinder head cooling.

Other advantages of the 3-valve layout were seen as a more central spark-plug location (thus shortening flame travel), and that valve-inertia force would be reduced by virtue of a lower weight of the individual exhaust valves. However, the three valves also made for an over-complex actuating mechanism which was to prove a major headache. A later version (never actually raced) employed shaft and bevel gears. This latter design was coded 7R3B, whereas the original type was known as the 7R3A.

The bottom half followed conventional 7R practice, except for a change in the crankcase

The design philosophy which prompted Hatch to plump for his 3-cam, 3-valve layout, was of course made in light of engineering principles of the period. And interestingly the Japanese, in the shape of Honda, used 3-valves-per-cylinder technology some three decades later, but employed a pair of inlet valves and a single exhaust component. Hatch carried out his design work on the AJS 3-valve single in late 1951 and early 1952, before his death in 1954.

Another reason why Hatch opted to use two exhaust valves and a single inlet was the major problem of valve spring breakage. This saw the 7R3 equipped with triple coil springs for each exhaust valve, whilst the single inlet retained the much stiffer hairpin type found on the single overhead cam 7R production model. The reason for the coil springs was that these allowed the pair of exhaust valves to be fitted, whereas the much wider hairpin variety would have never fitted into the confined area.

As already recorded, in the 7R3A, the chain drive of the production 7R was retained, but re-routed to drive the rear inlet camshaft. This in turn drove a parallel layshaft positioned forward of it (by means of spur gears) from which the two exhaust cams were disposed at 90 degrees and driven by bevel gears. This allowed cooling air to sweep over and through the cylinder head, whilst the use of twin sodium-cooled exhaust valves aided heat dispersal.

Racing the 7R3A

The 7R3A was raced in its original guise during 1952 and 1953. Initially it was reasonably reliable, if not over-fast, and the riders were Bill Doran, Rod Coleman, Jack Brett and the French star Pierre Monneret. During the 1952 season Coleman gained a couple of runner-up positions at Berne in Switzerland and Monza, Italy, whilst also finishing third in the Isle of Man TT, Dutch TT and Ulster GP. This gave him and AJS fourth place in the 350cc World Championship table.

As noted in Chapter 10, later in 1952 Coleman, together with Doran and Monneret, took a 7R3A to the Montlhéry circuit, just south of Paris, and broke no less than thirteen world speed and distance records, including the one-hour at 115.66mph (186.21km/h) and the seven-hour at 98.62mph (158.78km/h). Distance records were set for the 50 and 100km and 50 and 100 miles.

Into 1953 and with virtually no development over that winter, the 7R3A languished against the latest developments from chief rivals Norton and Moto Guzzi. The best position that year was second by Pierre Monneret in the French GP, and a couple of third places by Coleman at the Ulster round (where Bob McIntyre on a production 7R finished second!) and the Italian GP at Monza.

Development Leads to the 7R3B

Then for 1954, the 3-valver underwent more development. This centred around the cycle parts and carburation. The frame was lowered by 1.57in (40mm) at the steering head and a new larger Porqupine-style fuel tank specified. This was of the saddle-type shape to accommodate the rider's legs, virtually hiding two-thirds of the engine assembly. A remote float chamber was retained, but with a fuel pump driven by the offside exhaust camshaft. This fed fuel from the tank (which extended well below the level of the fuel bowl) to the header tank. The engine's power output had also increased, to 40bhp at 7,800rpm.

The freshly updated 3-valver got off to a brilliant start, winning the first two rounds of the 1954 World Championship series. The first of these was a huge home victory by Pierre Monneret at the French GP at Reims. A few weeks later, in June Rod Coleman repeated the experience by winning the Junior TT in the Isle of Man, and in the process gave the AJS marque its first TT win for almost a quarter of a century.

Spurred on by these successes, Ike Hatch was authorized to carry out further development

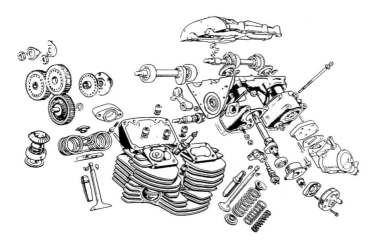

In the final version of the AJS 3-valve single (1954), the upper bevel operated a combined gear from which the drive went up to the cross-shaft serving the exhaust camshafts, then back to the inlet camshaft.

work on the triple knocker. The main change in what was to emerge as the 7R3B, was the substitution of the chain drive by shaft and bevel gears. This meant that any alteration to the compression ratio could be accomplished simply by inserting shims under the cylinder barrel and varying the thickness of the Oldhams couplings to adjust the length of the vertical shaft. The drive to the three camshafts was also altered slightly but the general layout remained basically unchanged. Sadly, Ike Hatch died before serious testing of the 7R3B could get under way, with Jack Williams taking his place as chief development engineer.

Bob McIntyre hurtling down the fearsome Bray Hill aboard his factory-entered works 3-valver, during the 1954 Junior TT.

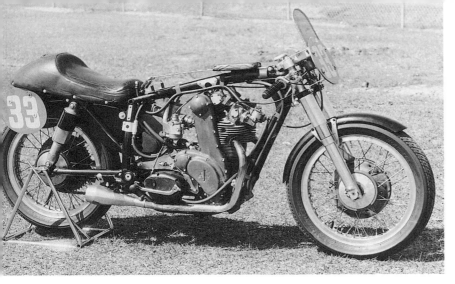

The 1954 3-valver with the fuel tank removed, showing both frame and engine details.

Jack Williams Takes Over

Williams did a limited amount of additional work on the 7R3B, but it was never raced. This was partly due to Williams' opinion that the elaborate valve mechanism was not worth the additional complexity for the small amount of additional power compared to the 2-valve production 7R. In addition, AMC announced, in February 1955, that both AJS and Norton were quitting Grand Prix 'specials' to concentrate their efforts on production models such as the 7R and Manx Norton.

Plans to market a production version of the 7R3 were studied, but it was soon realized that production costs and tooling would have been prohibitive. So instead, Jack Williams carried out a major (and highly successful) update of the standard 7R – which included using the shorter-stroke dimensions from the 3-valvers!

As for the 7R3, this quietly faded from the scene until an example of the A series 3-valver was brought back to life in the 1980s by the American classic racing team owner, Rob Iannucci. It is generally believed that only four 7R3A bikes were built, plus a number of experimental prototype engines.

Testing the Iannucci Machine

When racing journalist Alan Cathcart tested Rob Iannucci's 7R3A, he found the triple knocker accelerated rather sluggishly compared to a standard 7R (the latter fitted with an aftermarket six-speed 'box and with a rider of equal weight aboard). However, in the mid-

Classic Fest, Donington Park, July 1986. Team Obsolete brought over the only surviving 3-valve model for rider Dave Roper to race.

*The Team Obsolete 7R3,
photographed at Knockhill, Fife,
Scotland, in summer 1987.*

*The 7R3 (the Team Obsolete machine)
on show in the national Motorcycle
Museum; circa 1990s.*

range and top-end, the 7R3A was significantly faster, although less stable under braking. But as Cathcart went on to say, in comparing the triple camshaft model with a late-type short-stroke sohc 7R of the type it gave birth to, there was simply no comparison with the older long-stroke bike that it was designed to supplant.

With the benefit of hindsight, the author's opinion is that the 7R3 was a 'halfway house' sort of machine, full of compromises, and with Hatch only doing half the job in designing the cylinder head – a 4-valve type would surely have proved to be far more effective. In

addition, AMC policy at that time forbidding any form of streamlining for the AJS racers meant that performance potential was restricted. This is in stark contrast to Moto Guzzi, who for example, was already gaining several miles per hour on top speed through efficient streamlining. Finally, there were two other major failings: a 4-speed only gearbox and AMC's less than satisfactory 'Jampot' rear shock absorbers.

Even with all its faults the 7R3 was still an interesting motorcycle and an important piece of British racing history – and of course a GP and TT winner.

7 Four-Stroke Trials

Although the golden era for AJS in trials was the immediate post-Second World War period, mention must be made of George Rowley who, riding exclusively AJS machines, competed from 1925 until 1939 with great distinction. But Rowley was not just a trials man. He was equally at home taking part in road races, scrambles, hill climbs and even grass track. In road racing his greatest achievement was runner-up in the 1928 Senior TT. He also gained many victories both in Britain and in Continental Europe. Rowley also rode in many International Six Day events, gaining not only a strong of gold medals, but also helping Great Britain to win the coveted Trophy plus the Manufacturers team award for AJS.

Rowley Moves to Plumstead

When the Collier brothers took over AJS in 1931, Rowley moved south to Plumstead and not only continued to ride but also played a vital role in bringing AJS back into motorcycle sport. Also it was George Rowley who was the driving force in getting the overhead singles back into production.

He was also meticulous in the preparation of his machines. In Gregor Grant's 1969 book *AJS The History of a Great Motorcycle*, Rowley was described as 'fussy', saying that 'He would experiment with various shapes of cam and different weights of flywheel to obtain maximum torque at low engine speeds which suited his method of trickling up muddy and rocky sections.' His influence on trials bikes in general was considerable and he was the man

in the background who communicated his ideas and riding technique to the AJS team riders who succeeded in the post-war era.

C for Competition

As related in *Matchless: The Complete Story* (The Crowood Press, 2004), the post-war AMC competition bikes (both Matchless and AJS) had their origins in the wartime Teledraulic-forked Matchless G3/L. The AJS 348cc (69 × 93 mm) ohv single, the Model 16C, was the competition version developed by the AMC engineering team and George Rowley.

Unfortunately in the immediate months after the end of the conflict British riders could not get their hands on production roadsters, as everything was being exported. However, for the so-called 'production' competition mounts, things were very different, even though at first glance they were very much modified roadsters, less lighting equipment.

The Motor Cycle in its 14 March 1946 issue announced: 'A Small Number of Special Trials Mounts in Production'. These consisted of fifty AJS and fifty Matchless machines, thirty of each being three-fifties, the balance five-hundreds. The official AMC works line was 'The special competition models will not be catalogued, but will be sold to trials enthusiasts on the recommendations of local AMC agents.' This was also a way of getting around the 'export only' agreement.

The general layout of these early post-war AJS Competition models (the 348cc 16C and 497cc 18C) came in no small part from

George Rowley, who had not only his vast pre-war experience to draw upon, but who had personally carried out much of the extensive test programme. One notable alteration from the stock roadster specification was a special steering-head angle for the frame, together with revised trail to suit.

The 'C' models came with a low-level exhaust system with the header pipe tucked in close to the timing chest, and the silencer upswept. At the time, AMC also claimed that specially selected engines were being fitted, the gear ratios for the 16C three-fifty being 6.13, 7.93, 12.91 and 19.58:1, and for the 18C five-hundred 5.49, 7.1, 11.55 and 17.52:1. All unnecessary lugs had been removed from the frame. The 'C' models featured painted lightweight (duralumin) mudguards with tubular stays, security bolts (two per wheel), heavy duty spokes for the front wheel, a folding kickstart lever, duplicated (spare) clutch and throttle cables. Tyres were 2.75 × 21 front and 4.00 × 19 rear, and ground clearance was 7in (178mm). Lighting equipment was available by request as a cost option.

Because of what was referred to by AMC sources as 'the slipper-shaped lug' at the base of the front down-tube (a cradle frame being employed), no crankcase undershield had been seen as necessary.

Of course the specification also included many of the series production roadster's basics, including Teledraulic front forks, rigid frame, single sprung saddle, 4-speed Burman foot-change gearbox and clutch, and ohv engine with iron head and barrel. That these Competition bikes were only destined for a carefully selected clientele is clearly evident from the following statement in the 7 November 1946 issue of *The Motor Cycle*:

A limited number of competition models, both Matchless and AJS are being manufactured. The factory insists on knowing the name and past competition record of the prospective purchaser of one of these machines. The underlying reason is that otherwise some might find their way into the hands of ordinary road users, and since the number of machines is limited, various good trials riders might possibly have to go without.

As for prices, the 16C three-fifty cost £111 plus (in the UK) £29 19s 5d purchase tax, whilst the 18C five-hundred model was £121, plus £32 13s 5d tax. Speedometers and lighting equipment were available at extra cost.

The 1947 16MC	
Engine	Air-cooled, ohv single with vertical cylinder; iron head and barrel; vertically split aluminium crankcases; fully enclosed valve gear; coil valve springs; built-up crankshaft; roller bearing big-end; gear-driven cams
Bore	69mm
Stroke	93mm
Displacement	348cc
Compression ratio	6.3:1
Lubrication	Dry sump, two-start oil pump
Ignition	Magneto, Lucas
Carburettor	Amal 76 lin
Primary drive	Chain
Final drive	Chain
Gearbox	4-speed, foot-change, Burman wide ratio
Frame	Diamond type with single front down-tube
Front suspension	AMC Teledraulic oil-damped forks
Rear suspension	Rigid
Front brake	5.5in, SLS single-sided drum
Rear brake	5.5in, SLS single-sided drum
Tyres	2.75 × 21 front; 4.00 × 19 rear
Wheelbase	53in (1,346mm)
Ground clearance	6.5in (165mm)
Seat height	32.5in (825mm)
Fuel tank capacity	3gal (13.5ltr)
Dry weight	300lb (136kg)
Maximum power	16bhp @ 5,600rpm
Top speed	65mph (105km/h)

The 1947 18C

Engine	Air-cooled, ohv single with vertical cylinder; iron head and barrel; vertically split aluminium crankcases; fully enclosed valve gear; coil valve springs; built-up crankshaft; roller-bearing big-end; gear-driven cams
Bore	82.5mm
Stroke	93mm
Displacement	497cc
Compression ratio	5.9:1
Lubrication	Dry sump, two-start oil pump
Ignition	Magneto, Lucas
Carburettor	Amal 89 1⅛in
Primary drive	Chain
Final drive	Chain
Gearbox	4-speed, foot-change, Burman
Frame	Diamond type with single front down-tube
Front suspension	AMC Teledraulic oil-damped forks
Rear suspension	Rigid
Front brake	5.5in, SLS
Rear brake	5.5in, SLS
Tyres	2.75 × 21 front; 4.00 × 19 rear
Wheelbase	53in (1,346mm)
Ground clearance	6.5in (165mm)
Seat height	32.5in (825mm)
Fuel tank capacity	3gal (13.5ltr)
Dry weight	307lb (139kg)
Maximum power	23bhp @ 5,400rpm
Top speed	70mph (113km/h)

A Trio of Scottish Six Days Victories

The legendary Scottish Six Days Trial, which was one of the very toughest tests of man and machine, certainly on mainland Britain, ever to be devised – even though the organizing Edinburgh Club insisted on calling it 'A Sporting Holiday in the Highlands'. The Scottish was destined to become something of a happy hunting ground for AJS between 1947 (when the trial resumed after a break of some

eight years due to the war) and the end of the big 4-stroke dominance which continued until the mid-1960s. The AJS post-war success story in the Scottish began with a trio of victories in 1947, 1948 and 1949 – all by works star Hugh Viney.

On Sunday 4 May 1947, some 96 competitors presented themselves for signing on in Fort William, where the trial was to be centred. The trial proper got underway the following morning. As Tommy Sandham described in his book, *The Scottish 1900–62* (Willow Publishing, 1998):

Fine drizzle made the section greasy for the solos but the evening's results showed eight men still on clean sheets. One of these men was to become a Scottish idol with the fans, but that Monday evening he was not very well known. His name was Hugh Viney. Then 32 years old, Hugh had enjoyed only moderate success in Open-to-Centre trials, with his best ride being a fifth place in the British Experts. Like many of the others he had ridden bikes before the war and during the hostilities had become an instructor in the Royal Signals, riding an M20 side valve BSA. Hugh had never ridden in a six day event before, and that morning was just another rider on a 350cc AJS, one of 24 entered. Now he was joint leader.

And so Viney continued to show just why veteran AJS man George Rowley had taken him under his wing by going on to win with only 6 marks dropped; Artie Ratcliffe was (Matchless) runner-up with 25 marks lost and Bob Ray (Ariel) third (32 marks).

There is absolutely no doubt that Viney's and AJS's dominance of the event in the late 1940s not only created big publicity for AJS but also helped the development of the AMC competition models in general. In addition the majority of the year-to-year changes made to the works trials bikes found their way into the single-cylinder roadsters. When the 1948

Scottish Six Days Trial 1932–64					
1932	G. Rowley	497cc	AJS	3rd	12 marks lost
1937	F. Povey	348cc	AJS	3rd	13 marks lost
1947	H. Viney	348cc	AJS	1st	6 marks lost
1948	H. Viney	348cc	AJS	1st	27 marks lost
1949	H. Viney	348cc	AJS	1st	18 marks lost
1950	H. Viney	348cc	AJS	2nd	21 marks lost
1952	G. Jackson	348cc	AJS	3rd	33 marks lost
1953	H. Viney	348cc	AJS	3rd	35 marks lost
	G. Jackson	348cc	AJS	2nd	38 marks lost
1954	G. Jackson	348cc	AJS	3rd	31 marks lost
1955	G. Jackson	348cc	AJS	3rd	22 marks lost
1956	G. Jackson	348cc	AJS	1st	16 marks lost
	G. McLoughlin	348cc	AJS	3rd	33 marks lost
1958	G. Jackson	348cc	AJS	1st	6 marks lost
1959	G. Jackson	348cc	AJS	2nd	20 marks lost
1960	G. Jackson	348cc	AJS	1st	16 marks lost
1961	G. Jackson	348cc	AJS	1st	1 mark lost
1962	G. Jackson	348cc	AJS	2nd	18 marks lost
1963	M. Andrews	348cc	AJS	2nd	20 marks lost
1964	M. Andrews	348cc	AJS	2nd	38 marks lost

Also AJS won the Manufacturers Award four years running in 1953, 1954, 1955 and 1956, as detailed below:

1953	Hugh Viney,	Gordon Jackson,	Bob Manns
1954	Hugh Viney,	Gordon Jackson,	Bob Manns
1955	Hugh Viney,	Gordon Jackson,	Bob Manns
1956	Gordon Jackson,	Bob Manns,	Gordon McLaughlin

models were launched in October 1947 it was also seen that the roadster could benefit the competition bikes. The competition bikes had benefited from new brakes adopted by the roadsters (*see* Chapter 4) and other improvements, together with a special short-wheelbase frame which measured 52⅜in (1,329mm) with the rear wheel spindle in the mid-position, a reduction of 1⅛in (28mm). *The Motor Cycle* in its show issue dated 4 December 1947 reported:

So popular are the competition models that the factory will be unable to accept orders for probably at least a year.

Much of this was the vast demand from the United States of America, in particular from California, where the handling, traction and reliability of both AJS and Matchless models was highly rated for all forms of off-road sport including desert racing, green lanes and scrambles. The importer for AJS in the USA at that time was the Indian Sales Corporation of Springfield, Massachusetts, but for California there was a special concession held for that State by Los Angeles-based Cooper Motors.

The 1949 Model Year

When the Earls Court Show took place in London during November 1948, Hugh Viney had won the Scottish Six Days for the second time – so the AJS stand was a popular place.

As covered in detail in Chapter 4, the alterations to the overhead-valve singles for the 1949 model year included redesigned cylinder heads, hairpin instead of coil valve springs, and

During the late 1940s the 'C' Competition models were a big success for AMC, being built in both AJS and Matchless guises and in 350 and 500cc engine sizes. Basically the same bike was used for trials and scrambling at that time. This is a 1949 Model 16C three-fifty.

redesigned frames. Those changes only applicable to the competition models were a separate and thus detachable crankcase undershield, and an improved carburettor intake shield. The 16C and 18C models retained their rigid frames, even though the 1948 London Show saw the introduction of the new spring (swinging-arm) frame, which was a standard fitment on the new Model 20 twin (*see* Chapter 8) and an optional extra on the series-production roadster singles.

1950 Changes

The big news for fans of the AMC Competition models, was the introduction of alloy engines. As *Motor Cycling* outlined in its 13 October 1949 issue:

> The four competition models, 348 and 497cc 'Ajay' and Matchless of similar capacities, strike a new note in the programme. These machines have alloy barrels with cast-iron liners (and alloy cylinder heads) making for lightness – both competition models in the region of 300lb [135kg].

Other innovations for the competition models that year were the introduction of a Lucas Wader magneto, five-spring clutch and front brake torque arm.

During this period the American market began to make its influence on the dirt bikes, this having led to what Stateside enthusiasts referred to as 'chopped jobs'. AMC responded by providing a shorter wheelbase and a specification which *Motor Cycling* referred to as 'abbreviated to purely sporting requirements'. As offered, the Competition machines were fitted with tyres of 'suitable size for trials and scrambles' and a speedometer and bulb horn, but without lighting, the latter being an

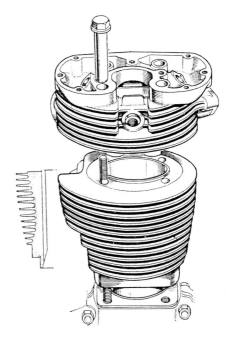

The 1950 model year saw the introduction of an alloy cylinder head and barrel for the competition models.

additional £9 10s (inclusive of the dreaded UK purchase tax). In the place of the 2¾gal (12.5ltr) fuel tank then specified on the roadster singles, the 'C' models had a peanut-shaped 2gal (9ltr) tank attached to the frame by improved quick-release bolts. The saddle was raised to 32½in (825mm), and in place of the conventional toolbox a much smaller tubular container with a quickly detachable cap was located beneath the saddle. The aluminium mudguards were now left unpainted and were polished.

ISDT Medals

In the 1950 ISDT held in Wales, AJS riders were extremely successful, gaining the following medals:

FIM Gold Medals

B.H.M. Viney	348cc AJS
A.B.N. Taylor	348cc AJS
D.M. Murdoch	497cc AJS
T.H. Wortley	348cc AJS
A.W. Burnard	348cc AJS
T. Hawkins	497cc AJS

FIM Silver Medals

H. Kelly	497cc AJS
A.F. Philip	348c AJS

FIM Bronze Medals

W.A. Roberts	497cc AJS

Designated Trials and Scrambles Models

For the first time, the 1951 AMC model range created separate model types for trials (coded C) and scrambles (coded CS). The subsequent CS ranges are covered in Chapter 12.

Essentially the Competition bikes were still manufactured in what AMC termed 'limited quantities', and were constructed in two batches, one in the autumn and one in the spring. The new spring-frame models for scrambling (or the ISDT) were built with a silencer as standard, but for motocross a straight-through open pipe was an option. The trials variants were largely as before, in other words with a rigid frame. And also as before, various improvements (including revision to the Teledraulic front forks) were incorporated.

The 1952 Model Year

There was a new Burman-made gearbox for the 1952 model year. Based on the racing AJS 7R unit, it was manufactured in three guises: B52 standard (roadster), B52 close (scrambles) and the B52 trials. The latter had wide ratios; the international ratios were: 1st 3.11; 2nd 2.02; 3rd 1.422; top 1:1. A particularly practical modification for both the competition models and the touring bikes was the provision of a circular inspection cover, held in place by three screws, for the primary chaincase.

From then on until the end of 1953, virtually no real development occurred on the Competition models, except those changes introduced across the single-cylinder range.

In May 1953 Hugh Viney won the Scottish Six Days for the fourth and final time on his works AJS Model 16MC, with Gordon Jackson on a sister machine finishing runner-up. After that it was very much a case of roles reversed, with Jackson, rather than Viney, victorious in the Scottish.

Big Changes for 1954

All models, including the trials models, received quite significant changes for the 1954 season. The most noticeable was the full-width alloy front hub with straight spokes. The off-road models were given internal gearbox changes, improved gearbox-to-chaincase seal, an altered oil-filler cap, and an alloy fuel tank. The rigid-frame models had an all-welded front frame, whilst the spring frame had new rear shocks and a dual seat (on the scrambler only).

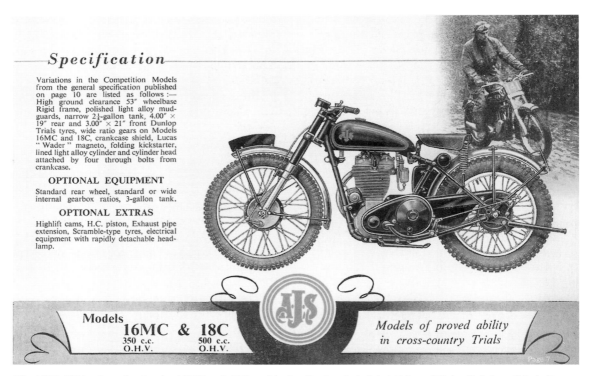

Specification

Variations in the Competition Models from the general specification published on page 10 are listed as follows :— High ground clearance 53″ wheelbase Rigid frame, polished light alloy mudguards, narrow 2¼-gallon tank, 4.00″ × 19″ rear and 3.00″ × 21″ front Dunlop Trials tyres, wide ratio gears on Models 16MC and 18C, crankcase shield, Lucas "Wader" magneto, folding kickstarter, lined light alloy cylinder and cylinder head attached by four through bolts from crankcase.

OPTIONAL EQUIPMENT

Standard rear wheel, standard or wide internal gearbox ratios, 3-gallon tank.

OPTIONAL EXTRAS

Highlift cams, H.C. piston, Exhaust pipe extension, Scramble-type tyres, electrical equipment with rapidly detachable headlamp.

Models 16MC & 18C
350 c.c. O.H.V.   500 c.c. O.H.V.

Models of proved ability in cross-country Trials

The 1953 AJS brochure showing the 16MC and 18C models. Specifications included rigid frame, Teledraulic forks, polished alloy mudguards, 21in front and 19in rear tyres, crankcase shield, Lucas 'Wader' magneto, plus much more.

AJS star Hugh Viney won the Scottish Six Days Trial three years running (1947, '48 and '49). Then, in 1953 (see here) Viney won for a fourth and final time. This view shows some of the difficult going in this legendary event.

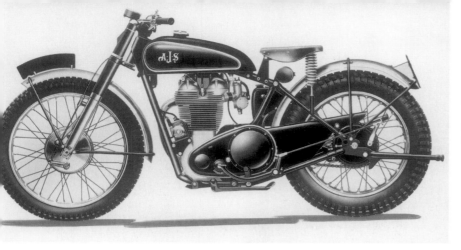

November 1954 saw the launch of the 1955 Model 18C. There were now separate C (trials) and CS (scrambles) machines.

The spring-frame roadster singles and competition models had been given a larger timing mainshaft, lighter flywheels and a modified oil tank. And an AMC bike, albeit a Matchless, with A.L. (Artie) Ratcliffe aboard won the Scottish Six Day's.

There was little change to the trials mount for 1955, except the adoption (together with the other singles that year) of a full-width alloy rear hub.

A New Trials Model for 1956

For the 1956 model year AMC introduced a new 348cc trials bike with a swinging-arm

AJS also did well in the ISDT (International Six Day's Trial). Here John Bassett with his ex Gordon Jackson 1955 AJS Model 30 six-hundred twin, tackles the Manor Parsley section during the 1982 End-to-End Trial, organized by the Cornwall Centre of the ACU.

frame. This frame, together with the roadster (and also the scramblers), was new, with a vertical seat tube (detailed in Chapter 4). Another component shared by both on- and off-road machines was the new alloy full-width rear hub assembly. (It should be noted that the trials machine was only offered as a three-fifty, whereas the scrambler came in both engine sizes.) However, the roadster and trials frames were not identical. The main portion of the frame of the trials bike was somewhat similar to that introduced for the 1954 rigid-frame models, being of welded construction with a single tube forming the front down and top members, and a wrap-around gusset plate at the steering head. But unlike the latest roadster frame, the main tube now extended back under the seat, to link up with the pivot lug.

Although the pivot lugs of the roadster and trials frames bore a resemblance to one another, there was an important difference: the pivot axis of the roadster frame was offset ½in (13mm) to the rear of the seat-tube centreline, whereas that of the trials frame was offset ahead by the same amount, thus providing a 1in (25mm) difference in wheelbase.

The 1956 AJS trials model price (15 September 1955) was: 348cc Model 16MC £212 8s; lighting equipment £9 18s extra (including British purchase tax).

This was also the year in which Gordon Jackson scored his first win for AJS, in the Scottish Six Days. Before this he had been placed second in both 1952 and 1953, and third in 1954 and 1955.

Production version of the AJS Model 30 six-hundred enduro bike; it sold particularly well in the USA. Girling units date it to being a 1957/58 bike.

In the 1956 ISDT in Austria, AJS works rider Bob Manns riding a specially prepared 506cc AJS single not only gained a Gold Medal but was also a member of the British Trophy team who finished third behind winners Czechoslovakia and Italy.

An AMC Gearbox

The big news for all AJS models, including the trials mount, for the 1957 season was an AMC gearbox and Norton-type clutch, to replace the previously Burman-sourced components. Also there was now no engine shock absorber and a smaller dome in the primary chaincase. There is no doubt that this move came as a major commercial set-back to the Birmingham-based transmission specialists, Burman, as AMC was probably its biggest customer.

For 1957, the AJS Model 16MC (and Matchless G3LC) was the only machine in the range to utilize a welded frame. In addition, the integral structure comprising the duplex engine cradle and the rear frame loops was raised with the result that ground clearance (with the bike unladen) was increased from 7in (178mm) to 10in (254mm). The altered sweep of the tubes permitted the exhaust pipe to be tucked in more closely, with the result that it was no longer necessary to employ an exaggerated outward crank for the kickstarter pedal. The trials engine, unlike the scrambler, remained unchanged from the previous year.

A nicely prepared 1957 16MC photographed by the author at the Stafford Classic Mechanics Show in October 2004. This is essentially stock except for the aluminium low-level oil tank.

AMC race shop man Tom Mortimer with an AJS 16MC trials bike; circa 1957.

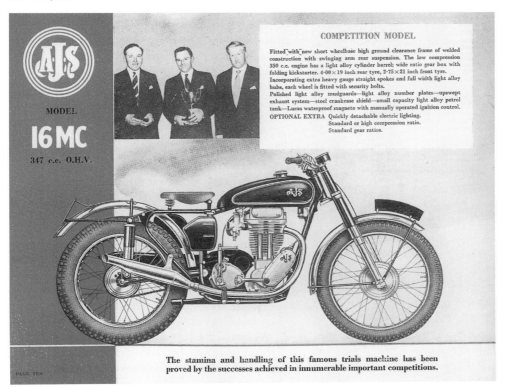

AJS

MODEL

16 MC

347 c.c. O.H.V.

COMPETITION MODEL

Fitted with new short wheelbase high ground clearance frame of welded construction with swinging arm rear suspension. The low compression 350 c.c. engine has a light alloy cylinder barrel; wide ratio gear box with folding kickstarter. 4·00 × 19 inch rear tyre, 2·75 × 21 inch front tyre. Incorporating extra heavy gauge straight spokes and full width light alloy hubs, each wheel is fitted with security bolts.

Polished light alloy mudguards—light alloy number plates—upswept exhaust system—steel crankcase shield—small capacity light alloy petrol tank—Lucas waterproof magneto with manually operated ignition control.

OPTIONAL EXTRA Quickly detachable electric lighting.
Standard or high compression ratio.
Standard gear ratios.

PAGE TEN

The stamina and handling of this famous trials machine has been proved by the successes achieved in innumerable important competitions.

The new 1957 16MC 347cc ohv trials mount was fitted with a new short wheelbase frame, but at this stage still retained much of the roadster components including the full-width alloy brake hubs.

The Magneto Remains

Although coil ignition with an alternator was adopted for the 1958 season on the single-cylinder roadsters, the trials bike (and scramblers) remained faithful to the magneto, a competition (gold) Lucas assembly. Meanwhile, the AMC gearbox-change had been lightened by the employment of a lower-rate selector spring (this applying to both the competition bikes and the roadsters).

The price of the Model 16MC had risen to £243 5s 3d, whilst in May 1958, Gordon Jackson made it win number two on his works three-fifty AJS, in the Scottish Six Days.

A Much Improved Trials Mount for 1959

For 1959 customers were offered what amounted to a production version of Jackson's

All-alloy top end of 1957 16MC and Lucas competition magneto.

1958 Scottish winning machine, or at least as far as cost terms would allow.

Although, as before, the 1959 model-year AJS 348cc trials model retained the long stroke (69 × 93mm) bore and stroke dimensions it shared with its roadster brothers (even though it was strongly rumoured that the works bikes had at least tested a new short-stroke trial motor), there were differences to the touring bike. These were a lower compression ratio, softer cam profile, a light-alloy cylinder barrel and magneto ignition. In other vital areas the 1959 production trials mount was considerably updated – and improved.

To start with the wheelbase was shortened by no less than 1¼in (32mm) to 52¼in (1,327mm) by the simple expedient of fitting a rear fork of different design. Previously, this had resembled that of the roadsters, with a massive malleable casting at the swinging-arm pivot with a bridge member ahead of the wheel. It had been replaced by an unbridged fork which, as on the new two-fifty roadster (*see* Chapter 11), had one arm integral with the pivot spindle and the other clamped and cottered thereto. This modified construction had contributed significantly to a total weight-saving of some 25lb (11kg), whilst a further reduction had come from discarding the malleable cast fork ends in favour of trapped ends to the tubes forming the arms.

The rear subframe was also new, being of much lighter construction, again based on the two-fifty design. The diagonal struts bracing the horizontal tubes were bolted to the seat tube above the fork-pivot lug, and the long, Girling rear-suspension legs were inclined forwards (at the top) by a considerable degree. Since these tubes were shorter, it had been possible to employ smaller-diameter material without sacrificing strength.

Of welded construction, with gussets at the steering head, the main frame was as before, but the Teledraulic front fork had been lightened by way of smaller diameter stanchions, heat-treated to compensate for their reduced tube section. Further weight had been saved

This was the ultimate development of the production 16MC trials model. A 1961 model is shown, but the new frame with long inclined Girling rear shocks, revised swinging-arm and small offset brakes had first appeared for the 1959 season. Only small changes were introduced thereafter.

by using a small 2¾pt (4ltr) oil tank and fabricated 5.5in (140mm) diameter single-sided hubs in place of the much larger (and heavier!) roadster-type full-width 7in (178mm) assemblies of the previous trials bike.

This, then, was the definitive AMC trials mount, which the man-in-the-street could buy, and which was to remain a highly effective mud-plugger from its introduction until the British 4-stroke trial models were finally ousted by the new breed of lightweight 2-strokes, led by the likes of Bultaco and Montesa from the mid-1960s onwards.

The Jackson Glory Years

But before this, came what were to become known throughout the trials world as the 'Jackson Glory Years'. This was the period which straddled the end of the 1950s and the beginning of the 1960s, when AJS works star Gordon Jackson dominated the Scottish Six Days, just as his predecessor Hugh Viney had done in earlier years.

Besides Gordon's debut victory in 1956, he also won in 1958, 1960 and 1961 (plus runner-up in 1959 and 1962) – some record. But the most famous performance came in 1961, when Gordon Jackson scored his fourth and final Scottish victory by only dropping a single point. This was the first and only time this has ever been achieved in the Scottish.

There were very few changes to the production 16MC trials mount until it was finally retired in late 1964, except for having short-stroke (72 × 85.5mm) engine dimensions for its final year and a few modification to the rear subframe and seat base. But by then the writing was on the wall and the 2-stroke invasion had already begun, something from which the British heavyweight 4-stroke was never to recover. But one has to say that if one takes out Sammy Miller's incredible Ariel HT5, the AJS (and Matchless) three-fifty was in many ways the definitive trials bike of the first two decades after the end of the Second World War.

The 1960 16MCS	
Engine	Air-cooled, ohv single with vertical cylinder; alloy head and barrel, vertically split aluminium crankcases; fully enclosed valve gear; hairpin valve springs; built-up crankshaft; roller-bearing big-end; gear-driven cams
Bore	69mm
Stroke	93mm
Displacement	348cc
Compression ratio	6.5:1
Lubrication	Dry sump, two-start oil pump
Ignition	Magneto
Carburettor	Amal Monobloc 376 1¹⁄₁₆in
Primary drive	Chain
Final drive	Chain
Gearbox	4-speed, foot-change, AMC wide-ratio
Frame	All-steel construction, full cradle with single front down-tube
Front suspension	AMC Teledraulic forks
Rear suspension	Swinging arm with twin Girling shock absorbers
Front brake	5.5in, SLS, single-sided drum
Rear brake	5.5in, SLS, single-sided drum
Tyres	2.75 × 21 front; 4.00 × 19 rear
Wheelbase	52.2in (1,326mm)
Ground clearance	10in (254mm)
Seat height	32.5in (825mm)
Fuel tank capacity	2gal (9ltr)
Dry weight	319lb (145kg)
Maximum power	18bhp @ 5,750rpm
Top speed	67mph (108km/h)

The Pre-1965 Classic Trials Scene

However, even when the two-stroke had taken over, many enthusiasts still hankered after the lusty torquey four-stroke. In response, the trials scene started running a separate class for four-strokes beginning as the 1970s dawned. This in turn became the basis for the

Pre-1965 Classic Trials Scene from the late 1970s onwards.

One famous AJS (Gordon Jackson's 1960 Scottish winner, VYW 659, which had first been registered by AMC on 11 December 1958) had survived and was purchased 'in poor condition' by Isle of Wight farmer and trials rider, Aubrey Attrill. Aubrey then carried out a total rebuild, which included fitting a standard 16MC (69 × 93mm) engine. When purchased it still had the original works short-stroke motor (72 × 85.5mm) with 7R flywheels, modified scrambles cylinder head and a 7R clutch.

It also featured a works-fitted later type frame and wheels, special alloy brake plates and central alloy oil tank. First time out Aubrey Attrill won the Gordon Jackson Four-stroke Class at Hungry Hill, near Petersfield during 1974. The only modification on the meticulously built replacement long-stroke engine was that the valve timing was a ½ tooth out from standard. The bike, with both the standard 'replacement' engine and the works short-stroke unit, survives to the present day and is still in Attrill family ownership.

Gordon Jackson's 1960 Scottish Six Days' winning 16MCS (VYW 659). First registered by AMC on 11 December 1958 it was sold to Comerfords on 9 December 1962. Purchased by Isle of Wight farmer Aubrey Attrill in 1973, it was subsequently totally rebuilt (see story in main text). Photograph shows the bike as it is now.

8   Twin-Cylinder Roadsters

Triumph and Edward Turner had begun the trend during the late 1930s with the legendary Speed Twin. Then post-war, Royal Enfield, followed by Norton and finally AMC launched brand new 500cc-class vertical twins within weeks of each other during autumn 1948. The announcement from AMC of its new AJS and Matchless twins came as an eve-of-show surprise for the London Earls Court exhibition which opened on the 18 November 1948. However, although great excitement was generated by their arrival it remains a fact that, for potential British buyers, the AMC twins were not to be available for some considerable time, as all initial production was destined for overseas markets, notably the British Commonwealth and North America.

The Model 20 'Spring Twin'

The new AJS Model 20, named the 'Spring Twin', received the following write-up in *The Motor Cycle* Show Issue, dated 25 November 1948:

> Although British motor cyclists have no chance of buying an AJS vertical-twin, these models capture the attention of the crowds on the AJS stand. This is not surprising, because the design embodies the most advanced technical features, including a three-bearing cast-iron crankshaft, separate cylinder castings and light-alloy cylinder heads. Many favourable comments were to be overheard regarding the attention given to detail points, such as the absence of external oil pipes, the use of chromium plated domed nuts, and the general neatness of the power unit. Wide interest was also aroused by the spring-frame which, fitted as standard on the twin and available as an extra for the single-cylinder models, is also in the 'export only' category. The layout of the swinging rear fork with Teledraulic legs for controlling the 3in of wheel movement follows racing practice.

Besides having a sprung saddle/pillion pad and traditional AMC fluted silencers (and of course a different finish), the AJS Model 20 Spring Twin was priced at £209 11s (including UK purchase tax) compared to its Matchless brother, the G9 Super Clubman which featured megaphone silencers and a dual seat and a higher price of £212 1s 10d (again including taxes).

The Engine Design

A heavy-duty cast iron was employed for the crankshaft of the new engine. This was a one-piece casting including the bobweights between the outer main bearings and the big-end bearings, and the flywheels between the big-ends and the main bearing in the centre. This use of a middle bearing was unique amongst British ohv twins of the era. The outer mains were of the journal roller types and the shafts measured 1⅜in (34mm) diameter at the journals. In the centre there was a Vandervell shell white-metal bearing of 1⅝in (40mm) by 1¼in (32mm) width. Bearings for

The early AJS Model 20, the 'Spring Twin' which first appeared in time for the 1949 season differed from its Matchless brother, the G9 Super Clubman, in details such as seating arrangements, silencers, price, colour scheme and of course badges.

the big-ends were of a similar type and diameter but were 1⁵⁄₁₆in (33mm) wide.

Location of the crankshaft was affected by the central bearing. This was a split bearing and was carried by a light alloy diaphragm plate bolted to the driving-side half of the crankcase; the plate was also spigoted into both halves of the crankcase, and thus could not be seen when the crankcase was assembled. To allow for crankcase expansion the outer roller bearings were not shouldered and therefore permitted lateral movement of the case relative to the crankshaft.

Light alloy- RR56 was employed for the connecting rods. These were particularly robust in the area of the big-end eyes, and were polished to remove surface scratches (thus decreasing the possibility of premature breakage).

An unusual type of fixing for the bearing-cap retaining studs was used. Steel rods, which formed trunnions, were pressed into the conrods. Into these screwed the big-end cap studs, and thus the cutaway necessary to accommodate the head of the usual form of retaining bolt (sometimes a source of weakness) was avoided.

There were no separate small-end bushes; instead the con-rods operated directly on the gudgeon pins. Each small-end eye was provided with a quartet of holes, two at the top and two at the bottom, for lubrication purposes.

Pistons were of the split-skirt, wire-wound

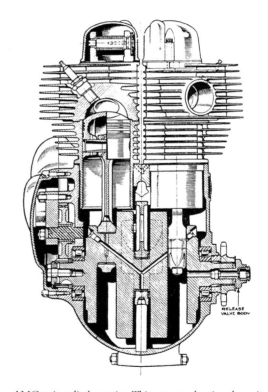

AMC twin-cylinder engine. This cutaway drawing shows its separate cylinders and heads, crankshaft with central bearing, pistons and con-rods.

variety, and had already proved their worth in the AMC single-cylinder engines. Each piston featured two compression rings and one slotted scraper ring. The piston crown was domed and had flats to clear the valves. Of ¾in (19mm) diameter, the gudgeon pin was tapered at the

A 1930 Wolverhampton-built overhead camshaft AJS single photographed by the author at the VMCC Founders' Day, July 2002.

AJS water-cooled, supercharged V4 five-hundred, the first motorcycle to lap the famous Clady circuit in Ulster at 100mph. The rider was Walter Rusk, the year 1939. The bike is now on show at Sammy Miller's Museum at New Milton.

A 1946 AJS three-fifty 16M. This was one of the first post-war bikes from Plumstead, and was based around the successful WD Matchless G3/L.

An extract from the 1948 AJS brochure, showing highlights of the firm's racing successes over the decades.

In 1949 Les Graham and his AJS Porcupine twin became the very first holders of the 500cc Road Race World Championship title.

AJS rider Hugh Viney won the prestigious Scottish Six Days' Trial in 1947, 1948, 1949 and 1953.

The cover from the 1953 AJS brochure.

A November 1953 advertisement showing the 1954 model-year heavyweight ohv single and highlighting the marque's continuing sporting successes.

An AJS advert promoting the company's stand at the 1953 Earls Court Show – the latest Model 18S 500cc ohv single with swinging-arm rear suspension, dual seat and new-for-1954 alloy front hub.

March 1954 and springtime means the return (hopefully!) of motorcycling weather.

November 1954 and the latest Model 20 Spring Twin 498cc vertical twin is shown against the backdrop of the Isle of Man Junior TT victory that year by Rod Coleman and the AJS 3-valve works single the previous June.

The 1956 AJS brochure proclaiming the arrival of two new motocross Models.

A 1957 model year 592cc Model 30 twin with AMC gearbox and Girling rear shocks; this was the last year of small, separate headlamp-mounted pilot lamps.

A mid-1950s 7R with Burman gearbox, owned by Dumfries enthusiast and classic racer Colin Dunbar.

The 1960 AJS 31CSR, a sports model with siamezed exhaust, alloy mudguards and small dual seat.

The author seated on the 7R he raced at the Snetterton Combine's National Road Races, Snetterton, summer 1967. His brother and mechanic, Rick, is standing alongside.

American film and TV actor Richard Wyler raced various bikes on the British short circuits during the early 1960s. He is seen here on his 7R at Snetterton in 1964.

The cover of the 1962 factory brochure with a Model 14 two-fifty single.

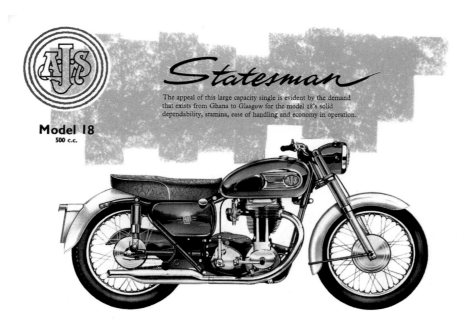

Statesman

The appeal of this large capacity single is evident by the demand that exists from Ghana to Glasgow for the model 18's solid dependability, stamina, ease of handling and economy in operation.

Model 18
500 c.c.

A 1962 AJS Model 18 500cc Statesman. 'The appeal of this large-capacity single is evident by the demand that exists from Ghana to Glasgow for the Model 18's solid dependability, stamina, ease of handling and economy in operation.' All true, except the word 'demand', as during the mid-1960s sales plummeted, leaving the once-great company in dire straits.

ends and retained by spring circlips. With bore and stroke dimensions of 66 × 72.8mm respectively, the five-hundred twin engine was slightly long-stroke and displaced 498cc.

The cylinders were separate cast-iron castings and were sunk to a depth of approximately 2½in (63mm) in the crankcase mouths. And except for the segment below the cap of the middle crankshaft bearing, the diaphragm plate separated the crankcase into two compartments.

Cylinder heads were in light alloy, and again were separate castings. These castings included the inlet and exhaust valve-spring wells and support for rocker spindles. A quartet of studs screwed into the crankcase to retain each cylinder head and barrel; on these studs were fitted chromium-plated, domed retaining nuts, and below them, waisted distance pieces. This waisting was provided so that airflow was not impeded. Bolted to the two cylinder heads above the exhaust ports was a flat head-steady, described by the AMC launch technical bulletin as a 'tie-plate'. Between each cylinder (which had a spigot) and its head was a gasket.

Each combustion chamber was hemispherical in shape and had shrunk-in valve seats. The iron inlet valve-guide and a bronze guide for the exhaust were a press fit in their bosses, and were prevented from being forced too far by spring circlips. Cylinder-head finning was conventional except at the crown, between the valve spring wells, where the fins were of diagonal shape from the outside at the front to the inside at the rear. The valves featured semi-tulip heads and hardened stem ends to resist wear from contact with the rockers.

Inlet and exhaust valves were in silchrome and KE965 steel respectively. The inlet valve had a $\frac{9}{32}$in (7mm) diameter stem with 1in (35mm) diameter head, and the exhaust valve had a $\frac{5}{16}$in (8mm) diameter stem with 1¼in (31mm) diameter head. Each valve was equipped with a pair of inner and outer springs, concentric in shape, with split collets seating in a groove in the stem retaining the valve-spring collar.

The 1949 20	
Engine	Air-cooled, ohv twin with vertical cylinders; separate alloy heads; separate cast-iron barrels; three main bearings (one central); one-piece crankshaft with split big-ends and Hiduminium RR56 con-rods; gear-driven camshafts fore and aft; coil valve springs; separate rocker boxes (four)
Bore	66mm
Stroke	72.8mm
Displacement	498cc
Compression ratio	7:1; 1956–58, 7.8:1; 1959 onwards, 8:1
Lubrication	Dry sump, twin gear-oil pumps
Ignition	Magdyno, Lucas, 6-volt
Carburettor	1949–54 Amal 76 1in; 1955–61 Amal Monobloc 376 1in
Primary drive	Chain
Final drive	Chain
Gearbox	4-speed footchange, 1949–51 Burman CP; 1952–56 Burman B52; 1957 onwards AMC
Frame	Two-part with single front down-tube, branching into twin tubes under engine; single top (tank) tube
Front suspension	AMC Teledraulic oil-damped forks
Rear suspension	Swinging arm, with oil-damped twin shock absorbers
Front brake	7in, SLS drum, single-sided; 7in full-width 1954 onwards
Rear brake	7in, SLS drum, single-sided; 7in full-width 1955 onwards
Tyres	3.25 × 19 front; 3.50 × 19 rear
Wheelbase	55.2in (1,402mm)
Ground clearance	5.5in (140mm)
Seat height	30in (762mm)
Fuel tank capacity	3gal (14ltr); 1954, 3.75gal (17ltr); 1959, 4.25gal (19ltr)
Dry weight	394lb (179kg)
Maximum power	29bhp @ 6,800rpm; 1956, 30.5bhp
Top speed	87mph (140km/h)

The rockers were one-piece forgings, and were each fitted with a pair of ⅝in (16mm)-long, phosphor-bronze bushes; the tips of the rockers bore directly on the valve stems, and the integral ball-ends were hardened. Rocker spindles were ½in (13mm) in diameter, and were mounted eccentrically in the supports in the cylinder head. This eccentric mounting was to provide rocker clearance adjustment, and followed the practice adopted on the 7R three-fifty ohc single-cylinder racing engine. Each spindle had a wide, flat, circular head with a segment ground back, and a small clamp-bolt located in the inner rocker support bore on this segment and held the spindle when the correct rocker setting had been obtained. Each rocker assembly had its own light-alloy cover, and there was a sealing washer between the face and the face around the valve-spring well. Four bolts, with extended heads for accessibility, clamped down the cover and thus ensured an oil-tight joint.

The inlet ports of the two cylinder heads were joined by a light-alloy manifold on which was fitted the single Amal Type 76 1in (25mm) carburettor. The exhaust pipes were a push-fit into the exhaust ports.

The Timing Gear

The timing gear was described by *The Motor Cycle* as 'noteworthy', long life and quietness in operation having been a priority in the design. Spur gears were employed with teeth of %₆in (14mm) width. Above the half-time pinion on the crankshaft was an idler pinion; this meshed with the inlet and exhaust camshaft pinions. The inlet camshaft drove a Lucas flange-fitting magneto, which had manual timing control and a cut-out. The exhaust camshaft pinion drove a 3in (75mm) diameter Lucas dynamo at 1⅕ engine speed. The dynamo was retained in a cradle formed in the crankcase casting by a clamping band, and also by screws from the timing chest into the end cover.

The one-piece forged camshafts, of ¹³⁄₁₆in (20mm) diameter at the bearing journals, each ran in three ⅝in (16mm)-long phosphor-bronze bushes. Two bushes were placed between the pinion and the cams, and the third bush was at the end remote from the pinion. The cams operated single-arm followers that were mounted directly on steel spindles; these spindles located in each half of the crankcase and acted as dowels. Formed in the followers were cups to take the ball ends of the pushrods.

Twin Gear-Oil Pumps

Twin gear-oil pumps were employed for the lubrication system. These were bolted to the crankcase inside the timing chest, by way of an aluminium plate. One pump was for supply, and the other for the return feed. The mounting plate also provided an outer support for the idler pinion. The oil pumps were driven by tongues mating with slots in the ends of the two camshafts, the exhaust cam operating the supply sump and the inlet cam the return.

From a ½gal (2ltr) tank next to the seat tube, oil was transferred by a flexible pipe to a banjo union on the crankcase and then to the supply pump. In the crankcase casting was a spring-loaded ball valve to prevent overloading of the pump gears. If the pressure exceeded a predetermined limit the valve opened and allowed oil to pass back into the feed line. From the pump the lubricant went via a filter chamber positioned laterally in the front of the crankcase casting.

The oil filter featured a fabric element and was provided with a spring-loaded relief valve to ensure that the element would be bypassed should it become choked. Access to this filter element was gained by removing a cap on the offside (right) of the crankcase. Within the filter chamber cap there was another non-return ball valve to prevent oil draining from the tank into the crankcase when the engine was not running.

From the filter chamber the oilway in the

crankcase split into two. The main outlet conveyed lubricating oil by means of a diaphragm plate to the crankshaft centre bearing, and thereafter via the crankshaft to the big-end bearings. Then from the big-ends, the oil was flung to the small ends, the pistons and the cylinder bores, plus the crankcase bearings. The small outlet led to a ported distributor at the end of the exhaust camshaft. This was located in the nearside (left) of the crankcase, and its boss was sealed by a detachable chromium-plated cap. This distributor directed oil to the upper and lower grooves round the deep spigots of the cylinder barrels.

Passages within the cylinder head and barrel castings led oil from the upper grooves in the inner rocker spindle of each rocker box. Again they split two ways, one along the centre of the rocker spindle with an outlet between the two bushes, the other directing or, more correctly, squirting oil into the pushrod-end cup in which the rocker ball-end was seated. Surplus oil lubricated the valve guide and then drained down the pushrod tunnel in the cylinder head and barrel castings into the camshaft chamber.

From the lower grooves in the cylinder barrel spigots the oil was directed to the camshaft chambers, and the supply was enough to enable the camshafts to operate in an oil bath. After circulating under pressure from the supply pump, the lubricating oil drained down to the base of the crankcase, whereafter it was drawn by the return pump through a cast-in pipe and forced back to the tank.

In the drive side of the crankcase and operated by the inlet camshaft was a mechanical release valve. A cap similar to the one that sealed the oil distributor was screwed into the crankcase wall. The release pipe led back to the oil tank.

The Transmission

A separate Burman 4-speed gearbox with a five-spring multi-plate clutch (also of Burman manufacture) and positive stop foot-change

mechanism, was specified for the Model 20 Spring Twin (and the Matchless G9 Super Clubman). In addition a cam-type engine-shaft shock absorber was fitted; primary drive was courtesy of a simplex chain and encased in the already well-known AMC pressed-steel oil-bath case.

The New Spring Frame

A feature of the new AMC twins was their new spring frames – a first on a standard production motorcycle from the Plumstead factory. In laying out this new assembly, its creators had retained the steering head, front down-tube and saddle tube of the existing rigid frame already in use on the single-cylinder machines. In addition, the famous hydraulically-damped Teledraulic front forks and the brakes, except for a small detail, were also identical to those found on the singles. The exception was that on the twins, a long front-brake torque arm was used in place of bolts attaching the shoe plate to the fork leg.

For the spring frame (as AMC liked to describe its swinging-arm chassis), the twin cradle tubes that passed under the engine and gearbox were attached by a transverse bolt – the cradle tubes being gusseted for additional strength at this point – to the base of a light alloy bridge casting, which extended from the base of the seat tube and curved around the rear of the gearbox. The cradle tubes extended beyond the transverse bolt and provided anchorage for the pillion footrests and the silencers.

A 1in (25mm)-diameter steel tube acted as the swinging-arm pivot point, and the twin AMC 'Candlestick' suspension unit provided both comfort and good road-holding. The pivot tube operated on sintered bronze bushes 1in (25mm) long. Lubrication was achieved very simply by filling the tube with oil on assembly. The tube featured end plates which in effect sealed the oil reservoir, the oil feeding round the ends of the tube to the moving surfaces, between the inner ends of the fork eyes and the bridge casting of the swinging-arm fork casting with felt sealing washers.

The rear wheel spindle was of a larger diameter than the one employed with the rigid frame. Another difference was that the adjustment was carried out by cams on the spindle bearing against projections on the swinging-arm lugs.

Based on the type already fitted to the 7R racing model, the rear shock absorber design, nicknamed 'Candlestick', contained a coil spring and a hydraulic damping device. These units were rubber-bushed at top and bottom. Factory sources gave a total movement (at the wheel spindle) of 3in (75mm).

Other details of the new Model 20 Spring Twin's specification included centre and side stands, a headlamp with the latest Lucas fixed-focus bulb, a pair of elongated toolboxes, 19in wheels, with 3.25 front and 3.50 rear section tyres, and a 3gal (14ltr) fuel tank with twin taps.

More Development

With the Model 20 (and Matchless G9) proving so popular that orders outpaced supply, it was perhaps unsurprising that when the 1950 model range was announced in mid-October 1949, the AMC twin-cylinder design remained unchanged, except for detail modification shared with the single-cylinder touring models; the rear brake pedal and mudguards had been redesigned, and the rear brake hub had been made wider.

Almost a year later, in September 1950, there were quite significant changes for the entire 1951 AJS range, including the Model 20 Spring Twin. On all touring and competition bikes there was a new clutch, its design based largely upon experience gained in road racing with the 7R ohc single. Another more visible alteration was the introduction of new, fatter rear suspension units, soon dubbed 'Jampots'. Again, these assemblies had benefited from the firm's participation in sporting events, this time on the dirt, rather than the tarmac. AMC claimed that the new shocks 'permit slightly

less fork arm movement than has been the case heretofore, but this definitely avoids all tendency towards "bottoming" when the machine is used on really rough country.'

For the 1951 range, AMC gave chaincase sealing a revision. The long-established V-section rubber band used by the company gave way to what AMC described as a 'mushroom'-section sealing band, this (at least in theory) forming a gasket between each half of the chaincase, and fitting into the light alloy retaining strap. However, both this seal design and an improved seal for 1953 still proved prone to leakage, and it was only an entirely new aluminium case several years later that finally solved the problem.

Also new for the 1951 model year was an entirely redesigned front suspension. Still of the Teledraulic type, AMC claimed 'considerable improvement' over what had gone before, saying: 'this gives complete freedom from oil leaks, the loading on the hydraulic seals on the forks having been considerably reduced'. The London firm were also able to point out that one of *Motor Cycling*'s staff members had recently completed a 900-mile (1,500km) Continental Europe test, during which the journalist had 'found that the manufacturers' claims with regard to these components (including the forks and rear shock absorbers) are fully justified'.

The new front-fork sliders featured recessed drain plugs. This was a departure from a decade of established practice, and was dictated largely by the requirements of the Australian importers, following damage sustained by several owners to the existing drain plugs when parking their machines against the unusually high kerbs existing in some parts of that vast country!

An air filter was now included, and to accommodate the filter the frame of the Model 20 (and its Matchless brother, the G9) had been slightly modified. Since the twins' introduction at the 1948 London Show the magneto cut-out had been handlebar-mounted, and this now took the form of a simple push-button situated on the Lucas magneto contact-breaker cover.

In the words of an official factory press release, 'With a view to making the range yet more attractive, a considerable number of minor "cleaning-up" innovations have been carried out.' For example, there was a provision on the twin for longer centre-stand legs, giving higher lift – important for tyre changes.

On all the swinging-arm frame models, the rear mudguard joints were now shrouded to prevent water and mud flung up by the rear wheel from trickling through on to the outer side of the mudguard. All models now featured a flexible horn mounting, since the older, rigid type had proved prone to fracturing. Improved production methods at the AMC Plumstead works had been responsible for the introduction of a forged steel steering crown member in place of the fabricated assembly previously employed. Finally, the fuel tank of the Model 20 (still smaller than the G9) received oval metal 'AJS' badges.

1952 AJS Model 20 498cc twin with alloy heads and cast-iron barrels, single front down-tube frame and pressed-steel primary chaincase with aluminium band.

Model 20
THE SPRINGTWIN
500 c.c. O.H.V. VERTICAL TWIN

The acknowledged leader of its class

For full specification see page 10

Page 3

1953 AJS brochure, showing the five-hundred Model 20 twin.

1954 Model 20 Spring Twin with full-width alloy front hub, small pilot lights, chrome tank and 'Jampot' rear shocks.

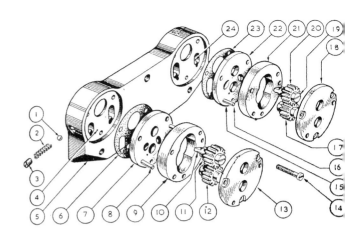

The twin oil pumps of the twin-cylinder family; together with their mounting plate.

Additionally, *Motor Cycling* was able to report in its 21 September issue:

> Particular good news for those who aspire to owning either the luxurious Matchless G9 Super Clubman twin or the AJS counterpart, the Spring Twin, is that both these models will definitely become available on the home market in 1951 – that is to say, from now onwards.

When the 1952 range was announced in late September 1951 there was another raft of changes. All models, including the Spring Twin, were given the new Burman B52 gearbox, as well as a clutch access cap in the primary chaincase, an aluminium front brake plate, and a malleable iron top fork crown. There was also an underslung pilot light, flexible-mounted voltage-control box, positive earth and colour-coded wiring. The only 'twins-only' feature to be introduced that year was the introduction of an engine breather in the crankshaft drive end.

More Changes for 1953

Early in 1952 a curious pillion seat, linked at its forward section to the saddle, made its bow on the Spring Twin, but this was superseded for the 1953 season by the adoption of a dual seat (which it now shared with the G9 Matchless).

AMC's policy of year-by-year improvements

Fabled AMC 'Jampot' rear shock absorber; unfortunately, although good looking they were prone to lose their damping efficiency all too early.

saw many other innovations when the 1953 range was announced in mid-1952. Actually, the standardization of the dual seat across the range of road-going swinging-arm models (referred to above) was the most noticeable

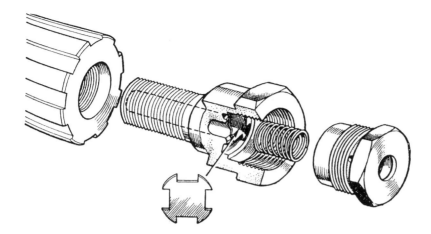

The engine breather introduced for the twins from 1952 had a flap valve in the end of the crankshaft.

1953 model-year feature, if not the most important. This seat was similar to, though not the same as, the seat which had been used on the Matchless G9 Super Clubman since its introduction in late 1948; the 1953 seat was narrower, now measuring 11in (280mm) across the top. The length remained the same at 24in (608mm), and the general seat design was unchanged. Blue piping was a feature of the AJS seat, whereas red was used on Matchless models.

Otherwise, a cursory glance might have led one to believe that both the AJS and Matchless machines were unchanged. That, however, would have been totally incorrect, because although it was true that there were no major changes and no new models, there were numerous detail refinements, including the twin-cylinder bikes.

Although still single-sided – and single leading shoe – the front brake had been modified to provide increased stopping power. There was very little that was different in the appearance of the newly-revised brake compared to the assembly it replaced. The shoe plate had been moved anti-clockwise through a number of degrees, whilst the cam lever had been turned relative to the camshaft, so that the lever projected forwards instead of to the rear, the cable stop having also been moved to the front of the fork. The new position for the

cam lever provided maximum mechanical efficiency on the leading shoe instead of the trailing shoe, and thus provided improved braking performance.

Also provided was 'a simple, thief-proof lock' (*The Motor Cycle*) – an indication that even in the early 1950s, motorcycle security was a potential problem. For this, the lower steering-head lug was drilled vertically in the vicinity of the nearside (left) tank stop.

For 1953, all AJS (and Matchless) models were given a new primary-chaincase sealing band. This new item was an endless, synthetic rubber moulding, wider than the one it replaced. AMC sources claimed that 'frequent removal and replacement of the band will in no way impair the oil tightness of the chain case'; although in practice, once it had been disturbed, its sealing abilities were never of the same quality as when new. In fact primary-chaincase leakage was to plague the AMC twins and singles until the introduction of the all-alloy 'case' for the 1958 model year.

A new Lucas rear lamp, the Diacon, made its debut on all the roadster models. This was manufactured in moulded plastic, the lens being oblong in shape with a white section underneath. It had been designed not only to provide more light at the rear, but also to permit a stop-light to be incorporated, which was available as a cost option.

Other modifications which applied to all 1953 models were the incorporation of a short length of flexible tubing in the fuel pipe, and an alteration to the top covers of the fork legs. The covers to which the headlamp brackets were welded were now free to pivot on the main fork tubes, and a tight fit was achieved by the insertion of a rubber washer at the base of each cover tube. This change had been introduced to enable the headlamp brackets to be turned through 90 degrees when bikes were packed for export, thus meaning the motorcycle was far less likely to be damaged in transit. So that there was no unsightly gap when the fork was fully extended, the slider extension tube had been lengthened. Allen screws instead of studs were employed to clamp the fork stanchions in the lower steering-head lug.

Another modification was that the rear mudguard was now fully detachable. Previously, both the mudguard and its hinged extension had been dipped in the enamelling bath together, but occasionally this resulted in a series of 'runs' in the vicinity of the hinge and rivets. Thereafter both sections of the guard were dipped separately. To remove the detachable portion, four ⁵⁄₁₆in BSF bolts had to be slackened off; these screws mated up with captive nuts in the welded pockets, which were, in turn, welded to a mild steel bridge-piece on the underside of the guard. The bolt holes in the detachable guard were slotted to facilitate removal.

Another feature introduced across the range of AJS and Matchless machines for 1953 was the fitment of a chromium-plated piston ring in the top groove. AMC said it had 'carried out extensive tests which showed that the use of a chromium-plated ring reduced cylinder-bore wear by two-thirds.'

The engines of the AJS Spring Twin and Matchless G9 were now of a slightly different appearance. The rocker-box covers were now retained by one or two studs, instead of the four fitted previously, and the pair of cylinder-head steady tubes employed before had been superseded by a triangular ⅛in (3mm)-thick, mild steel plate. This plate was joined to a pair of extensions on the cylinder head, and a lug brazed to the front down-tube of the frame.

The cam followers were now slightly longer, this having been achieved by moving the follower fulcrums further away from the cams. The reason was to improve the angle between the cam and follower, thus lengthening the life of the follower.

Finally, there was the provision of a small, neoprene rubber sealing ring in the carburettor joint face of the inlet manifold. This was needed because of service experience where AMC had discovered that the carburettor joint face of their twin-cylinder engine could become distorted after even a very low mileage. Factory sources saying the basis of this problem was that: 'the carburettor actively bends as a result of torque reversals in the engine, and the joint face, as a result, becomes slightly concave'. The company's engineering team solved the problem with what, in effect, was an 'O' ring. This idea was later taken up by Amal and introduced into their carburettor design.

The 1954 Model Year

A year later, when the 1954 AJS range was announced in September 1953, the big story was a brand new full-width, light alloy, die-cast front brake hub (sand-cast hubs, fully machined, being used on the initial batch of machines to avoid production delays). A feature of this hub was the use of straight spokes which, because they were inherently stronger than the angled variety, enabled a slight reduction in gauge size.

The flanged 7in (178mm)-diameter cast-iron brake drum was shrunk on to the hub shell and bolted through the flange. Waterproofing of the brake was achieved by incorporating, on that side of the hub, a conical face on the inside of the spoke flange. The conical face acted as a water flinger; in addition there was a step between the braking surface of the drum and the shell, which

A Model 20 of 1954 vintage superbly restored by a Scottish enthusiast, Ingleston, Edinburgh, August 2003.

Nearside view of 1954 Model 20 showing AJS badge on crankcase (just below cylinder barrel), cylinder head steady, valve covers, front-mounted generator and rear-mounted magneto.

further helped to keep water out. At the same time a new cast-aluminium brake plate was adopted, with a slightly domed exterior and with a grease nipple for the cam spindle. The shoes themselves, and their operating mechanism and anchorage, were largely as on the existing single-sided brake. A light alloy disc with concentric corrugations closed the offside (right) side of the hub.

Only one modification to the twin–cylinder engine was introduced for the 1954 model year: the oil holes in the big-end journals were repositioned to eliminate any build-up of sludge in the oilways. This meant that de-sludging of the crankshaft at 20,000 mile (32,000km) intervals, which AMC had formerly advised, was no longer needed.

On all models, including the Model 20 Spring Twin, the bottom front engine mounting bolt, which also connected the cradle to the front down-tube, had been increased in diameter from ⁵⁄₁₆in (8mm) to ³⁄₈in (9mm) in the interests of rigidity.

A new fuel tank with a capacity of 3¾gal (17ltr) was now fitted to all 500cc touring models (twins and singles); this meant that for the first time the AJS and Matchless twins both shared the same tank. In order to improve the accessibility of the oil filter, the filter-element was now located in the outer half of the tank. Another modification, also made for the purpose of accessibility, was to transfer the voltage regulator unit to a position between the seat stays under the saddle; this meant that the air filter could be changed much more easily. As has already been mentioned, on the twins the horn was rubber-mounted from a lug on the front down-tube to which the cylinder-head steady stays were bolted, this lug having now been redesigned.

There were a couple of changes made to the electrics, which were applicable to all models: a new dip switch (much easier to operate than the one it replaced), and the underslung pilot light was abandoned in favour of a pair of small lamps, one on each side mounted on the outside of the headlamp supports. In addition, the leads which emerged from the dynamo were enclosed in a rubber sheath, giving increased protection and a much neater appearance.

The development team had also improved access to the clutch, so that the primary chaincase outer half no longer had to be removed first. A domed cover which embraced the entire clutch and was held on by eight screws replaced the small inspection cover panel. In addition the clutch was now lined with a new friction material. AMC sources claimed that this provided superior grip when oily, rather than dry, but did not suffer from the usual 'sticking' problems which were evident with cork-lined plates running in oil. As a result of the improved frictional qualities, it had been possible to reduce the number of plates without increasing the danger of suffering clutch slip.

With the relaxation of nickel restrictions, chromium plating was reintroduced for the wheel rims. The wheels had enamelled centres, with gold lining for AJS machines and silver for Matchless models. The list price of the Model 20 Spring Twin in September 1953 was £240 (including British taxes).

More Development for 1955

When the 1955 model year AJS bikes were launched in early September 1954, *The Motor Cycle* called it 'evolutionary development'. And although there were no new models or any really startling changes, there were nonetheless numerous refinements to the ten-strong AJS range, which included the Model 20 Spring Twin.

But it was the Matchless G45 racing model which helped both the AJS Spring Twin and the Matchless G9 Super Clubman, with detail modification to the 498cc twin-cylinder engine including improved lubrication at the pushrod end of the overhead rockers. In the top of the rocker arm was a groove which was fed with oil via an oilway leading from the bore of the plain rocker bearing to the inboard end of the groove. The oil was carried to the outer end of this groove by centrifugal force, and then ran over the rocker end into the pushrod cup. This copied what was already employed on the G45 unit.

A shallower and more attractive cap nut was now fitted over the oil-filter element in the front of the crankcase, whilst there was an improved exhaust pipe lower mounting specified. The former double-cranked brackets from the header pipes to the front engine plates had been replaced by tubular pillar nuts which connected to the forward cradle bolt.

Several modifications were introduced, and were common to all engines. Formerly, air filters (still an optional extra) had been of different types on singles and twins, but now one type was adopted across the entire AJS and Matchless ranges. And, surprisingly in that it had been announced in the press only a week earlier, the new Amal Monobloc carburettor was fitted as standard equipment. On the Model 20 this was a 1in (25mm) 376 instrument with, as originally supplied (for the UK market), a 220 main jet and a number 4 slide.

The Lubrication System

The lubrication system had been tidied up across the entire AJS range, including the Model 20 twin, by repositioning the main feed and return pipes below the oil tank. Previously those pipes when viewed from the offside (right) of the motorcycle, lay side-by-side, but in the revised layout one pipe sat in front of the other.

Following the success enjoyed by the full-width hub fitted to the front wheel of 1954 models, for 1955 AMC introduced this type on the rear wheel too. Full-width hubs now fore and aft, as *The Motor Cycle* said, gave a 'greatly improved appearance' – thanks in no small part to the redesign of the 1955-type hubs. These featured a reduction in width, achieved by increasing dishing on the brake shoe plate and end cover, and by providing the die-cast hub shell with a more barrel-like appearance. This latter feature was achieved by making the middle cooling fins deeper than the outer fins. The rear hub did not, however, embody the brake drum, which was still in unit with the rear sprocket. On the spring-frame bikes (which of course included the Model 20 twin), the hub was QD (Quickly Detachable) in which guise it was equipped with a pull-out spindle.

The front mudguard on all the AMC roadsters for 1955 had been redesigned following feedback from owners and factory testers who had complained that much of the water and road filth thrown back on to the machine came via the front mudguard stays. The new guard, therefore, had no stays except at its very base. *The Motor Cycle* described the new mudguard thus: 'It is undoubtedly a good-looking guard, and is claimed to be as effective as a heavily valanced component.' To provide adequate rigidity, the mudguard extensions attached to the fork legs were radiused into the mudguard and were equipped with a stiffening bridge member spot-welded in place.

The front fork stanchion tube diameter had been upped from 1⅛in (28mm) to 1¼in (30mm). The reason for this change was not to improve handling, but rather to give greater resistance to damage in the event of an accident. The upper covers, between the steering head yokes, were tapered to make up the larger diameter spring covers; and the welded-on headlamp brackets, instead of providing a triangular form, now featured a horizontal top edge.

Both the upper and lower fork yokes had been redesigned, the lower one now a forging clamped to the fork tubes by means of socket-head screws; the speedometer cable passed through a rubber-grommeted hole in the web of the yoke. The overall height of the steering head was lowered, the steering column having been reduced, whilst the handlebar shape had also been altered to provide increased tank clearance for the riders' fingers on full lock.

The 'Jampot' rear shocks had been modified, so that the bottom spring abutment was no longer screwed to the slider, and was now a shell moulding located by a circlip. An internal modification to the damper assembly had eliminated problems surrounding the damper fluid experienced in the original set-up when under extreme conditions.

The frame now had a hole for an air filter tube, pressed steel lugs for the pillion footrests, and there was a deeper chain guard together with a simplified oil tank and battery carrier mounting. Yet another change was to a deeper headlamp shell, carrying the speedometer.

A Six-Hundred Twin

In September 1955, AMC launched its new six-hundred twin – known as the AJS Model 30 and Matchless G11. These were identical to the existing 498cc models except for tank finish and engine displacement.

The newcomers had been created in response to the demand for increased power from AMC's chief export customers, notably the United States of America. Additionally, this increase in engine size would benefit the sidecar enthusiast at home who required more torque than was available from the five-hundred twins. Additionally, as *The Motor Cycle* pointed out:

> For the solo rider in Britain, too, whether he required extra speed or not, there are advantages accruing from the use of increased capacity. Improved torque means better low-speed pulling; and reduced engine wear and tear is likely to be achieved since the power unit, for most of its life, is operating comfortably within its limits.

Displacing 592cc, the larger engine capacity had been achieved by increasing the bore size of the engine from 66mm of the 500 to 72mm, the stroke remaining at 72.8mm. This meant the new 600 was almost square. Engine modifications to the latest 498cc Model 20, and incorporated also of course on the new 592cc Model 30, were oil scraper rings and the replacement of the oil tank fabric filter by a crankcase magnetic filter. Additionally, thanks to improving supplies of higher octane fuels, the compression ratio of the Model 20 had been raised from 7:1 to 7.8:1; the ratio for the new 600 Model 30 being 7.5:1.

There was also a new frame (also fitted to the latest singles), featuring a vertical, instead of diagonal, seat tube. AMC also claimed that lateral rigidity had been improved by locating the swinging-arm pivot in a malleable iron lug clamped between the cradle tubes and brazed to the lower end of the seat tube; previously the pivot spindle had been carried in a light alloy casting linking the seat tube with the rear of the cradle. In general terms the mixed brazed and bolted-up construction of the frame had not changed, but by minor alterations to the rear subframe, the horizontal line of the fuel tank base was now continued through to the rear of the motorcycle.

Developments for 1956

For the 1956 model year the AMC engineering team had continued development apace. One modification concerned the strengthening of the fabricated sidecar attachment brackets on both sides of the rear subframe (on all roadster models). These brackets, which also supported the silencers and pillion footrests, were previously fillet-welded to the subframe tubes, but this had led to a number of owners experiencing distortion problems. This had been tackled by employing a one-piece pressing on each side of the machine, both of these brackets being wrapped round the tube and brazed to it, with the two meeting edges being subsequently welded together.

The 1956 Model 30	
Engine	Air-cooled, ohv twin with vertical cylinders, separate alloy heads; separate cast-iron barrels; three main bearings (one central); one-piece crankshaft with split big-ends and Hiduminium RR56 con-rods; gear-driven camshafts fore and aft; coil valve springs; separate rocker boxes (four)
Bore	72mm
Stroke	72.8mm
Displacement	592cc
Compression ratio	7.5:1
Lubrication	Dry sump, twin gear-oil pumps
Ignition	Magdyno, Lucas, 6-volt
Carburettor	Amal Monobloc 376 1in
Primary drive	Chain
Final drive	Chain
Gearbox	4-speed foot-change, Burman B52; 1957 onwards, AMC
Frame	Two-part with single front down-tube, branching into twin tubes under engine; single top (tank) tube
Front suspension	AMC Teledraulic oil-damped forks
Rear suspension	Swinging-arm, with oil-damped twin shock absorbers
Front brake	7in, SLS full-width alloy drum
Rear brake	7in, SLS full-width alloy drum
Tyres	3.25 × 19 front; 3.50 × 19 rear
Wheelbase	55.2in (1,402mm)
Ground clearance	5.5in (140mm)
Seat height	31.5in (800mm)
Fuel tank capacity	3.75gal (19ltr)
Dry weight	394lb (179kg)
Maximum power	33bhp @ 6,800rpm
Top speed	92mph (148km/h)

A distinctive feature between the 1955 and 1956 AJS (and Matchless) touring bikes was the introduction of a much longer and thinner oil tank. There was also an increase in capacity, from 4 to 5½pt (2 to 3ltr). A new toolbox on the nearside (left) matched the new oil tank design; both assemblies were bridged at the front by a detachable cover. If the optional (at additional cost) air filter was fitted, it was concealed behind this cover. Because of the higher oil temperature of the twins, a shield was mounted to the face of the oil tank, separated from it by a ¼in (6mm) air gap.

Featuring a lid hinged at its lower edge, the new toolbox housed the battery in its forward section, secured by a quick-release rubber strap, and was separated from the tool compartment by a bulkhead. At the upper rear section of the toolbox was located the automatic voltage-control assembly; this sat in what *The Motor Cycle* described as 'an anti-vibration, sponge-rubber nest', and was in fact taken from a similar layout adopted for the factory's ISDT models.

The horn was now concealed under the dual seat. The length of this seat was increased by 2½in (62mm) in order to provide, as the AMC press release described, 'additional accommodation for adults of above-average stature.'

Another alteration introduced for 1956 models, both twins and singles, concerned the primary-chain adjuster. Although perfectly accessible before, the development team felt it was 'rather unsightly', and moved it to an equally accessible new location between the gearbox plates, where it was neatly concealed by a snap-on cover.

Whilst the full-width alloy hubs with their straight spokes, and the internals of the brakes remained unchanged, there were changes to the brake-operating mechanism. In order to achieve 'a cleaner appearance' (*The Motor Cycle*), the front brake had, in effect, been rotated through 180 degrees so that the cam lever now lay above the wheel spindle and aft of the fork leg. At the rear, the brake adjuster had been transferred to the forward end of the operating rod so that it was accessible from the saddle.

The offside (left) of the machine was enhanced by a polished aluminium rear brake-shoe plate which replaced the previous back-plate assembly. In addition, a modified rear brake pedal was fitted; this featuring a straight shank, whilst the shorter arm was inclined at approximately the same angle as the subframe tube. The cotter-type retention of the pedal to its spindle and the concealed return spring, introduced the previous year, was still employed, but the adjustable stop was now clamped between the pedal spindle and the frame.

Minor detail modifications had also been made to the Teledraulic front forks, including attention to the wheel-retaining cups at the lower ends of the sliders and to the fork top cap nuts. There were also now holes on either side of the top yoke for cables to pass through. Another detail improvement, this time concerning the electrical equipment, was the introduction of a Lucas combined horn button/dip switch.

To distinguish between the 500 and 600 twins, the fuel tank of the larger was equipped with chromium-plated side panels. These were fixed to the tank by two screws retaining a plastic badge; two more screws held the knee-grips in position. Plastic beading round the outer edge of the panel sealed the gap between it and the side of the tank.

The major news of 1956 for both the AJS and Matchless ranges was the arrival of a new 'in-house' AMC-manufactured gearbox. This was announced in May of that year, and was thereafter incorporated on all models for the 1957 season. When reviewing the AMC range in the 27 September 1956 issue, *The Motor Cycle* said:

Tourists, racing men, trials riders and scramblers can all find models to whet the appetite in the AJS and Matchless ranges, which are, of course, basically similar. All models have pivoted-fork rear springing and telescopic front forks. The roadsters – comprising singles of 347 and 498cc and parallel twins of 498 and 592cc – are renowned for their comfort, high quality finish and mechanical quietness.

Uprating the Engine

Although the general performance of the AJS roadster twins had always been good, the demand from potential buyers for more speed and acceleration led to the introduction of modified inlet and exhaust cams on its twin-cylinder models.

The desire to eliminate oil leakage had been responsible for a slight modification to the end cap of the pressure oil filter situated in the near-side (left) crankcase. This cap was now manufactured as a one-piece assembly instead of two, thus eliminating a joint that had been subject to oil pressure. Although the spring retaining the filter element was different from that for the by-pass ball-valve, it had been possible with the old ball-cap to interchange them – with disastrous results. The end-cap modification

made the interchange impossible. Finally, neo-prene push-on oil pipes were adopted, which meant that threaded unions became a thing of the past.

Chassis Changes

In adopting Girling rear shock absorbers, AMC became one of the last manufacturers to buy in, rather than make their own, in this field. Incorporating a three-position adjustment for load, these new units were similar to those fitted to several other motorcycle companies, but the upper and lower attachments were specially made for the south London factory.

At the base of each shock absorber assembly was a rubber-bushed, cast-alloy yoke. The top fixing point took the form of a single eye containing a rubber sleeve. As the AMC shocks embodied yokes at both ends, the plain upper attachment ears originally welded to the frame loops had been superseded by box-section lugs. Thus the new shock absorbers were not interchangeable with the old. Another departure from conventional Girling practice was

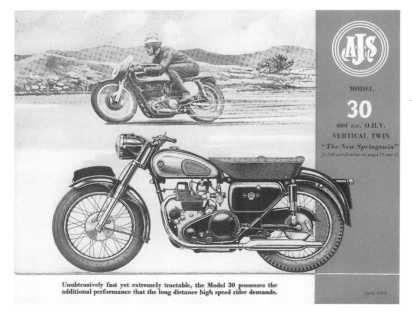

Unobtrusively fast yet extremely tractable, the Model 30 possesses the additional performance that the long distance high speed rider demands.

The 1957 Model 30 six-hundred twin was newly introduced for that year. The engine displaced 592cc (achieved by increasing the bore size from 66 to 72mm). Engine pulling power was considerably improved on the existing five-hundred.

the use of polished alloy for the split collects which retained the upper spring shroud.

To provide additional frame strength for sidecar work on both the twins and singles, the bolt which clamped the rear frame loops to the top of the seat tube was increased in diameter to ⅝in (16mm). Additionally, the attachment point was moved forwards slightly so that the lug on the main-frame member was formed integrally with the rear tank support lug (previously, two separate lugs had been employed).

In mid-1956 the front-fork damping was altered so that on both shock and recoil movements the hydraulic control was now more progressive in operation; AMC claimed that this eliminated front-end pitching. To prevent the possibility of chatter occurring after an extensive mileage had been covered, and to provide an additional degree of resilience in the transmission, a considerable change had been carried out to the 5-pin drive of the QD rear wheel on all the touring models. Previously, the driving (and braking) torque had been transmitted to the solid pins bolted in the full-width, light-alloy hub by their engaging with the five holes drilled in the cast-iron assembly, which doubled up as a brake drum and chain sprocket. The radius at which the pins were disposed from the hub axis had been doubled, whilst the pins themselves were hollow and of much larger diameter than before, each pin being rubber sleeved externally. In the brake-drum casting the holes the pins engaged with took the form of tubular bosses some ⅞in (22mm) long, connected by an annular rib.

A year earlier the toolbox, battery and voltage control regulator had been grouped together in a long box, which matched the equally extended oil tank on the other side of the machine. But this had presented a problem, because when attached to a sidecar (on the British side; i.e. with the chair mounted on the left) the hinged toolbox lid could not be opened fully, because it was too close to the upper rear sidecar mounting connection. To solve this problem, the lid was no longer hinged to the box, and instead, two ears

were formed at the lower edge of the lid, which engaged with slots in the box. Now the lid could be completely detached despite its close proximity to a sidecar connection.

A black moulded-rubber strap replaced the endless red rubber band that had held the battery in place on the 1956 models; for 1957 the lower end of the strap carried a metal peg which hooked into slots in the battery platform.

On the twins, a separate cover was attached to the side of the oil tank to match the toolbox lid. Both cover and lid had a trio of horizontal ribs embossed on them to minimize the possible effects of chafing by a pillion passenger's riding gear and also as a styling tool.

The ongoing saga of oil leakage from the primary chaincase led to a number of modifications being carried out to the rear section of the pressed steel case. First, the edge of the hole through which the engine shaft protruded was turned outward, and a composite cork washer was placed between the crankcase and chaincase at that point. Next, a sliding oil thrower, consisting of two dished plates riveted together one on each side of the slotted hole in the case, was located on the gearbox mainshaft and moved backwards or forwards with the gearbox during primary-chain adjustment. The singles had additional changes in the search to improve oil tightness in this area (*see* Chapter 4).

The shielding of the final-drive chain had also been improved by extending the chainguard further downward to the rear of the drive sprocket to cover the chain where it ran on to the gearbox sprocket.

The 1958 Model Year

When the 1958 models were announced in mid-September 1957, the main innovation was a newly designed primary chaincase across the entire AJS and Matchless ranges (excluding of course the racing models). This was an aluminium, two-piece affair, but the twins featured a different version to the one found on the singles, the main difference being that the bulge on the crankshaft axes was less pronounced, since there was no generator to be accommodated.

The two halves of the chaincase were polished and held together by a total of fourteen screws. There were also two flush-fitting plugs in the outer half. One of these threaded plugs was for checking chain tension and filling the case with oil; the other provided access to the clutch adjuster in the centre of the pressure plate.

Introduced the previous year, the AMC gearbox was retained, but the gearchange action had been made lighter by the fitment of a lower-rate selector spring; this modification applied not only to the roadster twins, but also to the singles and competition models.

There were two more small alterations applicable to both the twins and the singles: a ½in (13mm) reduction in seat height (as a result of shortening the shock absorber length); and chromium plating of the middle of the wheel rims in addition to the side. AMC had its own chroming vats at its huge Plumstead works.

The Model 30 CS and CSR

Apart from the list of minor changes catalogued above and the introduction of the aluminium chaincase, the existing twins were unaltered. However, there were two new twin-cylinder models for the 1958 season: the Model 30 CS scrambler (*see* Chapter 12); and the Model 30 CSR sports roadster, introduced in January 1958. Basically, the CSR was similar to the CS scrambler, the latter having been launched the previous September and exported to North America, Scandinavia and other markets.

Located in a modified motocross-type frame, the CSR featured a tuned engine with 8.5:1 compression pistons, and a siamezed exhaust header pipe which terminated in a single silencer on the offside (right) of the machine. It used the same 3¾gal (17ltr) fuel tank of the standard Model 30 tourer, with chromium-plated side panels. The covers of the front fork and the rear shock absorbers were also chromium plated.

The handlebar for the CSR was of the conventional roadster shape, and the standard wheels (with full-width alloy hubs) were equipped with 3.25 × 19 and 3.50 × 19 front and rear tyres respectively. Polished aluminium mudguards were fitted, as was the competition-pattern dual seat. Lighting equipment was of the quickly detachable type.

The price of the Model 30 CSR (and its Matchless counterpart the G11 CSR) in January 1958 was £299 8s, including British purchase tax, the basic (export) price being £240. In April 1958 journalist and former racer Vic Willoughby rode one of the Matchless versions of the CSR at the MIRA test circuit near Nuneaton, Warwickshire, putting no fewer than 102.9 miles (175.4km) into one hour. This not only proved the design's sporting credentials, but also its reliability.

1958 Model 20 with new cast alloy chaincase, but still fitted with dynamo and magneto.

The 1958 30 CSR	
Engine	Air-cooled, ohv twin with vertical cylinders, separate alloy heads; separate cast-iron barrels; three main bearings (one central); one-piece crankshaft with split big-ends and Hiduminium RR56 con-rods; gear-driven camshafts fore and aft; coil valve springs; separate rocker boxes (four)
Bore	72mm
Stroke	72.8mm
Displacement	592cc
Compression ratio	8.5:1
Lubrication	Dry sump, twin gear-oil pumps
Ignition	Magdyno, Lucas, 6-volt
Carburettor	Amal Monobloc 376 1 1/16in
Primary drive	Chain
Final drive	Chain
Gearbox	4-speed, foot-change, AMC
Frame	Two-part with single front down-tube, branching into twin tubes under engine; single top (tank) tube
Front suspension	AMC Teledraulic oil-damped forks
Rear suspension	Swinging-arm, with oil-damped twin Girling shock absorbers
Front brake	7in, SLS full-width alloy drum
Rear brake	7in, SLS full-width alloy drum
Tyres	3.25 × 19 front; 3.50 × 19 rear
Wheelbase	55.2in (1,402mm)
Ground clearance	5.5in (140mm)
Seat height	31in (787mm)
Fuel tank capacity	3.75gal (17ltr)
Dry weight	381lb (173kg)
Maximum power	37bhp @ 6,800rpm
Top speed	100mph (160km/h)

An Increase in Engine Size for 1959

When the 1959 range was announced in September 1958 the most significant change was that the range of twins had been extended from three to four (or eight, if one includes the Matchless versions). For the first time a six-fifty was offered. This had been made possible by the use of a longer-stroke crankshaft, increasing the displacement from 592 to 646cc; the model code changing from 30 to 31. In fact the six-fifty was not strictly brand new, as a few examples had been exported to the USA over the preceding months. The 646cc engine closely followed the pattern of its predecessors, the only external difference being that the cylinder barrels were longer and had an additional fin.

With the existing cylinder centres the limit on bore size had, at 72mm, been reached on the six-hundred, so the required capacity increase had been achieved by lengthening the stroke from 72.8 to 79.3mm, the increase in cylinder-barrel length making it possible to employ the existing connecting rods and pistons. The size of the single Amal Monobloc carburettor had been increased from 1 1/16in (27mm) to 1 1/8in (28mm) for the new six-fifty.

There were Standard and De Luxe versions of the 646cc Model 31, both using a compression ratio of 7.5:1, whereas the sporting versions had 8.5:1.

Power output had been further increased on the CSR (and the CS scrambler) by a modification to the shape of the inlet tract; AMC's chief development engineer, Jack Williams, had been responsible for this.

Following its successful use on the 348cc and 497cc roadster singles, a Lucas RM15 alternator was fitted to 1959 Standard twins (in both 498cc Model 20 and 646cc Model 31 guises), but a separate magneto and dynamo continued to be specified on the remaining twins. Installation of the generator was exactly as on the singles, with the rotor keyed to the drive's main shaft, and the rotor located by a spigot in a bulge in the outer half of the

113

primary chaincase. The distributor took the place of the magneto behind the cylinders.

Another feature of the 1959 model-year twins (except the CS scrambler version) was a new, larger, 4¼gal (19ltr) fuel tank, replacing the previous 3¾gal (17ltr) one previously fitted. The new tank also differed in construction from the others, in that the welded seam was on the centre-line of the motorcycle, and not along its bottom edges. Oil-tank capacity was 4pt (2ltr), except in the CSR (and CS) which had a 5pt (3ltr) tank.

Although a black fuel tank was usual on the Standard twins, chromium-plated side panels (included in the specification of the De Luxe twins) were available at additional cost. The Model 20 and Model 31 machines were also offered with an alternative finish: the mudguards, oil tank and toolbox were in Mediterranean Blue (instead of black) with the choice of a Mediterranean Blue tank with chrome panels, or a two-colour white-over-blue tank. A chromium-plated strip separated the two tank colours where applicable.

Major Alterations for 1960

When the annual round of improvements was announced towards the end of 1959, it was apparent that considerable changes had been introduced for the twin-cylinder range of AJS (and Matchless) models. Chief amongst these, and shared with the heavyweight singles (*see* Chapter 4), was the introduction of a full cradle frame, with Duplex front down-tubes were taken back to pass beneath the engine and gearbox. A single 1½in (38mm) diameter, 12-gauge top tube and a vertical seat tube completed the main frame, which was built on the time-honoured principle of malleable iron lugs brazed into position. There were substantial cast lugs forming the steering head and rear fork pivot housing. The rear subframe was bolted to lugs situated just below the rear of the gearbox and the nose of the dual seat.

AMC claimed that greater rigidity of the new frame, plus an increase in the fork trail,

The 1959 Model 31	
Engine	Air-cooled, ohv twin with vertical cylinders, separate alloy heads; separate cast-iron barrels; three main bearings (one central), one-piece crankshaft with split big-ends and Hiduminium RR56 con-rods; gear-driven camshafts fore and aft; coil valve springs; separate rocker boxes (four)
Bore	72mm
Stroke	79.3mm
Displacement	646cc
Compression ratio	7.5:1
Lubrication	Dry sump, twin gear-oil pumps
Ignition	Magdyno, Lucas, 6-volt
Carburettor	Amal Monobloc 389 1⅛in
Primary drive	Chain
Final drive	Chain
Gearbox	4-speed, foot-change, AMC
Frame	Two-part with single front down-tube, branching into twin tubes under engine; single top (tank) tube; 1960 onwards, duplex cradle frame
Front suspension	AMC Teledraulic oil-damped forks
Rear suspension	Swinging-arm, with oil-damped twin Girling shock absorbers
Front brake	7in, SLS full-width alloy drum
Rear brake	7in, SLS full-width alloy drum
Tyres	3.25 × 19 front; 3.50 × 19 rear; 1963 onwards, 18in
Wheelbase	55.2in (1,402mm)
Ground clearance	5.5in (140mm)
Seat height	31in (787mm)
Fuel tank capacity	4.25gal (19ltr); 1964 onwards, 4gal (18ltr)
Dry weight	396lb (180kg); 1964 onwards 403lb (183kg)
Maximum power	356bhp @ 6,600rpm
Top speed	98mph (158km/h)

provided improved steering and handling over the outgoing single front down-tube frame. Previously only found on the new semi-unit ohv two-fifty single, a three-point fuel tank mounting was a feature of the new frame, with two mountings at the front and one at the rear.

On all models except the two-fifties and the new lightweight three-fifties, the gearbox internal ratios had been changed to provide more even spacing, and in particular reduce the gap between third and top. Bottom was now slightly higher, at 2.56:1 (formerly 2.67:1), second remained unchanged at 1.77 and third was raised to 1.22 (formerly 1.33). Top gear provided direct internal drive at 1:1. However, to special order, the previous ratio could be specified.

The cylinder head of all the twin-cylinder models had been redesigned. Thus the combustion chamber shape was now hemispherical, and flat-top pistons with small recesses for the valves were used – but the compression ratios were unchanged. The inlet tract could be best described as an arc between the carburettor and inlet valve. 'The object of this design,' said chief development engineer, Jack Williams, 'was to promote swirl in the gases' and another effect 'was that the valve stem and protruding portion of the valve guide are at one side of the tract where they offer less restriction to gas flow'.

A couple of external alterations on the cylinder heads of the 1960 model year twins were thicker lugs at the front for mounting of the head steady, and an additional fin. Cast into the underside of the extra fin were three small short fins disposed diagonally to the direction of the airflow; this had been incorporated by Jack Williams to improve cooling in the region of the exhaust port.

In conjunction with the new shape of the combustion chamber and inlet port, in the twin the valve included angle had been reduced to 40 degrees. In addition, the twin's bolted-on induction manifolds had also been modified to suit the redesigned ports.

Yet another change was that two-rate valve springs (the coil type still being used) were now featured on the twins, instead of the previous single-rate type. The former spring-loaded felt oil filter was superseded for 1960 by a type using wire gauze of two mesh sizes. A spring-loaded pressure-release valve was now fitted on the twins, this being located inside the front of the timing chest; oil released from this flowed into the timing chest, and then drained off into the crankcase.

A new Lucas 12-amp hour battery (still 6 volts) of a more compact design (still retained by a rubber strap in the combined battery and toolbox) was now a feature on all AJS models, except the two-fifty and new lightweight three-fifty. There was also a new, more compact headlamp (which still held the speedometer). Yet another innovation common to the heavyweight singles and twins was a two-level dual seat, this having been introduced to, so AMC said, 'provide additional comfort for the pillion passenger without making the rider's seating position over-high.'

1960 646cc 31CSR sportster with siamezed pipes, alloy mudguards, upswept silencer and rakish lines – a classic of its era.

115

Trevor King of Norwich, Norfolk with his superb 1960 31CSR, photographed at Snetterton CRMC/Combine Reunion, Sunday 19 September 2004. Trevor has owned the bike since 1971 and completed a full restoration during the 1990s.

… siamezed pipes, alloy chaincase, chrome tank panels and much more.

Close-up views of the Trevor King 1960 six-fifty 31CSR …

The 1960 CSR headlamp, showing Smiths 120mph speedometer, light switch (left) and amp meter (right).

Engine top, with plugs, single Amal Monobloc carb, magneto, dynamo and head steady all evident.

The 1960 31CSR	
Engine	Air-cooled ohv twin with vertical cylinders, separate alloy heads; separate cast-iron barrels; three main bearings (one central); one-piece crankshaft with big-ends and Hiduminium RR56 con-rods; gear-driven camshafts fore and aft; coil valve springs; separate rocker boxes (four)
Bore	72mm
Stroke	79.3mm
Displacement	646cc
Compression ratio	8.5:1
Lubrication	Dry sump, twin gear-oil pumps
Ignition	Magdyno, Lucas 6-volt; 1962 onwards, alternator; 1964 onwards, 12-volt
Carburettor	Amal Monobloc 389 1⅛in
Primary drive	Chain
Final drive	Chain
Gearbox	4-speed, foot-change, AMC
Frame	All-steel construction, brazed and bolted; single top (tank) tube, twin tube cradle, including front down-tubes
Front suspension	AMC Teledraulic two-way, oil-damped forks
Rear suspension	Swinging-arm, with oil-damped twin Girling shock absorbers
Front brake	7in, SLS full-width alloy drum
Rear brake	7in, SLS full-width alloy drum
Tyres	3.25 × 19 front, 3.50 × 19 rear; 1964 18in
Wheelbase	55.2in (1,402mm)
Ground clearance	5.5in (140mm)
Seat height	31.5in (800mm)
Fuel tank capacity	4.25gal (19ltr); 1963 onwards, 4gal (18ltr)
Dry weight	381lb (173kg); 1964 onwards, 390lb (177kg)
Maximum power	42bhp @ 6,600rpm
Top speed	106mph (170km/h)

Little Change for 1961

After the major changes introduced the previous autumn, Jack Williams and his team did very little to the twins for the 1961 model year machines.

The major technical change concerned the lubrication system. Previously, oil from the rocker gear drained into the camshaft tunnels and thereafter, by way of the timing chest, to the crankcase. This new arrangement permitted oil from the exhaust camshaft tunnel to drain direct into the nearside (left) of the crankcase, ensuring a more even distribution. Oil returning from the inlet camshaft tunnel alone had proved adequate for timing-gear lubrication.

On the high performance Model 31 CSR, the exhaust pipe had been remodelled so that it now ran below, instead of inside, the offside (right) footrest hanger. This change had been dictated by a modified footrest assembly. Previously the footrest brackets clamped directly to the frame tubes, but this meant that no height adjustment could be provided. The rests were now secured to a square rod, placed transversely at the rear of the engine, thus providing a choice of positions.

On the Standard and De Luxe Model 20 and Model 31 machines, the deeply valanced front and rear mudguards had been shortened. Tyre clearance at the leading edge of the front guard had been increased.

As for prices, in April 1961 they were as follows (all including UK purchase tax).

This example of a 1961 AJS Model 31 six-fifty touring model largely correct for year, except the indicators, carrier, top box and bar-end mirror.

498cc	20	Standard	£252 0s 0d
646cc	31	Standard	£256 0s 0d
646cc	31	De Luxe	£267 0s 0d
646cc	31	CSR	£280 0s 0d

These prices were in fact considerably lower then those of a year earlier when, for example, the range topping CSR was listed at £302 15s 5d.

Problems Mount

During 1961, falling sales (and of course profits) had seen AMC begin its slide into a financial morass from which it was never to recover. At the end of July that year shareholders revolted and demanded an extraordinary general meeting in central London. This was attended by around 150 shareholders. It was proposed that the joint managing directors, A.A. Sugar and J.F. Kelleher, should be removed from office, but this motion was defeated. The same meeting also rejected proposals to appoint three new directors. Many who attended this meeting openly voiced some serious complaints concerning the sales policy of the AMC Group. They urged a more energetic programme of expansion, allied to an extension of the company's activities to other fields of manufacture. This was in the same week that the British government put up purchase tax from 25 to 27½ per cent!

In addition, other taxes, including that on petrol, rose steeply, whilst interest rates also rose.

At the end of August 1961, AMC sales director Jock West resigned from the AMC board. The official reason at the time was that Jock had 'a divergence of opinion with his co-directors'. Actually, for once this was an accurate statement when someone left, rather than the more usual 'whitewash' of anything but the truth. Jock West's main reason for leaving was the failed policies of another board member, Donald Heather. For example, Heather had pushed through the James scooter project – which Jock West had been against from the start, and which was to prove a costly financial failure. There were other similar incidents within the AMC empire; which at that time not only included AJS and Matchless, but also James, Francis-Barnett and Norton.

As *The Motor Cycle* said upon his resignation: 'Jock is probably motor cycling's most notable road racer turned businessman'. In the late 1930s he had been with AFN, the British BMW importers, and he had competed in many races, including the Ulster GP and Isle of Man TT with considerable success. After the war he had been a member of the AJS works team. During his sixteen years with Associated Motor Cycles (he had been sales manager from 1945 until he joined the board in the late 1950s) Jock had travelled widely in search of exports, and was well-known around the world. During the mid-1950s he had also spent considerable time helping the James factory in Greet, Birmingham, and was largely responsible for that factory's resurgence. There is no doubt that with Jock's departure, AMC lost the services of its most 'hands-on' board member, and someone who understood the product he was selling and the industry he served.

Jock West's position at AMC was taken by W.J. (Bill) Smith, who until then had been general sales manager at Norton. He took over his duties as home and export manger for AJS and Matchless on 1 October 1961. A Scot, Bill had ridden as a member of the OK Supreme team in the pre-war days, and later became one of Scotland's most outstanding trials and scrambles riders.

During 1961 AMC had also considered moving its manufacturing base to a new factory at the Isle of Sheppey, Kent. However, this project was abandoned in mid-October that year. At the time the official reasons was primarily 'the possibility of labour shortage'. However, the existing workforce was far from being keen on the move – since finding new skilled workers appeared to be a non-starter, the whole project was abandoned. But it does provide an indication that even at that time AMC was looking at ways of 'downsizing' its operation.

The 1962 Range

A feature of the 1962 AJS and Matchless ranges (announced in September 1961) was that all models (except the AJS 7R and Matchless G50 road racers) were given a name as well as the existing catalogue code number. At the same time the last of the 498cc twins, the Model 20 Standard, was axed. This left only the 646cc Model 31. The De Luxe version of the touring Model 31 was no longer listed separately, although it could still be obtained by specifying magneto ignition and QD rear wheel when ordering. The Model 31 was known as the Swift, whilst the CSR version became the Hurricane.

Only minor changes had been made to the bikes. The front fork spring poundage on the Model 31 Swift tourer was increased in line with the CSR version. On the sportster, the pillion footrests were now carried on brackets extending rearwards from the subframe (as on the touring model) instead of being brazed directly to the subframe, AMC claiming this made the mountings stronger and better placed. Other changes were new fuel tank badges, a modified oil tank, softer rubber fuel-tank mounts, a stronger kickstart return spring, an extension to the centre stand, a new-pattern Lucas horn (which was smaller, lighter and louder) and a combined ignition/light switch. The battery had reverted to the original size.

From the 1962 model year the standard 31 six-fifty was known as the Swift.

Streamlining the Operation

With a continuing financial decline, 1962 was a year of streamlining for Associated Motor Cycles. First it was announced that Norton's Bracebridge Street, Birmingham factory was to close its doors at the end of the year, with production being transferred to the Plumstead works in south London.

When the AJS (and Matchless) model ranges for the 1963 season were announced at the end of September 1962, the number of models had been significantly reduced, although both the six–fifty twins (the Swift Model 31 and Hurricane CSR) remained. At the beginning of November 1962 AJS made some price increases, including the Swift tourer up to £276 18s and the Hurricane sportster to £306.

The 1962 31 CSR was very similar to the original 1960 bike, except for the fuel tank, large tank badge design and silencer position.

Optional factory headlamp fairing for the 1962/63 Hurricane 31 CSR.

A New Look for 1963

In an attempt to arrest flagging sales, the AJS range was given a new look for the 1963 season, including the two surviving twins. The Swift was affected most, with some of the revisions also appearing on the latest CSR Hurricane. First, wheel sizes had been reduced by 1in (25mm) to 18in (450mm), although tyre sections remained unaltered; and the steering-head angle was taken back 1 degree to restore the original fork trail.

The appearance of the aluminium full-width hubs had been revised; this having been achieved by tapering the sides and reducing the number of circumferential ribs from seven to five. The diameter of the brake drums was still 7in (180mm), but shoe width had increased by ¼in (6mm) to 1⅛in (28mm). A new cast-alloy brake-shoe plate was internally ribbed. The front and rear mudguards now featured a reduced radius to suit the smaller wheels, the makers having changed blade section from C to D and incorporated a rib along the middle.

The bolted-on rear subframe had been shortened. This, claimed AMC, provided a dual benefit, rigidity being increased, whilst the suspension units now sloped slightly forward. There were also small changes to the swinging-arm: the brazed-on wheel spindle lugs were now steel plates rather than the former malleable-iron castings, whilst two tiny cross-tubes were set into the nearside (left) fork arm to accept fixing bolts for a rear chain-case. This new fitment was of conventional design, comprising upper and lower steel pressings. The front end of the case was over-lapped by a pressed-steel sprocket cover, meaning that no section of the final drive chain was left exposed.

The contours of both the oil tank (on the offside) and matching battery/toolbox (on the nearside) had been totally revised, with an entirely new, more rounded style. Knee recesses with stuck-on rubber grips reduced fuel-tank width between the rider's thighs. The tank filler cap had moved to the centre line, whilst a single two-level tap replaced the previous two separate tap assemblies. The dual seat had been narrowed at the rear and the depth reduced at the front. In concert with the smaller wheel size, this dropped the seat height by a useful 1½in (38mm).

In an attempt to satisfy the anti-noise lobby, a brand new silencer design was introduced. 'Cigar'-shaped and considerably quieter than the one it replaced, it nonetheless had somehow lost the character of the outgoing component. The size of the number-plate holder was increased to accommodate seven-digit registration numbers. The rear light was now also increased in size, and there was a new stop-light switch with an enclosed spring to tidy up appearance. The sole engine modification that year was to the oil-pump, with the width of the gears being doubled to step up the circulation rate.

Of all the changes and modifications described above, the CSR Hurricane only received the new fuel tank, silencer and oil-pump gears. For endurance racers the works offered a speed kit for the CSR, comprising twin Amal 389 Monobloc 1⅛in (29mm) carbs, 10.25:1 pistons and hi-lift cams.

A no-cost option on the Model 31 Swift tourer (when ordered on a new machine, ex-factory) was sidecar suspension and gearing, together with a siamezed exhaust system (the latter to make fitting a left-hand chain easier). AJS also listed the following as cost options on the Model 31 Swift:

- air filter £2 6s 2d;
- rear carrier £3 16s 6d;
- pannier set £9 5s 3d;
- steering damper £1 4s 0d;
- safety bars £5 2s 6d;
- steering lock 2s;
- two-tone colour finish £4 8s 2d;
- magneto ignition £10 1s 7d;
- high-compression (8.5:1) pistons £1 12s 10d;
- rear chain enclosure (price to be announced).

For the CSR Hurricane the following cost options were offered:

- speed kit (h.c. pistons, twin carburettors, hi-lift camshafts): price to be announced;
- headlamp cowl (with rev counter £18 18s 0d; or without rev counter £7 4s 0d);
- rev counter separately £11 15s 0d.

1964 and Rising Financial Woes

The need to cut costs to counter a rising burden of debt, plus the fact that now Nortons, as well as AJS and Matchless models, were all being produced in the same Plumstead works, led to standardization across the range for the 1964 model year.

A major change was the employment of Norton front forks and brake hubs, for both AJS and Matchless in the twins (and Heavyweight) roadster singles, in place of the previously used AMC items. This meant the famous 'Road-holder' forks and alloy, full-width hub assemblies of 8in (203mm) front and 7in (178mm) rear respectively. However, the duplex AMC frame was retained, slightly modified to allow fitment of the Roadholders. Notable was the switch from 6 to 12 volt electrics (together with two sets of contact-breaker points) for both the Swift and the Hurricane. The latter now received 18in wheels, the altered subframe and gearing, plus the rounded oil tank and toolbox assemblies, as the touring model had been given a year previously.

The Model 33

Towards the end of 1964 came the Model 33 (also sold as the Matchless G15). This was powered by the 745cc (73 × 89mm) Norton Atlas engine, mounted in the AMC duplex frame, but as on the six-fifty twins, using the Norton suspension and brakes. The Atlas engine ran on a compression ratio of 7.6:1, producing maximum power of 49bhp at 6,400rpm. A prototype of this bike had first been seen back in 1963 and was inspired, primarily for ever more power and displacement, from AMC's Stateside importers, the Berliner Corporation of New Jersey.

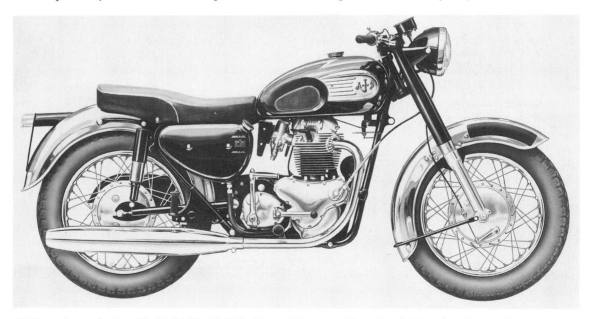

1965 saw the introduction of the Model 33 with 745cc Norton Atlas engine, Norton Roadholder forks and Norton hubs, but still with the AMC frame.

But if AJS (or Matchless) hoped that sales would improve, they were doomed to disappointment, because in fact sales continued to

Diamond badge found on some AJS twins from the 1965 model year.

slide. The fact was Norton fans would buy an Atlas, but only in a Norton Featherbed frame and with a Norton badge; whilst AJS enthusiasts preferred AMC engines – even if it meant having a six-fifty instead of a seven-fifty.

The 33 CSR

Following in the wheel tracks of the touring Model 33 came the 33 CSR. Launched at the Earls Court Show in November 1964, this came laden with all the customary goodies so beloved of the café racer brigade. Actually, this was ironic, because only a few months before AMC had decried these very same sixties youths by saying it had 'no intentions of pandering to the tearaway culture of the café racer'. But the once proud (and great) AMC had been forced to eat a big helping of humble pie after experiencing yet more bad news from a balance sheet laid down with red ink.

In April 1967 The Motor Cycle *tested this six-fifty Model 31 CSR with a chair attached; one of the very last AJS models with the AMC engine to be produced.*

But again the buying public did not take the bait, even though the 33CSR had masses of bright, shiny chrome and polished alloy, low handlebars, swept-back exhausts, matching instruments, fork gaiters, rear-set footrests and controls – and much, much more. Just how bad things had become is illustrated by the fact that someone within the fast dwindling AMC Plumstead works came up with the idea of having a new chrome-plated diamond-shaped tank badge for the AJS marque. Unfortunately, not only was this creation exceedingly garish, but it made no difference to a sales trend which was pointing ever more downwards.

For 1966 there was no change to the twins, except for raising the gearing on the CSR versions. Mid-year the axe fell on all the 650s, finally bringing the AMC-engined models to an end, leaving only the Norton-powered models in the twin-cylinder line-up.

Then in late 1966 the Official Receiver was called in as insolvency seemed inevitable. Although the AJS name survived through the efforts of Dennis Poore and Manganese Bronze, this signalled the end of the traditional Ajays, both in single- and twin-cylinder guises, as the new company (Norton Villiers (NV)) only built AJS models powered by 2-stroke Villiers-type engines, the full story of which is catalogued in Chapters 13 and 14.

The 1965 33CSR			
Engine	Air-cooled Norton ohv twin with vertical cylinders, one-piece cylinder head, one-piece barrel, plain bearing big-ends, coil valve springs	Frame	Duplex
		Front suspension	Norton Roadholder forks
		Rear suspension	Swinging-arm, twin oil-damped Girling shock absorbers
Bore	73mm	Front brake	8in, SLS full-width alloy drum
Stroke	89mm	Rear brake	7in, SLS full-width alloy drum
Displacement	745cc	Tyres	3.25 × 18 front; 3.50 × 18 rear
Compression ratio	7.6:1	Wheelbase	56.5in (1,435mm)
Lubrication	Dry sump, Norton oil pump	Ground clearance	5.5in (140mm)
Ignition	Battery/coil 12 volt; alternator	Seat height	33in (838mm)
Carburettor	Pair Amal Monoblocs 389 1⅛in	Fuel tank capacity	4gal (21ltr)
Primary drive	Chain	Dry weight	398lb (181kg)
Final drive	Chain	Maximum power	49bhp @ 6,400rpm
Gearbox	4-speed, foot-change, AMC	Top speed	110mph (170km/h)

9   7R – The Boys' Racer

The Second World War finally came to an end in the summer of 1945 after six long years of global conflict.

Subsequently, the sports governing body, the FIM, banned the use of supercharging, which effectively ended the career of the 1939 water-cooled V4 on which Walter Rusk had become the first man to lap the Ulster GP's Clady course at 100mph. Not only this, but as recorded in Chapter 5 it was also to put a spanner in the development of the new E90 Porcupine parallel twin which had originally been conceived with a blower in mind. The Porcupine finally made its debut in 1947, but perhaps of even more importance to AJS's history – and this book – the following February saw the announcement of AJS's most famous and highly regarded design, the classic 7R 'Boys' Racer'.

A New Design

Compared to the pre-war R7 the new bike shared very little with the older version apart from some very basic design principles, such as being an ohc single with the camshaft drive by chain, the latter with a Weller tensioner.

As for the newcomer's frame, this was largely copied from the works E90 Porcupine, being a wide-spaced double cradle layout in welded steel tubing. The front forks were modified AMC Teledraulics, whilst at the rear the fashionable swinging arm was controlled by a pair of oil-damped spring-controlled shock absorbers. In the braking department conical hubs were employed, both with cast-iron liner and 8in (205mm) diameter.

A New Engine

However, the real centre of attraction was the new 74 × 81mm 348cc single overhead cam engine. As with the earlier ohc single, this was the work of Yorkshire engineer, Phillip Walker, then aged 47, who had worked with both AJS and Matchless for many years, apart from a move to the Handley-Page aviation concern for the duration of the war.

To keep weight to an absolute minimum, extensive use was made of magnesium castings and these were finished in a highly distinctive gold-coloured, corrosion-inhibiting paint.

The engine was one of the truly classic motorcycle designs of the twentieth century. Not only could it trace its roots way back to the original cammy Ajay singles of 1927, but it was to remain in production for fifteen years as the 7R, and perhaps even more significantly

The first 7R model was produced in spring 1948 and this is as it appeared that year. It was powered by a 348cc (74 × 81mm) ohc engine, the work of engineer Phillip Walker.

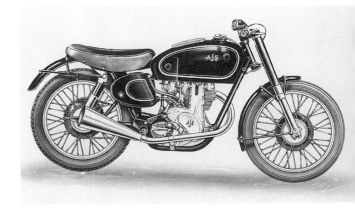

it was to give rise to an enlarged version, the 496cc (90 × 78mm) G50 Matchless in 1958. Even at the beginning of the twentieth century it remains in production as the Seeley

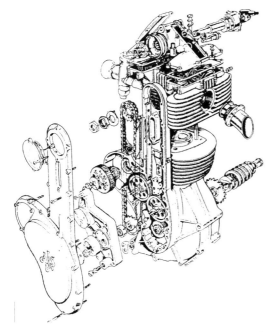

Line drawing of the 7R engine, showing its chain drive to the single overhead camshaft.

The very first customer for one of the new production 7R models was Fergus Anderson.

G50 for classic motorcycle racing events at club, national and international level.

An Alloy Cylinder Barrel

The aluminium alloy cylinder barrel had a shrunk-in iron liner and was held in position by four long bolts which passed from the crankcase right through to the cylinder head.

A forged 3-ring piston was employed, together with a massive I-section steel connecting rod, the latter component featuring a bushed small-end and a duralumin caged single row big-end bearing. Circumferential webs to the eyes of both the big and small-ends provided additional strength.

The solid steel crankshaft flywheels were drilled and recessed on their inner faces to accommodate the big-end bearing, thus keeping lateral width of the assembly to a minimum. The crankpin, following normal company practice, consisted of a toughened aluminium-steel pin on which a hardened race was pressed. The timing-side mainshaft featured a single large-diameter journal ball-race whilst on the drive-side there was, first, a double-caged roller-bearing and then on the outside a further single roller-bearing. At the extremity of the shaft came a conventional cam-type shock absorber.

Magnesium Crankcase

The magnesium crankcase (vertical split) had strengthening webs, arranged in such a manner as to best withstand the extreme stresses of prolonged racing use.

The timing cover encased the gear-type oil pumps, both of which had cylindrical bodies. Each pump took its drive co-axially from a pinion in the timing gear train, the delivery pump being driven from the magneto-drive idler pinion and the scavenging pump from the main half-time wheel. There were only two external pipes which were short ones running between the oil tank and the pumps. The main feed from the delivery pump went directly to the big-end; another feed went via a pipe cast integrally with the magnesium alloy chaincase straight to the overhead camshaft which was drilled so that oil was led to the lift faces of the cams. The single crankcase breather valve was located in the drilled drive-side mainshaft and exited on to the simplex primary chain.

The timing case featured a small cover plate, which provided access to the magneto-drive pinion.

Vernier Adjustment

The timing of the strap-mounted Lucas racing magneto had a Vernier adjustment produced by an AJS method of using a pegged locking washer and a pinion boss, each of which had a different number of radially disposed drillings with which the pegs mated. This same type of adjustment was also employed for the camshaft.

The massive, but at the same time light, aluminium alloy cylinder-head casting had unusual finning. Around the centrally disposed exhaust port the horizontal fins extended until they reached their maximum depth between the port and the ohc chaincase. They were squeezed in to accommodate this before swelling out again. Beneath the one-piece rocker-box casting there was finning, running diagonally at an angle of 45 degrees from the drive-side to the rear of the chaincase on the timing side. Both the rocker box and camshaft housings were in magnesium.

It was possible to remove the rocker box without first having to take the engine out of the frame or risking the problem of stripped threads. This was just one example of why the AMC sohc design was so much easier for the private owner to maintain than the equivalent double-knocker Manx Norton.

Camshaft and Rockers

The camshaft ran on twin ball-races and at its 'free' end there was provision for the tachometer drive.

As for the rockers, these were manufactured in toughened alloy-steel with deposited hard-metal bearing pads and were short to keep reciprocating weight to a minimum. The rocker spindles, which ran in plain bushes, were mounted eccentrically, allowing valve clearances to be set without recourse to screwed adjusters or shims. Incidentally, these clearances could be checked without disturbing the valve-spring covers. There were, in fact, no end caps to the valves, which received the same treatment as the rockers and had a chemically deposited surface of bearing metal on their ends. Fully enclosed (another notable advantage over the Norton design) hairpin springs were used, these being retained by circlip-type collets.

The two valves of KE 965 steel were set in the cylinder head at an inclusive angle of 79 degrees and the inlet port was not only down-draught but offset. Valve timing, obtained with no rocker clearance, was:

inlet: opens 68° BTDC, closes 76° ATDC;
exhaust: opens 72° BTDC, closed 50° ATDC.

Carburation and Transmission

Carburation was taken care of by an Amal 10TT 1⅛in instrument, whereas Burman supplied AMC with the close ratio 4-speed gearbox and dry multi-plate clutch. The standard, as supplied, gear ratios were 5.14, 5.84, 6.94 and 9.95:1, obtained with a 21-tooth engine sprocket and 54-tooth rear-wheel sprocket. With this top gear 6,600rpm represented exactly 100mph. The gearbox was mounted in light alloy plates, pivoting at the top and swinging at its base for primary-chain adjustment. The 4¾ gallon (21.6ltr) fuel tank was manufactured from aluminium, as was the oil tank.

A feature of the 7R engine was its clean and generally uncluttered lines and an air of quality. In the past its creation has generally been credited entirely to the efforts of one man, its designer Phillip Walker, then AMC's chief engineer, but in reality there is no doubt that racer and AMC sales boss Jock West had

The 1948 7R	
Engine	Air-cooled sohc 2-valve single with vertical cylinder, 79 degrees valve angle aluminium-alloy cylinder head, aluminium-alloy barrel with shrunk-in iron liner; 3-ring forged piston; I-section con-rod; built-up crankshaft, hairpin valve springs, vertically-split magnesium crankcases, enclosed valve gear; camshaft drive by chain with Weller tensioner
Bore	74mm
Stroke	81mm
Displacement	348cc
Compression ratio	8.45:1
Lubrication	Dry sump; twin gear pumps
Ignition	Lucas racing magneto
Carburettor	Amal 10TT 1⅛in
Primary drive	Chain
Final drive	Chain
Gearbox	4-speed Burman close ratio 7R gearbox
Frame	Steel construction; duplex
Front suspension	AMC Teledraulic oil-damped forks
Rear suspension	Swinging arm, with twin shock absorbers
Front brake	8in, SLS conical hubs, with cast-iron liners
Rear brake	8in, SLS conical hubs, with cast-iron liners
Tyres	3.00 × 21 front; 3.25 × 20 rear
Wheelbase	55.5in (1,410mm)
Ground clearance	5.5in (140mm)
Seat height	32.5in (826mm)
Fuel tank capacity	4.75gal (21.6ltr)
Dry weight	298lb (1,355kg)
Maximum power	31bhp @ 7,000rpm
Top speed	102mph (164km/h)

Note: Steel rims as standard; aluminium listed as cost option

a major part to play in its arrival. In fact, it was West who convinced the AMC board to authorize the project, even though Walker carried out the actual design work.

Introducing the 7R

It was Jock West who gave the 7R its first public outing, when he created a minor sensation by turning up with the new bike at Brands Hatch on Sunday, 14 March 1948.

By then the prototype had already covered several hundred miles on the king's highway. Brands Hatch in those days was still a grass circuit. However, this didn't stop the intrepid West from dong a 'hands-off' at full bore to prove the stability of his new charge. The large crowd left the Kent circuit that day suitably impressed with the new AJS product.

In the first year seventy-seven machines were produced, the British prices being £249 plus £67 4s 8d purchase tax with steel wheel rims or £255 plus £68 17s purchase tax for light alloy components. Either way the 1948 7R was supplied with mudguards and tachometer as standard.

Of the twenty Replicas awarded in the 1948 Junior TT, no less than ten were won by 7R riders. But the highlight of that TT was the inspired ride by Geoff Murdoch to annex fourth spot in the Senior TT on his Junior AJS, with a race average speed of 78.51mph (126.4km/h). Backing this up was Maurice Cann's fifth in the Junior TT and Phil Heath's second in the Junior Manx Grand Prix.

This set the new Plumstead-made single off to a flying start, and it was to record countless victories all over the world and at every level of competition including Grand Prix and the Manx GP, but strangely, never a TT. The nearest was probably in the 1961 Junior event, when the great Mike Hailwood led the race until a gudgeon pin broke a mere 12 miles (19km) from the finish on the final lap.

The First Production Batch

The first production batch of 7Rs (the 1948 model) put out 29bhp at 6,800rpm (on low octane 'pool' petrol) and for the first two seasons, apart from copper-plating the cams to counteract a rate of wear that was high on some engines, the power unit modifications were nil. However, that is not to say that these early bikes were entirely without fault. Foremost amongst these glitches was the poor damping qualities of AMC's own slimline 'Candlestick' rear shock absorbers. The action of these would usually deteriorate rapidly, due to excessive build-up of heat.

Another early problem centred around the somewhat restricted power range caused by the employment of an over-large megaphone exhaust. This restricted usable bottom and torque, and under 5,500rpm the dreaded megaphonitis was a real nuisance. This in turn showed up weaknesses in the Burman-made gearbox. Even so, the design's potential was clearly shown, when out of twenty-five examples which started the 1948 Junior TT, eighteen finished. In addition, Fergus Anderson used a 7R to excellent effect in Australia during the early months of 1949, in the process also breaking four Australian national records for the standing mile, both solo and with a third wheel attached.

Out of forty-one starters mounted on 7Rs in the 1949 Junior TT, thirty-two finished, another testament to the overall strength of the design. Unfortunately this did not include the works-entered model of Bill Doran, whose Burman gearbox gave up the ghost when in sight of victory with only a few miles to go.

Changes for 1950

Following various tests on the 1949 works bikes, the 1950 production model introduced a number of changes. The engine gained lightened crankshaft flywheels (also reduced in diameter to cut oil drag), a detachable finned sump fitted to the crankcase, the inlet valve head diameter decreased, valve timing altered

A 1949 7R at Cadwell Park, CRMC, spring 1992.

and roller rockers substituted for the slipper type. Both valves were given shorter stems, whilst their included angle was altered, together with more substantial collet-type spring retainers. The compression ratio was increased to 8.85:1 (thanks to improved, 80-octane fuel now becoming available). The piston was also modified by fitting double oil control rings in the scraper-ring groove. The connecting-rod was strengthened, whilst a revised crankpin design was introduced which featured end diameter shanks and castellated securing nuts. A roller bearing was also now specified on the timing side main.

Oil Pump Redesign

Of all the 1950 model year new features, the most important was a redesign of the twin oil pumps, the housings of which were manufactured in three sections. The AJS engineering team had given the delivery pump the ability to supply a greater volume of lubricant to the cambox, in an attempt to finally rid the engine of its premature camshaft lobe and rocker pad wear. In addition the power output had been upped to 31bhp, together with improved torque figures.

Externally there were more changes. Most noticeable was the redesigned exhaust system, which was now not only of a much neater appearance but employed a much smaller diameter megaphone (this change being largely responsible for the improved torque figures). The oil tank was now narrower, and featured a large diameter quick-action filler cap. The front brake had also been modified, having its iron liner flange bolted to the hub itself, rather than riveted as in the past. The clutch had been redesigned to provide a much more robust housing, having dispensed with the steel band previously fitted around its circumference in an attempt to prevent it falling apart!

Primary chain lubrication featured a timed breather in the shaft of the magneto drive idler pinion providing oil delivered under crankcase pressure. A needle adjuster controlled the flow, which was provided via drill-ways to the nearside crankcase and down a vertical drill-way to an annular boss surrounding the mainshaft. Small holes in the boss allowed the oil to drip into a circular face formed on the inner face of the engine sprocket in which radially disposed holes connected the groove with the sprocket teeth. Centrifugal force did the rest. A removable plug at the base of the crankcase allowed the rate of flow to be checked.

A New Exhaust System

Another obvious feature of the 1950 production bike was the new exhaust system. The effective length of the pipe had been reduced and the megaphone was of smaller dimensions. In order to set this latter component far enough to the rear to be clear of the footrest and gearchange lever, and at the same time obtain the critical, shorter pipe length, the header pipe now curved very sharply from the exhaust port and led to the rear inside the right-hand (offside) front down-tube. As it was impracticable to bend a pipe to this small radius angle, the curved portion was a separate section, made up of two half-pressings with welded seams.

A new light-alloy fork top-lug gave a handlebar position ½in further to the rear than formerly; and last but certainly not least, came a new Burman racing gearbox coded 7R50. This was in response to reliability problems experienced with the earlier design. In laying

out the new box, which weighed 30lb (13.6kg), Burman had five main requirements, namely to achieve a more sturdy, shorter gear train, an improved and simplified foot-change mechanism, improved clutch-lift operation, better oil sealing and an improved clutch mechanism. The ratios of the 7R50 gearbox were 1.87, 1.35, 1.09 and 1:1. Weight saving had been assisted by manufacturing the case (shell) of the new gearbox in magnesium-electron.

Racing Success

During 1950, not only did Les Graham win the Swiss GP on a works development 7R (beating the likes of Bob Foster and Geoff Duke, mounted on Velocette and Norton respectively), but also Don Crossley won the Junior Manx GP on a production bike.

Changes for 1951

Outwardly at least, the 1951 production 7R was as the 1950 model, except for the new AMC 'Jampot' rear shocks and an equally new primary chain guard. The latter was domed in section (previously being flat) and brought further round the clutch sprocket, the object being to prevent oil from being flung on to the rear of the machine, including most importantly, the rear tyre. There was also a new chain oiler, consisting of a tap with a calibrated jet.

Internally, the engine had several notable changes. The camshaft was identical to the works development machines campaigned the previous year by the likes of Les Graham, Bill Doran and Ted Frend. The same applied to the piston, which gave a compression ratio of 9.4:1. In addition, the oil feeds to the camshaft had been uprated.

As previously, oil was fed, under pressure, into one end of the camshaft, then by way of a radial drilling to an annulus in the camshaft bearing at the other end. From this bearing the oil travelled along a passage to a face hole in the end-cam, thereafter spurting onto the

Six national champions rode 7Rs to victory in 1950 – in Switzerland, Austria, Brazil, Belgium, Holland and France.

Edinburgh rider Jackie Campbell with his future wife, Margaret, 6 June 1953. His 1949 7R was used for both road and racing use at that time!

Jackie Campbell with his 1949 7R (with later exhaust) competing at Kinnell, early 1950. The other machine is a BSA Gold Star. Notice how close the spectators are to the action.

AJS works rider Mick Featherstone leading the 350cc race on his 7R at Brough Airfield, East Yorkshire, Easter Saturday, 1951. Number 12 is a KTT Velocette; number 2 a Manx Norton.

camshaft lobes. With this arrangement alone it was found that the inlet cam-lobe tended to be masked. Now, in addition, a radial drilling in the end-cam joined with a passage in the camshaft tunnel which emerged directly over the inlet cam, the latter receiving its own separate oil spray. Finally, the inlet valve was fitted with an 'O' ring seal to improve combustion chamber cleanliness, the head of the exhaust pipe was shortened and the timing side bearing was keyed.

Breaking the Thruxton Lap Record

The 1951 season got underway in encouraging fashion, when works rider Bill Doran broke the Thruxton lap record on his way to victory in the 350cc final, raising the speed to 77.42mph (124.6km/h). Although no official statement had been made regarding development to the works models during the winter months, some changes had occurred. New signing Mick Featherstone's machine at Goodwood in April sported a 19in front wheel (the original sizes having been 3.00 × 21 (front) and 3.25 × 20 (rear), the brake hub diameter remaining unchanged). There were also modified Teledraulic forks (to which the clip-on handlebars were attached directly). It also featured a hump-backed seat with a zip at the rear, in which a spare plug and spanner could be stowed away.

In the 1951 Junior TT, Featherstone was the first rider home on a 7R, in fourth. Once again the unfortunate Doran suffered his annual retirement when well placed. However, Doran came back to win the Dutch TT at Assen, backed up by team-mate Bill Petch in runner-up position. Other official teamsters that year were Irishman Reg Armstrong and New Zealander Rod Coleman. As far as privateers were concerned, the 7R (and Featherbed Manx Norton) had largely supplanted the by now ageing Velocette KTT. In September 1951 Robin Sherry won the Junior Manx GP on a 7R.

1952 Changes

The 1952 production 7R continued to benefit from the works development models and that year saw roller cam followers fitted to the rockers, whilst the compression ratio was bumped up to 10:1. In addition, during September 1951 Burman had announced the B52 gearbox. By employing shorter mainshafts, whip had been reduced, and the new 'box featured an improved selector mechanism which dispensed with the hold sliding dog set-up. Increased backlash in the dogs permitted a more positive gearchange. Even then things were not quite right, and Burman were forced to put in an additional bearing to provide greater reliability (in spring 1952).

South African Borro Castellani was into his late thirties before he became one of his country's top riders. He is seen here in 1952, winning at Argyle Road on his AJS 7R.

Period postcard showing 7R rider Robin Sherry and his machine; circa 1952.

Although the works-supported riders switched to the new 7R3A triple-valve model (*see* Chapter 6), the production 2-valve 7R continued to be competitive, even at the higher level. A notable event occurred during September 1952, when the Scot, Bob McIntyre, riding a 7R entered by Ayrshire dealer Sam Cooper, not only won the Junior Manx Grand Prix, but also finished runner-up in the Senior event on the same machine! It is also interesting to see that in the Junior Manx GP, 7Rs filled the first four places (McIntyre, H. Clark, D. Farrant and D. Ennett).

Major Changes for 1953

For 1953, the production 7R saw some major changes. Not only was the engine extensively updated, but there was an entirely new frame.

A November 1952 advertisement showing Bob McIntyre during his victorious Isle of Man Junior Manx GP victory that year on a 7R; Bob also finished runner-up on the same bike in the Senior event, a wonderful achievement.

Although superficially similar to what had gone before, the 1953 engine was considerably different. In fact, in many respects it was entirely new and thus the degree of interchangeability was quite small.

A new cylinder head (74 degrees included

The 1953 7R	
Engine	Air-cooled sohc 2-valve single with vertical cylinder, 74 degrees valve angle, roller rockers, revised bottom end including slimmer crankcase, stiffer crankshaft and reduced width for crankpin (and con-rod), drive side now featured a double-row cage for the drive-side main bearing (instead of the former two single-row assemblies); sodium-cooled exhaust valve
Bore	74mm
Stroke	81mm
Displacement	348cc
Compression ratio	10:1
Lubrication	Dry sump; twin gear pumps
Ignition	Magneto
Carburettor	Amal TT 1⅛in
Primary drive	Chain
Final drive	Chain
Gearbox	Revised 4-speed Burman coded B52
Frame	Duplex cradle, fully welded construction, of entirely new design.
Front suspension	AMC racing Teledraulic oil-damped forks (shortened)
Rear suspension	Swinging arm with AMC 'Jampot' rear shock absorber
Front brake	8in, 2LS, conical electron magnesium-alloy hub with cast-iron liner
Rear brake	8in, 5LS, conical electron magnesium-alloy hub with cast-iron liner
Tyres	2.75 × 19 front; 3.25 × 19 rear
Wheelbase	55.5in (1,410mm)
Ground clearance	5in (127mm)
Seat height	32in (813mm)
Fuel tank capacity	5.25gal (24ltr)
Dry weight	293lb (133kg)
Maximum power	35bhp @ 7,400rpm
Top speed	110mph (177km/h)

angle) featured a combustion chamber with a larger radius, with the valves which were now of larger diameter (inlet 1⅝in, exhaust 1⅜in – the latter now sodium-filled) having in effect been moved forward around the hemisphere, resulting in, it was claimed, improved down-draught and a superior inlet tract. Apart from crown modifications to suit the altered valve layout, the piston remained as before. The rockers had been increased in strength with roller cam followers replacing the slipper faces used previously.

The Bottom End

The bottom end was also considerably modified, with the crankpin (and connecting-rod) width having been reduced, resulting not only in a stiffer crankshaft assembly, but a slimmer crankcase and a narrower chain-line. Both main bearings were now carried in sep-arate housings spigotted into the crankcase halves on the inside. The drive-side main bearing featured a double-row cage, instead of the former two single-row assemblies, whilst the inner case was a sleeve pressed into the mainshaft; formerly rollers ran directly on the shaft. The external appearance of the electron crankcase had been altered by elimination of the stiffening ribs, which the AMC engineers had discovered to be unnecessary. Timing gear and camshaft drive continued virtually untouched.

A Massive, Cast-Alloy 'Bridge'

To improve the rigidity of the engine and gearbox assemblies, engine plates were axed in favour of a massive, cast-aluminium 'bridge'. This was bolted to the rear of the engine, forming an upper clamp for the Burman gearbox and, at the rear, was bolted to the frame cross-member. In addition, both the gearbox pivot bolt and the lower engine attachment bolt passed through the frame tubes and not the lugs. The tubes were drilled for this purpose and flanged bushes welded in;

the flanges were on the inside, and crankcase and gearbox lugs pulled up against them. Box-section lugs formed the front engine supports. The all-welded frame of circular-section tubing featured a shorter wheelbase than previously, with the engine cradle section considerably narrower. These cradle tubes were cranked outward behind the gearbox to provide a broad base for the rear suspension pivot. Allen screws, passing through the lugs and spindle, secured the pivot to the frame.

Smaller Wheel Rims

Another change for the 1953 production bikes, pioneered on the works machines, was the use of smaller diameter (19in) wheel rims, with tyre sections being 2.75 front and 3.25 rear. The small section front was claimed to assist handling (through a reduction in unsprung weight).

A new seat was specified, shorter than before and for the first time on a production 7R featuring a raised rear section. The capacity of the fuel tank remained at 5.25gal (24ltr), but the tank was no longer secured by horizontal through-bolts. In their place was a spring-loaded strap fixing; this was employed in conjunction with rubber supports both fore and aft. At the rear the supports comprised vertical pegs and rubber bushes which located into pockets in the tank. At the front, the supporting 'feet' were adjustable for height on the frame down-tubes to allow for any individual variation in tank shape. There was also a redesigned oil tank.

The primary drive had also been overhauled. A new chain guard offered better protection, and improved lubrication and less whip between the engine and gearbox (through the new mounting method) was said to considerably improve chain life. Final drive chain lubrication now mirrored the Porcupine twin: oil from the supply entered the gearbox mainshaft bearing housing then being fed to the rear of the gearbox sprocket and reaching the base of sprocket teeth via drillways. There

was also a new three-stud flange fitting exhaust header pipe arrangement. As for the result of the year, this was Bob McIntyre's astonishing runner-up spot in the Ulster Grand Prix – in front of Rod Coleman's works 3-valve model.

Little Change for 1954

For the 1954 model year the production 7R saw very little change. This was partly due to modifications which were carried out on the Matchless G45 twin, plus the continuing development time required on the works Porcupine and 3-valve single. The 7R detail work consisted of ventilation holes for the front of the primary chain guard, and at the rear of the guard an inclusion of a drain pipe for excess oil. The only other item was an improved gearchange thanks to a modification of the pedal linkage. Derek Ennett made history in September 1954, when he became the first native Manxman to win one of the races, when taking victory in the Junior Manx Grand Prix on his AJS 7R.

Williams Takes Over Development

In late 1954, Ike Hatch died and development of both the works 7R3 and production 7Rs passed to Jack Williams. A combination of

Cadwell Park, August 1954, with AJS 7R rider Fred Wallis approaching Hall Bends at the Lincolnshire circuit.

Derek Ennett, a 23-year-old Castletown engineer, made Manx Grand Prix history in September 1954, when he became the first native Manxman to win one of the races, by taking victory on his 7R in that year's Junior (350cc) event.

events meant that the development tempo of the 2-valve 7R picked up once again. The AMC group policy of axing specialized works-only machinery also came into force at the end of 1954: 'to concentrate on the standard production models'. However, it was not until the 1956 7R series that the full effect of Williams' arrival was to be felt – in fact the only change for the 1955 season was a twin-feed primary chain oiler. In addition, Jack Williams tested the changes on the works development 7Rs campaigned by selected riders during 1955.

The Redesign

Jack Williams' redesign, as that is exactly what it amounted to, saw for the first time since the original launch back in 1948, the adoption of new bore and stroke dimensions; these were 75.5 × 78mm respectively, giving a displacement of 349cc. The change, Williams said, was 'to permit an increase in engine revolutions without unduly augmenting piston speed'. Strangely, this change stemmed from theoretical, not practical, research as no works development 7Rs had previously used these new dimensions. However, together with a new reverse-cone megaphone exhaust, the

new engine had been extensively bench tested.

As for the cycle parts, the 1956 changes included knee cut-outs for the fuel tank, a narrower oil tank, works-type handlebars, footrests, brake and gear pedals and front brake adjuster. More changes saw local strengthening of the frame, a pair of entirely new rear shock absorbers and revised brakes, which now featured a larger air scoop for the front hub and improved ventilation for the rear unit. The torque arm anchorage for the rear brake saw the replacement of the original stud by a bolt set-up. The 1956 7R went on sale in spring that year costing £403 inclusive of UK purchase tax.

Not only did AJS win the Manufacturers' Team Prize at the 1956 Junior TT, but 7R-mounted Derek Ennett finished runner-up behind the race winner Ken Kavanagh (Moto Guzzi) and in front of several full works bikes.

Yet More Changes

For 1957, the development team, headed by Jack Williams, upped the power output to 37.5bhp, whilst the infamous 'Jampot' rear shocks were at last ditched in favour of the much superior Girlings.

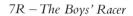

7R action at Brough in the summer of 1956. This photograph shows up all the main details of the machine including the frame, engine, brakes, suspension and exhaust.

A year later, when the 1958 7R arrived, there was another increase in power when, thanks to a new camshaft, modified inlet port and a new larger bore Amal GP carburettor, the figure was raised to 39bhp. A suspended float chamber was specified to prevent the possibility of fuel surge and frothing. There was also the replacement of the Burman-made gearbox with one of AMC's own design (which was also used on the Manx Norton, and later the new Matchless G50 single).

The compression ratio had been hiked to 10.25:1, with peak power being produced between 7,400–7,800rpm. Other modifications on the 1958 7R series included an external type of chain oiler which fed oil to the lower run of the final drive chain, and a timed engine breather working between the engine sprocket and the drive-side main bearing. The swinging arm pivot now served as the pick-up point for the rearmost sections of the alloy engine mounting plates, dispensing with the aluminium bridge-piece forging previously described. This, Williams found, helped reduce vibration at higher engine revolutions.

And although the 7R had a poor TT in 1958, the Manx Grand Prix saw an impressive victory by future star Alan Shepherd, who on Bill Bancroft's AJS, also set a new class lap for the Mountain circuit of 90.58mph (159.7km/h).

Australian Jack Ahearn aboard his 348cc 7R in the pits area in preparation for the 1958 Junior TT; he finished seventeeth, averaging 88.42mph (142.4km/h) for the 7-lap race.

German Karl Hoppe 7R (75) leads Fritz Klager's Horex twin at the Hockenheim circuit during a round of the German national championships, August 1958.

Bob McIntyre, 7R-mounted at Aintree in 1958.

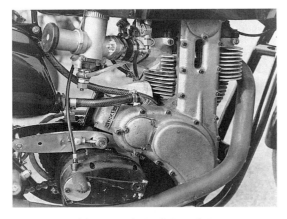

Engine room of the 7R, with Amal GP carb, Lucas racing magneto and AMC gearbox; this is a 1958 machine.

The 1959 Model Year

When AMC announced its 1959 range it was seen that a new larger engined single based on the 7R, the G50 Matchless, had been added to the lists. But everyone was left asking the question why had it taken AMC so long to come up with the bike? Displacing 496cc (90 × 78mm), the G50 was a much superior motorcycle to the road-based G45 twin which it replaced. There is no doubt that Jack Williams did not like the twin, but it had also been the excellent results gained by Bill Nilsson in motocross (*see* Chapter 12) where the Danish rider had won the 500cc World Championship in 1957 (Nilsson also finished runner-up in 1958), which had really proved the point.

As for the 7R itself, engine modifications

The 1958 7R	
Engine	Air-cooled sohc 2-valve single with vertical cylinder, light alloy head, light alloy barrel with cast-iron liner; valve springs, fully enclosed valve gears, camshaft drive with Weller tensioner, Dykes piston ring
Bore	75.5mm
Stroke	78mm
Displacement	349cc
Compression ratio	10.2:1
Lubrication	Dry sump; twin gear pumps
Ignition	Lucas SRR1 racing magneto, gear-driven with Vernier coupling
Carburettor	Amal 10GP 1½in
Primary drive	Chain
Final drive	Chain
Gearbox	AMC 4-speed, close ratio, foot-change
Frame	All-welded, Reynolds 531 steel tubular cradle with duplex front down-tubes and integral subframe and steering head bracing; cylinder head steady attachment points
Front suspension	AMC racing Teledraulic oil-damped forks
Rear suspension	Swinging arm, with twin Girling racing shock absorbers
Front brake	8in 2LS, conical electron magnesium-alloy hub with cast-iron liner
Rear brake	8in SLS, conical electron magnesium-alloy hub with cast-iron liner
Tyres	3.00 × 19 front; 3.25 × 19 rear
Wheelbase	55.5in (1,410mm)
Ground clearance	6in (152mm)
Seat height	31.5in (800mm)
Fuel tank capacity	5.25gal (23.9ltr)
Dry weight	287lb (130kg)
Maximum power	38.5bhp @ 7,600rpm
Top speed	116mph (187km/h)

were claimed to have produced a further 1.5bhp. This had been achieved by carrying out changes to the inlet port to improve volumetric efficiency and the use of a 1⅜in GP carburettor. As a result, Williams and his team had been able to increase top gear ratio from 5:1 to 4.85:1. To improve ground clearance when the machine was laid over, the rear frame had been narrowed, whilst the exhaust header pipe (the diameter being increased to 1½in) and megaphone were now tucked away to a greater degree. Although the steering head angle remained unchanged, the Teledraulic front forks had been given a slightly increased trail and their damping changed in order to provide improved handling and road-holding qualities. A fibreglass seat base had been adopted as standard, decreasing overall weight.

In the Junior TT in 1959, George Catlin was the first 7R rider home; placed tenth, with a race average speed of 91.38mph (147.1km/h).

1960 Programme

When the 1960 AMC racing programme was announced, it was seen that further changes had occurred to the ongoing 7R development regime. The engine saw closer adjustment of the vernier ignition timing, strengthening of the magneto retaining strap and more rigid float-chamber mounting brackets. Once more the AMC engineers had managed to improve

ground clearance. This had been achieved by shortening and re-tailoring the nearside (left) bottom frame loop and by narrowing the swinging arm fork to bring the exhaust megaphone closer to the bike's contra line. The gearbox end-cover was modified to suit and the opportunity taken at the same time to stiffen up the engine mounting plates. The rear brake operation was switched to full cable operation and the pedal redesigned, along with that of the gearchange lever. A cutaway in the aluminium oil tank permitted improved engine breathing and a smaller filler cap was now employed. The riding position was lowered by an inch, allowing the rider to adopt a more compact stance.

1960 Racing Results

As for the 1960 racing season, besides a whole host of British short circuit successes, which had even seen Mike Hailwood out regularly on a 7R, the Junior TT was to see Bob McIntyre put up a splendid performance to finish third, behind the four cylinder MVs of John Surtees and John Hartle. In the Junior Manx Grand Prix, Roy Mayhew came second, with Ron Langston on another 7R setting the fastest lap at 91.69mph (147.6km/h). Future Suzuki world champion Hugh Anderson put his 7R on the rostrum with a third in the Ulster Grand Prix.

Mike Hailwood said he preferred the 7R to the three-fifty Manx Norton, and rode one of the Plumstead-built bikes from 1959 until the end of 1961. This photograph taken in 1961 at Oulton Park shows his Ecurie Sportive machine with Oldani front brake and Peel 'Mountain Mile' fairing.

The 1961 Bikes

In spring 1961 AMC announced that it would be building sixty 7Rs and forty G50s – all one hundred bikes had been 'sold out' since the previous December. Most of the machines' list of updates concerned the chassis rather than the engine. Among the former, which applied to both models, was the replacement of the two springs formally used in each telescopic fork leg by a single, multi-rate component. Damping characteristics had been altered to match this change.

The front-fork oil seals were now of the double-lipped type, the outer lips wiping and cleaning the fork stanchion tubes to exclude any foreign bodies. The metal fork covers had been ditched in favour of rubber gaiters, both for weight saving and cost purposes; the fork travel itself was increased. In addition there were revised Girling shock absorbers which not only featured improved damping, but were now individually tested and matched in pairs prior to shipment to the AMC race shop in Plumstead.

Another change was to the front brake air scoop, which had been given more frontal area, whilst the brake shoe expander cam had an end-plate to locate the shoes on the cam. An alteration to the shape of the engine's timing chest had been made to enable the exhaust header pipe curve to be tucked in closer.

Revised Sprockets

There was also the fitment of a larger gearbox sprocket (twenty-two instead of twenty-one teeth) providing a lower gearbox running speed and temperature. Gear ratios had been maintained by fitting a smaller engine sprocket (twenty-two instead of twenty-three). The engine's compression had been upped yet again, from 11.7 to 12:1, by way of a modified piston.

The 7R's tyre size had been increased to match those of the G50: 3.00 × 19 front, 3.50 × 19 rear. The price in April 1961 of the 7R was £443 5s 11d, including UK tax.

Hailwood Misses Out

In June 1961 Mike Hailwood won three TTs in a week (125 and 250cc Honda; 500cc Norton), but it could, and should have been, four wins. Sadly, this was not to be the case, when within sight of victory on the last lap, Mike's 7R broke its gudgeon pin, robbing him of a historic victory. Even so, his performance had shown that the 7R could still lead a world championship race. Something of a consolation came three months later, when in September 1961, 7Rs scored a superb 1–2–3 in the Junior Manx Grand Prix when, in truly dreadfully wet conditions, Frank Reynolds, Robin Dawson and Arthur Newstead brought home the bacon. But after setting a record lap at 85.22mph (137.2km/h) and leading the race, Fred Neville, on another 7R, crashed on the final lap and was fatally injured.

The year of 1962 was not only to prove the 7R's final year of production (although a few more examples were subsequently built from

Welshman Selwyn Griffiths winning the 350cc final at Castle Combe on Saturday, 30 April 1963.

Rhodesian Bruce Beale during the 1962 Natal '100' races at the Westwood circuit on his very fast AJS 7R.

The later 7R models had these air scoops on both the front …

… and rear wheel hubs as shown here.

Surtees 7R Special

The Motor Cycle called it 'Fit for a Champion' and in many ways that's exactly what it was. We are of course talking about the very special 7R-engine machine which multi-world champion John Surtees completed in 1961, after two years of his by-now precious time.

The project stemmed from 1959 when John had intended to return to short circuit racing when his MV commitments allowed. Originally the plan called for a five-hundred Manx Norton (sold to Stan Hailwood in the spring of 1961) and a much more ambitious creation, powered by an AJS 7R engine. However, Count Domineco Agusta eventually vetoed John's plans and he quit motorcycle racing at the end of 1960. Because of the huge amount of work needed, the 7R wasn't finally completed until late summer 1961.

But it had certainly been worth the effort, as it was a masterpiece of design work. The frame was designed by John himself and manufactured in cooperation with Ken Sprayson of Reynolds Tubes. The 7R engine was modified by fitting twin spark ignition, a longer inlet tract with the carburettor rigidly mounted, with a modified Dell'Orto SS-type float chamber. The gearbox, a modified Manx Norton assembly, employed an electron shell and a one-off close ratio, stronger gear cluster. But it was the cycle parts which attracted most attention, giving the machine a much lower and compact feel than the standard AMC product.

The engine was mounted 1⅛in (26mm) lower than on a standard 7R. A trio of tubes, 1¼in (31.8mm) diameter and of 18 gauge, formed a rigid, lightweight structure.

Surtees 7R Special *continued*

Norton Featherbed fashion, the twin front down-tubes were connected to the top of the steering head; but in place of sweeping downward and backward in straight lines, they were bent approximately halfway down so that the lower sections were almost vertical. 'This', said Surtees at the time, 'gives better support for the steering head and allows the engine to be mounted further forward.' The pair of tubes passed beneath the power unit then swept upward behind the gearbox. The twin top-frame rails were joined to the base of the steering head, splayed outward around the front down-tubes, then continued rearward to join the upper extremities of the main loops. Gusset plates at the joints were used to form upper anchorage points for the Girling rear shock absorbers. The upper and lower tubes were both cross-braced by a pair of short tubes.

John had ensured enhanced rigidity by a third pair of tubes, extending from halfway along the upper tubes to the region of the swinging arm pivot pin. Oil for lubricating the primary chain was held in the nearside frame tube.

What appeared to be a small gusset plate was welded into the joint each side. In fact the 'plate' was actually hollow and fabricated from 16 gauge sheet steel. The pivot pin for the swinging arm passed through the above mentioned gussets, which also formed the footrest mountings.

The long, low, slimline aluminium fuel tank held 3½gal (16ltr) and was held in place by an aerolastic which passed over an ear at each end of the tank, clamping it down onto the rubber-covered frame top rails. Much thought was given to the triangular-shaped oil tank which, again in aluminium, sat lower in the frame than on the production 7R.

Weighing in at 265lb (120kg), some 25lb (11kg) lighter than the current 7R, the Surtees Special had spring poundages 15 per cent lower than the standard 7R front and rear suspension systems. A Manx Norton Roadholder front fork had been shortened by ¾in (19mm) and the sliders switched to take an Italian Oldani front brake. The forks also had their dampers modified and employed lightweight SAE 5-rate oil.

To further minimize unsprung weight the Girling racing rear shocks were mounted upside-down (with the internals suitably changed). The rear brake was a Manx Norton conical hub, whilst attention was given to raising components such as footrests and exhaust higher than normal, to permit, as John put it, 'the extreme cornering angles possible with the latest racing tyres.'

When asked what he would do with the bike once he had completed it the reply came back that 'I am loath to let anyone else straddle it and I'm certainly not interested in selling it.'

The 1962 7R

Engine	Air-cooled sohc, 2-valve single with vertical cylinder, die-cast light alloy head with pressed-in valve seats, sodium-cooled exhaust valve, light-alloy barrel with iron liner, eccentric rocker spindles, hairpin valve springs, fully enclosed valve gear, camshaft drive with Weller tensioner	Frame	Twin tube, cradle, welded construction, Reynolds, 531 tubing
		Front suspension	AMC racing Teledraulic oil-damped forks
		Rear suspension	Swinging arm, with oil-damped racing Girling shock absorbers
		Front brake	8in, SLS, conical electron magnesium-alloy hub with cast-iron liner
Bore	75.5mm		
Stroke	78mm	Rear brake	8in, SLS, conical electron magnesium-alloy hub with cast-iron liner
Displacement	349cc		
Compression ratio	12:1		
Lubrication	Dry sump; twin gear pumps	Tyres	3.00 × 19 front; 3.50 × 19 rear
Ignition	Rotating magnet Lucas 2MTT magneto	Wheelbase	55in (1,397kg)
		Ground clearance	6.75in (171mm)
Carburettor	Amal Grand Prix T5GP 1⅜in	Seat height	27in (686mm)
Primary drive	Chain	Fuel tank capacity	4.75gal (21.6ltr)
Final drive	Chain	Dry weight	285lb (129kg)
Gearbox	AMC 4-speed, close ratio, foot-change	Maximum power	41.5bhp @ 7,800rpm
		Top speed	118mph (190km/h)

Scot Denis Gallagher riding his 7R in the mid-1960s; the front brake has been modified with large air scoops and cooling rings.

Bill Ivy with the Kirby 7R short-stroke (81 × 68mm), during the 1965 Isle of Man Junior TT. Over the measured 176 yards at the Highlander, the bike clocked 120.4 mph (193.8km/h).

spares), but also, as described elsewhere it brought the onset of AMC's financial problems, which ultimately to lead to the group's demise only four years later.

Rights to the 7R (and G50) passed to Colin Seeley who, using frames of his own design, went on to remanufacture the two former AMC racing designs. But in truth the majority of the Seeley machines used the five-hundred G50 engine, so the 7R's story effectively ended with AMC's downfall. A somewhat sad end for a motorcycle which had achieved so much during its 18-year life.

Lincoln Club Cadwell Park meeting July 1966, with Brian (Snowy) Cammock heeling his 7R over to the limit.

Arthur Keeler (right) and Tom Mortimer with the Keeler ohc twin; much of the machine used 7R components. Note the Lotus Cars van and Lotus Elan in the background; October 1966.

The author racing a mid-1950s 7R at the national Snetterton Combine road races; summer 1967.

Lovely period shot of an un-named 7R rider during mid-1960s. The bike is largely stock except for the fibre-glass fuel tank and front-brake cooling muffs.

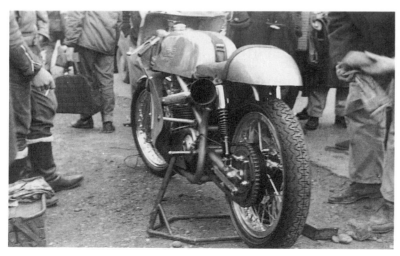

Easter Friday 1966; Brands Hatch. The Seeley 7R machine raced by Derek Minter that day.

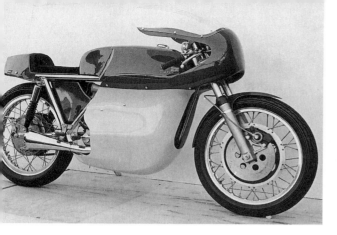

1967 Rickman Metisse road racer with 7R (or G50) engine. Specification includes: Lockheed/Rickman disc front brake, Fontana rear drum brake and nickel-plated frame.

Peter Williams on the Arter 7R at Brands Hatch 4 April 1969; he finished third.

Early 7R at the Snetterton Combine Reunion; Sunday 19 September 2004.

Frenchman Jean-Claude Castella's 1954 AJS 7R at Dijon, 23 May 2004.

Dave Hunt's 1962 7R at the CRMC races, Snetterton, August 1984.

Jim Porter with his Keeler 7R (92) leading the field at Lydden Hill, Kent circa 1970s.

Norman Francis racing at an early CRMC meeting at Oulton Park in 1982 on his 7R.

Arter Bros

Tom and Egerton Arter of Barham, Kent were the men behind the amazing 'Wheelbarrow' Matchless G50 which was ridden with such great verve by Peter Williams at the end of the 1960s and the beginning of the 1970s. Less well known is that the Arter brothers also entered Peter on an Arter 7R, which until the TR2 Yamaha became established, was equally successful. There again the formula was the same, the most power from the engine together with the lightest possible weight.

The list of riders entered down through the years by the Arter brothers was formidable and read like a Who's Who of racing talents, including: Ernie Lyons, Reg Armstrong, Dickie Dale, Bill Lomas, George Catlin, Peter Pawson, Frank Perris, Bill Smith, Syd Mizen, Hugh Anderson, Mike Duff, Fred Stevens and of course Peter Williams. The other interesting point is that the Arters had a brand loyalty, AMC – which meant AJS and Matchless.

So how did it all begin? In 1926, Tom Arter purchased an old Mackenzie 2-stroke for the princely sum of fifteen shillings (75p in today's UK coinage). Tom's interest in sport increased and in 1929, together with a few other enthusiasts in the locality, he became a founder member of the Barham Motorcycle Club. In 1930 the young Tom Arter began grass tracking with a 'big-port' AJS single and, on the same bike, began speed events and reliability trials. Motorcycles grew to become a passion and perhaps it was natural that Tom and his brothers should use the family agricultural business to fund the agency for AJS machines (1933).

In 1936 Tom acquired an ohc 350 AJS, to which a 500 version was soon added. And it was on this latter machine that he won the Brands Hatch Grass Track Championship title. Then in 1937 he attended his first Manx Grand Prix. For 1938 he rode a brand new R7 racer, ordered at the Olympia Motorcycle Show in the autumn of the previous year, following his Isle of Man visit. After outings at Brooklands and Crystal Palace Tom Arter rode the R7 in his first Manx GP, finishing an excellent thirteenth in the Junior.

Tragedy struck in 1939 when another brother, Donald, was killed in an accident. In May that year Tom sold all his machines and devoted himself to the business side of his life. During the war, he continued to work on the land, helping to produce essential home-grown food.

In 1946, motorcycle sport began to revive and he managed to obtain one of the ex-factory 350 AJS singles and at the same time became a sponsor for the first time. His rider was Irishman Ernie Lyons. On the pre-war Ajay, Lyons finished eighth in the Junior Manx GP. By 1948 the 7R had arrived and Tom's devotion to AJS ensured that he was one of the first to get the new bike. Ernie Lyons proved the newcomer's worth by winning the Leinster 200 as well as gaining numerous other successes on the Irish road circuits. Throughout the 1950s and 1960s 'Arter Bros' was a major entrant of AMC machinery, often fielding a team of two or three riders per season and winning races throughout Great Britain and Europe.

A major surprise came in 1963 with the reappearance of the magnificent Porcupine. Originally, this historic bike (a 1954 model) had been sent to Arter Bros to display in their showroom at Barham; but after discovering it to be fully serviceable, Tom and his rider, Mike Duff, took it to Brands Hatch 'to play', as he once described what happened. But after a few outings, including lapping in practice for the 1964 TT at over 100mph, it was put back on the shelf. Then, as described elsewhere in his book, the same Porcupine, together with a spare engine and other components, resurfaced at The Classic Motor Cycle Show at Stafford in the year 2000, and in the process set a new world price record of £157,700 (just for the bike!).

10   Record Breaking

As with all forms of motorcycle sport the earliest events were often ill-recorded and none more so than the outright speed record. It was often a case of claim and counter claim as these early speedsters attempted ever faster speeds. Finally in 1909, both the international body the FICM (the forerunner of the FIM) and several other bodies (including the British ACU) officially recognized the holder of the outright two-wheel speed record.

AJS were involved right from the off and set many records both before and after the First World War. Riders included the likes of Bert Denly and Nigel Spring. When the FICM published its official list of World Records achieved during 1929, no less than 117 of them were held by either Denly or Charlie Hough on AJS machinery. Also in 1929 a special 1,096cc ohc v-twin was created by Ike Hatch. Later this was used at Arpajon (France) and Southport Sands (England) before achieving a two-way average of just under 145mph (233 km/h) at Tát in Hungary. This compared with the outright World Record which then stood to Germany's Ernst Henne and BMW at almost 152mph (245km/h). Much of the testing for this unsuccessful record attempt was done on Southport Sands, prior to leaving for Hungary – in both cases the rider was Joe Wright.

Record Breaking

However, in the immediate post-war period AJS was to be much more successful in breaking records. It all began in October 1948,
when one of the new Porcupine five-hundred dohc racing twins, ridden by Ted Frend in that year's Senior TT, was earmarked for an attempt – at Montlhéry in France – to bag a number of World Records. In early November the machine, together with its attendant crew (including AMC race mechanics Matt Wright and Charlie Matthews) with Les Graham in charge, left the Plumstead factory for the Hotel du Chevel Blanc, at Montlhéry, on the outskirts of Paris. Jock West followed a couple of days later and by 11 November everyone, except the French officials (who were celebrating Armistice Day), were installed. Unfortunately the next few days saw the locality covered by fog. But by lunchtime on Friday 18 November the fog had at last cleared, to provide a bright, clear, but very cold day.

Keeping the engine lubricant warm enough for sustained high speeds was a major problem. This had been solved by covering the oil tank completely in brown paper, cut to size and neatly stuck on, before coating the paper with aluminium paint. The brown paper acted as an insulator and covered the air tunnels through the oil tank, and the bright exterior reduced heat radiation. The external oil pipes were also lagged to prevent additional heat loss.

Tests had also showed that by filling the engine with warm oil before starting, the temperature could be maintained high enough for safety. Even so it is unlikely that the most efficient engine temperatures were ever reached during the track sessions which were to follow.

The squad had been joined by the French champion, Georges Monneret (also the AJS importer), and after the early morning mist, the sun came out to dry the 1.69 mile (2.72km/h) concrete saucer, which comprised the Montlhéry track. Shortly after midday Jock West got the proceedings underway and he covered the first ten laps in 8 mins 38 secs – nearly 112mph (180km/h) from a standing start. He continued to lap steadily, but dropped to the pre-arranged 110mph (177km/h) average.

After an hour West came in to be replaced by Les Graham who, being lighter, suffered the circuit bumps better. When his riding stint was over the first record was safely in the bag – 223 miles (359km) in two hours at an average of 110.83mph (178.4km/h). Georges Monneret, a famous long-distance record-man in his own right, then took over, but only after the rear tyre had been changed (due to a cut, rather than excessive wear).

The 500km record mark was passed at 15.00 hours with Monneret in the saddle. It was found that the average was now 108.54mph (174.8km/h), despite the 3 mins 55 sec pit stop to change the tyre. Monneret had at one stage lapped at 116mph (187km/h).

Graham relieved West for the fifth hour, and with the light fading it was decided to call it a day when five hours had been completed. The four hours had been completed at 107.44mph (173km/h), the five hours at 107.14mph (172.5km/h). The 500 mile figure was 107.01mph (172.3km/h).

As a point of interest, the oil used for this successful record breaking spree (in which no fewer than eighteen new figures were set) was Mobiloil D, a mineral-based lubricant. Other equipment used included Lucas magneto, Amal carburettors, Dunlop tyres, Lodge sparking plugs, Smiths rev counter, Renold chains, Hepolite pistons, Salter valve springs, Wellworthy piston rings, Ferodo brake and

November 1948 advertisement, produced following success at Montlhéry, near Paris on Friday 12 November that year. Seated on the Porcupine record breaker is Les Graham, with Jock West (left) and Georges Monneret.

clutch linings, SKF ball race bearings, Vandervell big-end bearings and Esso fuel (a mixture of petrol and benzole).

Return to Montlhéry

AJS returned to Montlhéry on 20 November 1950, when a Porcupine ridden by Bill Doran and Mick Featherstone broke two World Records – the 2 hours at 115.04mph (370.4km/h) and the 500km at 115.03mph (185.2km/h). Bad weather then set in to stop further attempts. Almost a year later on 20 October 1951 AJS made another foray to Montlhéry and in the process captured no less than thirty-seven new World Records – which brought the number of records held by AJS at the time up to an impressive sixty-nine.

Many of the 1951 attempts were achieved by Bill Doran and Georges Monneret with a 348cc 7R and Blacknell sidecar. These included the 2/3/4/5/6/7 hours, 10/50/100/ 500 miles and 10/50/100/500/1,000 kilometres. In addition Doran and Rod Coleman averaged 109.44mph (176.2km/h) for the 2 hour distance with the machine in solo trim.

Finally, in mid-October 1952 the AJS equipe made a final visit to Montlhéry, this with one of the new 3-valve triple camshaft 7R3A model and a Porcupine. The result was another thirteen international World Records, gained over two days, 17 and 18 October.

On Friday, 17 October Georges Monneret's son Pierre took the 350cc 50 kilometres (115.76mph), 50 miles (116mph), 100 kilometres (115.96mph), 100 miles (115.75mph) and 1 hour (115.66mph) records. Then the following day Bill Doran, Rod Coleman, Georges and Pierre Monneret set the following: 500 kilometres (106.86mph), 500 miles (101.98mph), 3 hours (105.03mph), 4 hours (103.54mph), 5 hours (102.25mph), 6 hours (102.16mph), 7 hours (98.62mph) and 1,000 kilometres (102.25mph).

AJS then quit the record-breaking game in which, post-war, it had received considerable backing from the Mobil Oil company.

AJS 3-valve 7R3 single foreground; Porcupine at the rear. Montlhéry in October 1952, when more records were gained.

Rule Changes

On 1 January 1957 the whole system of creating and claiming World Records was revised by the FIM. This meant that in future only nine records in each class would be recognized, in place of the previous thirty-six. This change, the FIM claimed, was brought about to increase the value of individual records, as under the old scheme there were no fewer than 540 records, whereas the new regulations brought this down to 135.

The nine recognized record categories were:

- One kilometre flying start
- One kilometre standing start
- Ten kilometres
- One hundred kilometres
- One thousand kilometres
- One hour
- Six hours
- Twelve hours
- Twenty-four hours

This change left AJS holding only one World Record – the One Thousand Kilometre 30 wheel 350cc record set by Bill Doran in 1951 at 88.42mph (142.4km/h). Even so, AJS was able to claim that it had led the world on numerous occasions in the field of record breaking endeavour; and in the process won much international acclaim for the marque and for Great Britain.

V-Twin Record Breaker

Built for record breaking, the mighty eleven-hundred AJS V-twin was created during 1929, making its public debut the following year. The heart of the machine was its awesome 50-degree v-twin, which at first shared two of the existing five-hundred ohc singles 495cc, making 990cc. However, this was soon upped to 1,096cc.

The valve gear was a traditional AJS chain-driven overhead camshaft with a Weller tensioner. The cylinder barrels themselves were of steel, with hardened liners. The heads were aluminium, with cast-iron valve seats and bronze valve guides. A foot-operated 3-speed Sturmey-Archer gearbox was employed, with ratios of 3.2:1, 4.3:1 and 7.8:1, and a 4-plate clutch, together with Renold chain-driven primary and final drives completed the transmission specification.

The front forks were of the latest AJS TT-type, but specially constructed, using self-aligning ball bearings throughout and an Andre steering damper was fitted. The full cradle frame gave a wheelbase of 60in (1,524mm), its outstanding feature being a massive top tube of 2½in (64mm) diameter, hidden by a long, sleek fuel tank which, in its black and chrome finish, gave the bike a 'lean, rakish look' as described by *The Motor Cycle* in the 24 July 1930 issue.

But although it was certainly an imposing piece of machinery, its performance, at least at first was disappointing. With Captain Owen Baldwin at the controls the best it could achieve at Arpajon in France was 121mph (195km/h).

Then came the closure of the AJS works in Wolverhampton and subsequent takeover by the London-based Collier organization, which saw AJS join Matchless at Plumstead, south-east London. The giant vee lay for many months gathering dust in a corner of the Plumstead facilities. Then, in 1933 interest in the project was revived and the big twin was put back into commission. Percy Brewster fitted a Zoller supercharger and several test sessions were undertaken at the Brooklands circuit in Surrey.

Interviewed post-war Jock West stated that 'it was a brute to handle' and 'that a pair of Druid front forks might have made a lot of difference'. But at least Jock stayed aboard, as another factory rider, Reg Barber, who shared the testing with him got into a massive 'tank slapper' and came off the v-twin on the unyielding Brooklands concrete, resulting in some bad bruising and a broken collarbone.

The Mobil Oil company became involved in

The AJS v-twin record machine was created during 1929, making its public debut the following year. At first it displaced 990cc, before having its capacity increased to 1,096cc. In this photograph Jock West is sixth from left, with Barry Baragwanath fourth from left.

V-Twin Record Breaker *continued*

sponsoring AJS in another attempt on the world speed record. Following more development work, the big v-twin was hauled up to Southport on the Lancashire coast for former Zenith record holder Joe Wright to see if he could do any better.

At that time the outright motorcycle speed record was held by Germany's Ernst Henne riding a supercharged flat-twin BMW at 152mph (245km/h). Wright, wearing his famous streamlined helmet, carried out several runs up and down Southport Sands, then it was off to Tát in Hungary for an attack on the record. But even the great man could not make the Ajay go quickly enough, with a best one-way-direction speed of 145mph (233.5km/h), the mean average two-way coming out at 132mph (212.5km/h).

After this showing the bike was largely forgotten, before turning up over three decades later, in 1965, on the other side of the world in Tasmania, Australia! Many parts were missing and it was in a sorry state. Even so it was brought back to Great Britain and subsequently restored to concours condition. Lately visitors to various shows, including the Classic Motor Cycle exhibition at Stafford Showground, have been able to view this wonderful, but ultimately unsuccessful piece of motorcycle history.

Joe Wright (seated on bike) with the supercharged v-twin AJS at Southport Sands, 1933.

11 Lightweight Singles

The AJS Model 14

The Model 14 (and its twin brother, the Matchless G2) were launched at the Swiss Geneva Show in March 1958, the result of parent company AMC's decision to return to the popular 250cc class for the first time in the post-Second World War era.

Although the new quarter-litre AJS and Matchless machines were never viewed in quite the same way as their Heavyweight brothers (*see* Chapter 4) they were nonetheless important arrivals. Previously, the two marques had suffered because no such machines were available in their line-up; instead, newcomers to the world of two wheels had been forced to buy products from other British firms, notably BSA and Triumph. It was obviously important to encourage brand loyalty right from the start. Conversely the wily Japanese went about things differently, building small-capacity machines first – and following later with ever bigger models – and so keeping their customers happy.

In addition, there was considerable talk of likely new legislation restricting novices to smaller machines, and AMC thus needed to supplement its existing Francis-Barnett and James 2-strokes as both its AJS (and Matchless) models were of 350cc and above.

The 'Lightweight' Tag

So it was that the range of 'Lightweight' singles came about, ultimately encompassing not only touring, sporting and competition (scrambling) two-fifties, but also a three-fifty variant as well. At first sight the newcomer appeared to have followed the Continental European trend of unit construction. However, in truth, this was not the case, as the gearbox was a separate entity. The same could be said of the 'Lightweight' tag, because in truth, at 325lb (147kg) the new two-fifty was anything but that. However, the description stuck, and in any case the three-fifty model was a lot lighter than the long running Model 16 range.

The Motor Cycle's show report said:

> Around Geneva, as far as the eye could see, was draped a vast mantle of snow. Inside the Palais des Expositions man seemed to be challenging nature's spectacle with a glittering show of chromium plating and burnished aluminium.

AMC's sales director, Jock West, had this to say at the Geneva launch:

> We have tried to achieve that indefinable modern appearance without resorting to the excessive bulk and extreme 'one-ness' that costs money and often results in poor accessibility.

With bore and stroke dimensions of 69.85 × 64.85mm, the engine displaced 248.5cc. Of particular interest, the cylinder axis was offset ahead of the crankshaft axis. The actual crank throw was 32.385mm, the cylinder being offset 0.25in (0.6mm) forward – giving a *dé saxe* effect. Although this arrangement was rare on motorcycle power units, this was

Spring 1958 saw the arrival of the new 'Lightweight' AMC single cylinder models in the shape of the AJS Model 14 and Matchless G2, both with 248.5cc (69.85 × 64.85mm) ohv engines.

certainly not so in the car world. And there were two distinct advantages. The first of these was less piston slap and bore wear because the movement of the piston across from the non-thrust to the thrust side of the cylinder bore at the top of the stroke was gentler. This minimized 'slap', whilst the connecting-rod angularity at maximum combustion pressure was reduced. The other advantage was that there was better use of that portion of the power stroke, together with a small, but worthwhile, reduction in piston friction.

In creating their new two-fifty engine assembly, the AMC design team said that:

the degree of offset is not great, however, and the system was chosen not just for the benefits (as stated above) but also because it fitted in with the general geometry of the engine.

Engine Design

Although from first glance the new AMC power unit appeared radically different from

what had gone before at the Plumstead works, in practice the new engine followed familiar ground, with a built-up crankshaft and many of the traditional AMC features. So there were no exotic overhead cams. Instead there was the traditional ohv system. The actual layout featured a single camshaft, mounted in the crankcase on the offside (right) and featuring a pair of trailing lever-type followers; the pushrods themselves being positioned in 'crossed' form. The cylinder head and valve gear closely followed that found on the existing Model 16 heavyweight single. By positioning the cylinder forward and the camshaft behind the crankshaft axis, there was increased room for the cam lobes and their followers.

Another design requirement was that there should be a minimum of side thrust on the followers, which meant that the pushrods had to be as near as possible to vertical in front elevation. Rotation of the plane of the valves (through 21¼ degrees clockwise, viewed from above) made this practical without the use of rocker spindles of differing lengths. In addition it had the advantage of bringing the exhaust port and spark plug more directly into the cooling airstream.

Manufactured in DTD24 aluminium alloy, the cylinder head featured a part-spherical combustion space with cast-in valve seats of austenitic cast iron. In addition there were diagonal vertical fins on the nearside (left) to direct air over the combustion chamber and spark plug areas. The silicon–aluminium inlet valve was substantially larger than the exhaust valve, which was of Jessops G2 steel (valve head diameter was $1^{15}\!/_{32}$in (37mm) and $1^{3}\!/_{16}$in (29mm) respectively). Due to this significant difference, and the wish to avoid too sharp a bend in the exhaust tract, the valve-included angle of 75 degrees was split unequally: the inlet valve was at 35 degrees to the vertical, whilst the exhaust valve was set at 40 degrees.

The inlet tract was offset 10 degrees towards the right of the centerline of the head; the exhaust tract was also offset to the right, but this time by $11\frac{1}{2}$ degrees. This meant that, in effect, the cylinder head was skewed around $21\frac{1}{4}$ degrees, effectively bringing the exhaust to the right, and the carburettor to the left. The choke diameter of the latter was $1^{1}\!/_{16}$in (26mm), and the carburettor was an Amal Monobloc Type 376, with a down-draught angle of 12 degrees. There was a thick heat-insulating spacer between the carb and cylinder head.

With an alloy head the valve guides were manufactured in cast iron and were located axially by circlips and crossover hairpin valve springs. Four long thru-studs screwed into the crankcase held down the head and barrel; the separate die-cast rocker box was attached to the head by no fewer than nine bolts.

The rockers were of typical AMC built-up construction; on each, the arms were splined to the ends of what *The Motor Cycle* described as a 'live' spindle, and were separated by a hardened sleeve to which they were clamped by nuts on the spindle ends. Each rocker was supported by a pair of bronze bushes with an oil-retaining felt sleeve separating them. Owing to the unequal valve angles in the cylinder head, and the desirability of employing interchangeable pushrods, the exhaust rocker was mounted slightly lower in the box than the inlet component.

For both simplicity and quiet running, the single camshaft was driven directly by the crankshaft pinion. Both ends of the camshaft were supported in bronze bushes, one in the crankcase wall, the other in a light-alloy bolted-on case that surrounded the gears. On the outside of the case was the contact breaker assembly (including the condenser), the points being operated by an extension of the camshaft and incorporating centrifugal automatic control of the ignition timing.

The cam followers featured curved operating faces and moved directly on a common spindle ahead of the camshaft. Of light-alloy tubing, the pushrods were equipped with steel ends, the upper of which embodied the valve-clearance adjusters. The pushrods were quite widely splayed and operated in a single tunnel of figure-eight cross-sections in the cylinder barrel; at the head each pushrod had its own tunnel.

Yet another feature which followed conventional AMC design practice was the piston (with a compression ratio of 7.8:1). This was wire wound above the gudgeon pin and had a split skirt. The piston featured a single scraper ring and a pair of compression rings; the upper of these two was chromium plated and had a taper face for quick bedding in. The piston crown employed a shallow dome and flats, these providing valve-head clearance during the overlap period.

The connecting rod, of 1 per cent chromium steel, measured $5^{3}\!/_{8}$in (136mm) between centres; within the ribbed big-end eye was a hardened-steel sleeve, which formed the roller track. The small-end bush was of aluminium alloy. As for the big-end bearing, this comprised two rows of $\frac{1}{4} \times \frac{1}{4}$in ($6 \times 6$mm) rollers, ten in each, spaced by a Duralumin cage. Nominal crankpin diameter was 1.2in (19mm), whilst EN351 was employed for the hardened roller track sleeve, on a body of KE805. The crankpin was a parallel press fit in the cast-iron flywheels, the latter being 6½in (165mm) diameter by ⅞in (22mm) wide, and secured by nuts.

Manufactured of Ubas steel, and with a journal diameter of ⅞in (22mm), the main-shafts featured flanged inner ends and were a parallel interference fit in the flywheels, each being located by a woodruff key. A pair of ball-race bearings supported the drive-shaft, their inner races spaced by the keyed-in sleeve of the timed crankcase breather, which discharged to the rear of the case. The timing-side bearing, in contrast, was a long phosphor-bronze bush, cut out on its underside to accommodate the oil-pump worm drive.

The engine sprocket was splined on the drive-side mainshaft, and outboard of this was the rotor of the Wico Pacy AC generator. The stator was located in the outer half of the primary chaincase, and both sides of the inner chaincase were dowelled to ensure accuracy of alignment. The drive-side crankcase-half mated up with the primary chaincase, and the timing-side half blended into a domed cover which carried a circular plate providing access to the contact-breaker assembly.

The Lubrication System

A reciprocating plunger oil-pump worm, driven from the timing-side main, was similar in design and operation to the type already employed in other AJS (and Matchless) singles, such as the Model 16 and Model 18. This drew oil from a 2½pt (1.4ltr) oil tank (AMC referred to this as 'a container') which was bolted to the outside of the timing-side crankcase half, ahead of the timing case; the inboard wall of the tank was formed by the crankcase and the filler neck was situated at the very front of the crankcase.

Part of the lubricating oil picked up by the supply side of the pump was fed to the worm chamber and thereafter passed through holes in the base of the worm thread into the main-shaft and thence to the big-end bearing via drillways. The remainder of the lubricant trav-elled to the overhead rocker shafts via passages in the cylinder barrel and head. Grooves in the side of the valve-operating arms of the rockers led some of the oil to the valve stem ends, and there was also an adjustable bleed to the inlet valve guide.

Oil drained from the valve compartment down the pushrod tunnels to the timing gear. From the timing chest it overflowed into the crankcase to join the excess thrown out by the big-end. The scavenge pump picked up the oil from the base of the crankcase and passed it across the rear of the engine to the felt car-tridge oil filter, mounted longitudinally in the nearside (left) half of the crankcase and with access to this filter from the front. From the filter the oil returned across ahead of the cylin-der and, with the oil filler cap removed, could be seen re-entering the tank.

The Separate Gearbox

As *The Motor Cycle* said:

> The most ingenious single feature of the new models is the combination of the neatness of an integral gearbox with the ease of disman-tling or unit replacement afforded by a sepa-rate box.

Adjustment of the primary chain was achieved in the traditional British way, by drawbolts. The gearbox featured a cylindrical shell which matched up against a similar curvature at the rear of the crankcase; the offside (right) end cover of the gearbox fitted neatly within a hole in the engine side cover. Because the main-shaft lay considerably above the shell axis, rota-tion of the shell altered the position of the primary chain centres. The mounting was identical in principle with that widely used for belt-driven dynamos on automobiles.

A pair of substantial steel straps attached under the rear of the crankcase were responsi-ble for holding the gearbox in place. At the

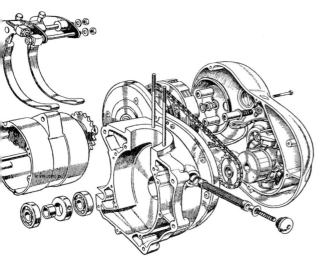

The drive-side of the AMC Lightweight engine, showing how the gearbox shell was clamped and the primary chain adjusted.

Primary Drive

The primary drive was taken care of by a ⅜ × 0.225in (9.5 × 5.7mm) simplex chain running on sprockets with twenty-one and fifty teeth. The clutch employed four friction plates with bonded-on oil-resisting material, and in its centre a vane-type transmission shock absorber embodying rubber blocks.

In the outer half of the primary chaincase were two large holes, with screw-in plugs. The most forward of these holes served as a combined inspection, filling and level orifice, whilst the other provided access to an adjuster at the centre of the clutch pressure plate. Final drive was by a ½in × 0.305in (12.7 × 7.75mm) chain running on nineteen (gearbox) and fifty-five (rear wheel) tooth sprockets, giving a top gear ratio of 6.9:1.

The Frame Design

The frame design for the 'Lightweight' singles is best described as being of the composite type, being a mixture of steel tubing and a fabricated pressed-steel box section that ran under the engine and gearbox assemblies. Actually, had the engine been of true unit construction it would then have been used as a stressed member of the frame and thus dispensed with the entire box section under the engine/gearbox on the AMC design; this would have also saved a considerable amount of weight.

The rear subframe was bolted on whilst the rear swinging arm had a pivot pin attached to the offside (right) leg and held by a collar on the nearside (left); this spindle ran on bronze bushes. Suspension was provided by a pair of bought-in Girling (adjustable) hydraulically damped shock absorbers at the rear, with a pair of lightweight AMC hydraulically damped front forks. The latter components were the same as used on the James and Francis Barnett two-strokes and the Norton 250 Jubilee twin.

In an era when the wheel size was almost always 19 or 18in, the 17in used for the new AMC two-fifties was notable – although, as *The Motor Cycle* noted, it was 'admirably suited

upper ends of these straps were eye bolts threaded to take tensioning bolts passing through a bar bridging the two steel plates which embraced the gearbox, and which bolted to the crankcase and frame-seat tube to form the rear mounting of the power unit. A draw bolt of conventional pattern rotated the gearbox after the straps had been loosened. Both the draw bolt and the strap bolts were readily accessible upon removal of a pressed-steel cover plate which was secured by two screws and curved well round the rear of the gearbox, provided a very neat appearance, giving no indication of what lay beneath. This, of course, only added to the appearance of a full unit-construction design.

Standardization had been achieved by cleverly utilizing the 4-speed gear cluster from the Piatti-designed, AMC 250 two-stroke single cylinder machine. These provided internal ratios of 1, 1.30, 1.85 and 2.95:1. The gear change and selector mechanisms were also similar to the two-stroke components, whereas the clutch thrust operation followed that of the heavyweight ohv singles, with the floating cable arm pivoting on a thrust ball, having on its other a cam profile bearing on a fixed-centre roller.

to the proportions of the machine'. The 6in (153mm) full-width brake hubs were also taken from the James/Francis Barnett/Norton Jubilee stock, but were generally agreed to be sufficient in providing decent braking performance for the 18bhp, 325lb (147 kg), 70mph (113km/h) motorcycle.

Wipac Headlamp

Included in the newcomer's specification was a 6in (152mm) Wipac headlamp, in which was mounted a speedometer, ammeter and separate ignition and lighting switches. Comprehensive mudguarding was also a feature. However, signs of economy showed in the way that the clutch and front brake pivots were welded to the handlebars – meaning that adjustment of these was virtually impossible.

Other Features

In standard guise the Model 14/G2 had a deep-section guard over the upper run of the final drive chain, but a fully enclosed chaincase was available as cost option.

This case was divided horizontally and embraced the swinging arm to which the upper and lower halves were bolted; the edges of the halves overlapped to prevent the ingress of road dirt and water. The front end of the case was shielded by a sheet-metal section bolted to the rear of the primary chaincase.

The frame, mudguards, stands, headlamp shell and the like were finished in gloss black, whilst the 2¾gal (12.5ltr) fuel tank was in Mediterranean Blue with silver lining or black with gold lining. The main tank colour was repeated in a flash on each side of the engine outer casings, which also carried a small replica of the tank badge.

It was anticipated that production would begin in May 1958, but initially only for export. Then in mid-June it was announced that production of the Model 14 (and Matchless G2) was underway for the home market. The basic cost of either machine was £157 10s;

with UK purchase tax added, this figure went up to £196 9s 8d; or with the optional, full enclosure of the rear chain, £199 12s (including purchase tax).

The 1959 Model 14	
Engine	Air-cooled, ohv single with vertical cylinder; alloy head; cast-iron barrel; vertically split aluminium crankcases; fully enclosed valve gear; hairpin valve springs; built-up crankshaft; single gear-driven camshaft; crossover enclosed pushrods; roller-bearing big-end
Bore	69.85mm
Stroke	64.85mm
Displacement	248.5cc
Compression ratio	7.8:1
Lubrication	Dry sump, plunger worm pump
Ignition	Battery/coil 6-volt; alternator
Carburettor	Amal Monobloc 376 1¹⁄₁₆in
Primary drive	Duplex chain
Final drive	Chain
Gearbox	4-speed, foot-change AMC, adjustable type
Frame	All-steel construction, brazed and bolted; single main and front tubes; pressed steel under-channel
Front suspension	AMC lightweight oil-damped telescopic forks
Rear suspension	Two-piece swinging arm, with oil-damped adjustable twin shock absorbers
Front brake	6in, SLS full-width iron drum
Rear brake	6in, SLS full-width iron drum
Tyres	3.25 × 17 front and rear
Wheelbase	53in (1,346mm)
Ground clearance	5.5in (140mm)
Seat height	30in (762mm); 1961 onwards, 30.5in (775mm)
Fuel tank capacity	2.75gal (12.5ltr); 1960 onwards, 3.25gal (15ltr)
Dry weight	325lb (147kg)
Maximum power	18bhp @ 7,200rpm
Top speed	72mph (114km/h)

Testing the Model 14

In the 26 February 1959 issue of *The Motor Cycle* George Wilson wrote an article entitled 'Hookey to the Seaside', subtitled 'Tale of a day's outing through fog to sunshine with a 248cc Model 14 AJS'. Wilson began his piece:

> since its [the Model 14] introduction in March last year, I have looked on it with mixed feelings. Technically the design is undoubtedly right out of the top drawer. But it has always seemed to me to be a modern machine in which the stylist had not gone far enough.

His first impressions were 'good – very good'. He considered that 'navigation was magnificent', and that both brakes were good (the rear one better than the front): they were smooth, and his feeling was that they would never lock the wheels. He also found that the 'engine is beautifully quiet mechanically', and that 'there is powerful punch low down on the rpm scale so that one can trickle in a highish gear'.

George Wilson went on to say:

> Power delivery could not have been more smooth. The lower three gears are well chosen and combined with the engine punch provide the sort of off-the-mark acceleration that makes Ford Consul drivers give.

Fuel consumption was impressive – George Wilson averaged around 80mpg (3.54ltr/100km). But the feature which impressed him most:

> was the utter cleanliness of the engine and gearbox side covers. They were free from oil in all respects and not much mud-dappled either – so that deep-section front mudguard really does its stuff as a mudguard should.

A More Comprehensive Test

A much more comprehensive test of a Model 14 subsequently appeared in *The Motor Cycle*, this time in the 20 April 1961 issue. The test was headed 'Attractive, Well-Finished, Economical Roadster with Snappy Performance, Good Roadholding and Excellent Handling.'

By now the rear chaincase was a standard fitment. With UK purchase tax the price was now £203 17s 2d; chromium-plating for the tank panels was £2 10s 2d extra. Maximum speed achieved was 77mph (124km/h). And it was found that:

> No particular drill for first-kick starting was required and the air lever could be opened immediately the engine fired. Even when cold, the engine was exceptionally quiet mechanically; there was no trace of piston slap and the valve gear was almost inaudible.

As for performance:

> Half-throttle allowed a comfortable 60mph [97km/h] which could be maintained indefinitely and, under favourable conditions, 70mph [113km/h] was possible for many miles without sign of stress from the engine.

Other positive points included a 'light clutch' and 'the gear change was excellent, "like a hot knife through butter" was the cliché which sprang to mind. All gear changes, upwards or downward, could be made quickly and noiselessly.' And 'Though heavier than the average two-fifty, the Model 14 has most of its weight low down; consequently handling on the move is not impaired.'

Less positive features were noted: 'Both brakes, though progressive in action, lacked rear power . . . Heavy pressure was required on the front-brake lever,' whilst the lighting 'restricted after-dark cruising to 50mph (80km/h) or so because the headlamp threw only a moderately well-defined beam.' Also the horn 'could, with advantage, have been louder.' And whilst the 'standard of the toolkit and instruction manual is very high the C-spanner for adjusting the rear suspension dampers bent in use.' Finally:

AJS trials and ISDT star Bob Manns sits astride a specially prepared Model 14 trials bike at the factory in early March 1959. To the right is a Matchless G2 road racer, specially constructed to a customer's order.

To open the toolbox lid fully, it is necessary to depress the kickstarter. When closing the lid, difficulty was sometimes experienced in locating the retaining screw thread.

The Model 8 Three-Fifty

In early September 1959, AMC announced a new 348cc (72 × 85.5mm) version of the by now firmly established Model 14 two-fifty. In the vast bulk of its technical details the newcomer followed its two-fifty ancestry (including its *dé saxé* cylinder), the cylinder axis offset forward from the crankshaft axis and a cylinder head in which the inlet and exhaust tract were oblique to the fore-and-aft line of the engine. The outward appearance of the new power unit was virtually the same as that of the Model 14, although a distinguishing feature was an exhaust-valve lifter operating on the exhaust rocker.

A major internal difference lay in the crank flywheels which were flat faced and, viewed in side elevation, appeared as right-angled triangles, each with a rounded apex and a semi-circular base. Cast iron was the material employed, and the thickness being $^{15}\!/_{16}$in (24mm). The flywheel faces were recessed to receive the crankpin nuts. Crankpin diameter was 1½in (38mm), and a Duralumin cage spaced out the two rows of rollers, their size and number being identical to the smaller engine.

The compression ratio was 7.5:1, instead of 7.8:1 on the smaller power unit. A larger inlet valve was specified – 1⅝in (40mm) – whilst the inlet port size was 1⅛in (28mm); otherwise the two engines were essentially the same. Other changes included new gear ratios, 3.25 × 18 front and rear tyres, and the more sturdy AMC Teledraulic front forks from the heavyweight singles and twin-cylinder models. There was also a duplex, rather than single primary chain, whilst the clutch had been given an additional plate.

Because of the changes outlined above, the dry weight had increased to 350lb (159kg), although this was still 32lb (14.5kg) lighter than the latest Model 16 single.

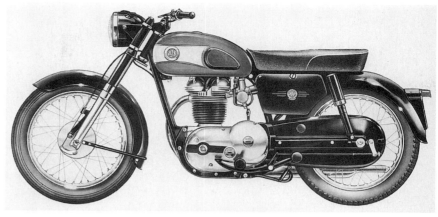

A larger 348cc (72 × 85.5mm) version, the Model 8, arrived for the 1960 model year. There were several differences between the 250 and new 350, notably the more robust Teledraulic forks and engine changes. Bike shown is a 1962 model.

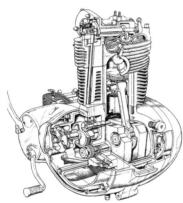

The Lightweight 350 engine, showing its internal details, including hairpin valve springs, piston, crankshaft, roller-bearing big-end, timing gears and pushrods.

Testing the Model 8

The Motor Cycle's George Wilson was back in frame when testing of the Model 8 three-fifty was undertaken by the journal (actually Wilson rode the Matchless version, the G5). This was in fact the first G5 to leave the Plumstead production line on a 500-mile-plus weekend ride to Llandrindod Wells in mid-Wales for the 25th British Experts Trial. These road impressions appeared in the 10 December 1959 issue.

Compared with the Model 14, the Model 8 not only had an additional 100cc, but was also of the long-stroke engine format. This, suggested Wilson, 'contributes largely to the excellent power characteristics.' He went on to explain what this low-speed punch meant: 'most important of all, you can change up early, and you can accelerate fairly hard without

causing offence to drivers being overtaken, or to inhabitants in towns and villages on your route.'

Nevertheless George Wilson still discovered that:

> when the whip was being used hard, the Matchless [remember he was riding the G5 rather than the AJS equivalent] spoke with an overloud tongue . . . my feeling is that better muffling would be a good thing.

Once again he was impressed by the quietness of the engine:

> Mechanical noise was virtually nil. Idling (which it did in true gas-engine style), the power unit is quiet to the point of being exemplary.

When George Wilson had ridden the bike at first there had been a 'marked low-speed roll', and after a gauge showed there to be only 15lb pressure in the front tube, he concluded that was the answer. However, as he wrote:

> Putting up the pressure brought no improvement. A check revealed the steering head bearing adjustment to be apparently just right, but after the bearing was slackened off by half a flat on the adjusting nut, the handling was transformed. In Wales, and on the swervery on the way there and back, the model could be cranked over hard on wet or dry. The steering was just heavy enough to be truly positive, so that I knew exactly what the front wheel was doing. Even so, I think the handling could be improved even further if the suspension were softer. Under my 10 stone [63.5 kg] load the

front fork was hard and, at the rear, the suspension legs appeared reluctant also to react at speeds below 50mph [80km/h].

With maximum speed in the region of 75mph (120km/h), and a mixture of good torque across the entire rev range combined with excellent handling, George Wilson was able to tuck 200 miles (320km) into four hours with relative ease. He observed that 'in order to keep down exhaust noise, I generally notched top at about 45mph (72km/h)'; but he also found a 'light, impossible-to-beat gear change, and sweet transmission.'

Unfortunately for AMC, new laws restricting novice riders to machines of 250cc and below virtually killed off the traditional British 350cc 4-stroke, and as the 1960s unfolded, this proved to be the case with the AJS Model 8.

Detail Changes for 1961

When the 1961 range was announced at the end of August 1960, it was very much a case of detail changes, rather than major alterations, to the entire AJS family, including the Model 14 and Model 8 singles.

One update concerned the crankcase breathing system. Previously the timed, rotary breather vented to the atmosphere via a hollow bolt in the nearside (left) crankcase half. This vent was now direct, and the hollow bolt replaced by a solid bolt repositioned to one side of the breather.

To improve top-gear engagement, the pin-type dogs on the sliding pinion, which mated with elongated holes in the fixed, output pinion, were exchanged for dogs with more normal segmental teeth. The side faces of the teeth had been given a slight reverse taper so there was less tendency for the dogs to slide out of engagement. In a further gearbox modification, a bronze bush had been fitted to the layshaft bottom-gear pinion, thus obviating steel-to-steel contact.

But a potentially far more worrying aspect of the Model 14 and Model 8-type gearbox

The 1961 Model 8

Engine	Air-cooled ohv single with vertical cylinder; alloy head; cast-iron barrel; vertically split aluminium crankcases; fully enclosed valve gear; hairpin valve springs; built-up crankshaft; single gear-driven camshaft; crossover enclosed pushrods; roller bearing big-end
Bore	72mm
Stroke	85.5mm
Displacement	348cc
Compression ratio	7:1
Lubrication	Dry sump, plunger worm pump
Ignition	Battery/coil 6-volt; alternator
Carburettor	Amal Monobloc 389 1⅛in
Primary drive	Duplex chain
Final drive	Chain
Gearbox	4-speed, foot-change, AMC, adjustable type
Frame	All-steel construction, brazed and bolted; single main and front tubes; pressed steel under-channel
Front suspension	AMC Teledraulic, two-way oil-damped forks
Rear suspension	Two-piece swinging arm, with oil-damped adjustable twin shock absorbers
Front brake	6in, SLS, full-width iron drum
Rear brake	6in, SLS, full-width iron drum
Tyres	3.25 × 19 front and rear
Wheelbase	54in (1,372mm)
Ground clearance	6in (152mm)
Seat height	29.5in (749mm); 1962, 30.5in (774mm)
Fuel tank capacity	3.25gal (15ltr)
Dry weight	340lb (154kg)
Maximum power	21bhp @ 7,200rpm
Top speed	76mph (122km/h)

design was never rectified. This was essentially due to the cylindrical nature of the shell itself and the location of the gears near the very top of this, which meant that anything less than the full 3 pints of lubricating oil could spell trouble. Another weakness was an appetite for gearchange springs. All this was a great pity, because when operating normally, the gearchange quality was excellent.

Previously only supplied as a cost-option, the rear chaincase was now fitted as standard equipment. In addition, all AMC single-cylinder models had benefited from a modification intended to strengthen the drive to the rotary-reciprocating oil pump. Both the crankshaft worm and the pump-drive pinion featured a redesigned tooth, which brought them into closer engagement.

Prices on 27 August 1960 were £203 17s 2d for the 248cc Model 14, and £221 19s for the 348cc Model 8 (including UK purchase tax).

Then in November 1960, on the eve of the London Earls Court Show, came a sports version of the Model 14, the 14S – although in truth there were no significant differences, apart from lower handlebars and an excess of chrome plate.

Names Arrive in 1962

For the 1962 model year AMC came up with names for its various models. The two-fifty

Model 14 became the Sapphire, whilst the Model 8 assumed the Senator tag. All this was really just another ploy by a beleaguered AMC to generate more sales interest in a depressed market. And in retrospect it did little or no good whatsoever.

To prevent the rider's foot from fouling the footrest when starting, a longer kickstart lever was now fitted to the Model 14/Model 8 series. On the three-fifties there was an improved crankcase breather, and a change from ball- to roller-type bearing for the inner drive-side main bearing. For the sports version of the two-fifty Sapphire there was a redesigned handlebar, reducing the overall width to 24¾in (629mm); this was known as the 'ace-type', with long straight portions at the downward ends of the central curved section.

Prices (including UK taxes) as at 14 September 1961 were £204 19s 2d for the Model 14 Sapphire, £212 5s 7d for the Model 14S Sapphire Sports, and £220 4s 2d for the Model 8 Senator.

The Model 14 CSR

In May 1962 AMC at last did the decent thing and launched a sporting two-fifty: the CSR.

The Model 14S was the forerunner of the CSR, and was only offered in 1961 and 1962.

A Model 14 CSR Sapphire 90 out on road test in January 1965. Note the cigar-type silencer.

This was sold either in AJS guise (14 CSR) or Matchless (G2 CSR). And compared to the soon-to-be-axed 'S', the newcomer had a much superior specification. Not only was there more power, but revised braking, and the more robust Teledraulic front forks from the Model 8. There was also a larger carburettor (a 1⅛in Amal 389 Monobloc), bigger inlet valve, longer induction tract, higher compression ratio (8:1), stronger valve springs, steel fly wheels and stiffer con-rod and crankpin.

As a result of the changes catalogued above, it had been necessary to raise the gear ratios. The front brake was now a smart British Hub Company light-alloy hub with a cast-iron drum shrunk in. This new 6in (152mm) front brake was still of the SLS (Single Leading Shoe) type, but the shoe plate featured cast-in air scoops. However, 'as delivered' these slots had not been opened up so air could not assist the cooling! Although it looked nice, the British Hub Co unit was not the most efficient

unit around and tended to suffer fading during heavy applications.

During performance testing by *The Motor Cycle* a highest one-way speed of 75mph (120km/h) was achieved, this being virtually the same as the Model 8 three-fifty. But the bigger engine scored on superior torque, which manifested itself by way of superior pulling power in the lower and mid-range.

Although a considerable improvement on the outgoing 'S' model, the CSR was still no match for the latest foreign machinery such as the Aermacchi Ala Verde, Ducati Daytona or Honda CB72. However, when compared to the vast majority of home-grown rivals of the period the AJS (and its Matchless brother) stood up well. There were other advantages too – as *The Motor Cycle* said 'this is no cramped lightweight', with a 'man-size riding position', and went on to point out that:

> The handlebar is virtually flat and slightly downswept at the grips – this was felt to be a good compromise between sporty styling and practicability, and results in a forward lean rather than a semi-crouch.

So the AJS 14 CSR was a bike which provided plenty of room and probably more comfort than could normally be expected of a light-weight sportster. *The Motor Cycle* tester ended his report by summing up in the following manner:

> The G2 CSR (he was testing the Matchless version) is not temperamental and is a lively, attractive mount. It will undoubtedly appeal to the rider who wants sporting lines plus useful performance.

End of the Road

It was seen that several models in the AJS/Matchless range had been axed when the 1963 range was announced towards the end of September 1962. Chief amongst these were four lightweight singles: the AJS 14 Sapphire

The 1965 14CSR	
Engine	Air-cooled ohv single with vertical cylinder; alloy head; cast-iron barrel; vertically split aluminium crankcases; fully enclosed valve gear; coil valve springs; built-up crankshaft; single gear-driven camshaft; crossover enclosed pushrods; roller bearing big-end
Bore	69.85mm
Stroke	64.85mm
Displacement	248.5cc
Compression ratio	9.5:1
Lubrication	Dry sump, plunger worm pump
Ignition	Battery/coil 6-volt; alternator
Carburettor	Amal Monobloc 389 1⅛in
Primary drive	Duplex chain
Final drive	Chain
Gearbox	4-speed, foot-change, AMC, adjustable type
Frame	All-steel construction, brazed and bolted; single main and front tubes; pressed steel under-channel
Front suspension	AMC Teledraulic, two-way oil damped forks
Rear suspension	Two-piece swinging arm, with oil-damped adjustable twin shock absorbers
Front brake	British Hub Co full-width alloy, SLS, drum
Rear brake	British Hub Co full-width alloy, SLS, drum
Tyres	3.25 × 17 front and rear
Wheelbase	53in (1,346mm)
Ground clearance	6.5in (165mm)
Seat height	30in (762mm)
Fuel tank capacity	3.25gal (14ltr)
Dry weight	328lb (149kg)
Maximum power	20bhp @ 7,400rpm
Top speed	78mph (125km/h)

Sports, the Matchless G2S Monitor Sports, the AJS Model 8 Senator and the Matchless G5 Matador.

The two-fifties had been dropped in favour of the much improved CSR variants, whilst the three-fifties had become victims of a major drop in sales following the introduction of the new laws which restricted new British riders to a maximum of 250cc. A few months later, in July 1963, the axe fell on the standard Model 14 two-fifty. This left only the sporting CSR.

In June 1964 came a class victory in the prestigious Thruxton 500-mile endurance race. This feat was achieved by an AJS 14CSR and came in the teeth of severe foreign competition. The riding was shared between Peter Williams (son of the factory's chief development engineer, Jack) and Tony Wood. Visually, the only major change was the fitment of a 7R racing seat; internally, however, there were serious questions as to just how far from stock this particular engine was. Not only was this victory totally unexpected by the opposition, but the bike had a fair turn of speed and lasted the distance.

There were a few changes for the 1965 model year, with only the CSR two-fifty remaining in the lightweight family. The compression ratio was increased to 9.5:1, coil-valve springs replaced the hairpin type, closer ratio gears were specified, and a cigar-shaped silencer, with no tailpipe, was used.

A year later, when the 1966 AJS range was announced, the 14 CSR was mechanically unchanged, but now came with alloy mudguards and a swept-back 'Gold Star' pattern exhaust header pipe. In mid-July 1966, the final 14 CSR left the Plumstead production line, its departure bringing down the curtain on the story of the lightweight single-cylinder family which had begun back in the spring of 1958 with such excitement and promise at the Swiss Geneva Show.

12 Four-Stroke Motocross

The sport of scrambling (now universally known as motocross) began in England on 29 March 1924, when the Camberley Club decided to modify the rules of their popular Southern Scott Trial by deleting the gymkhana section and concentrating on a timed trial section, with some eighty competitors assembling for the start of what was to prove an historic event. The winner was to be the rider who recorded the fastest time over two heats. And thus a brand new form of motorcycle sport had been born.

Scrambling Develops

For the next few years scrambling developed, together with its own set of regulations – although it was still very much a mixture of existing motorcycle sporting activities and did not become clearly defined until after the Second World War. The sport really became established when it crossed the channel to continental Europe, preceded by the fame of several British riders. The first internationally organized event was staged in France during 1939, at Romanville on the outskirts of Paris, just prior to the outbreak of war.

The annual Motocross des Nations was inaugurated in 1947, and the first five years saw a titanic struggle for supremacy between Belgium and Great Britain, with the score three-to-two in the latter's favour. Early stars from the British side included the likes of Bill Nicholson (BSA) and Harold Lines (Ariel), plus trials specialists such as John Avery (BSA) and Hugh Viney (AJS).

In 1952 the FIM established the European 500cc Championship series. The top AJS rider during this period was Geoff Ward, with a best placing of 6th in 1953. Also with the establishment of the European 500cc Championship, the Swedes joined the battle in earnest, the newcomers making an impression when they won the Motocross des Nations in 1955 (held at Randers, Denmark). For 1957, the European title was changed to World. The first winner was Sweden's Bill Nilsson on his AJS machine (based on a 7R road racer). Backed by the Swedish Crescent firm, Nilsson went on to finish runner-up the following year, and again in 1959.

As far as the British Championship scene was concerned Geoff Ward dominated the early 1950s, taking the title in 1951, 1953 and 1954.

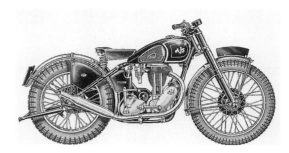

When the first competition models were offered for the 1946 season it was very much a case that, in the UK at least, they would only be sold to riders with a proven sporting record. Built in 348 and 497cc engine sizes, the same bike was sold at that time for both trials and scrambles. This is a 1948 machine.

A 1949 advertisement showing one of the AJS Competition bikes in a scrambles event.

Specialized Scrambles Bikes

For the 1951 model year, AMC offered specialized trials and scrambles bikes for the first time. Previously, a one-model-does-all policy existed (*see* Chapter 7) with C (Competition) machines being offered in 347 and 498cc engine sizes, in both AJS and Matchless guises. But now there were to be the trials (coded C) and scrambles (coded CS). Essentially, these were still manufactured in what AMC termed 'limited quantities', being constructed in two batches, one in the autumn and one in the spring. The new spring-frame models for scrambles (or the ISDT) were manufactured with a silencer as standard, with a straight-through (open) exhaust as an option. Both the trials and scrambles models benefited, as before, from various improvements (including a revised Teledraulic front fork assembly).

The B52 Model Year

There was a new Burman-made gearbox for the 1952 season. This, coded B52 (Burman 1952), was introduced in August 1951. It was intended to replace the existing BA (heavy) and CP (light) assemblies. AMC had been closely connected with its development, the design being similar to the 'box used on the AJS 7R racer.

Like the 7R unit, the B52 had as its centre a very short and sturdy gear train. And as was traditional amongst British motorcycles of the time, the new Burman 'box was 4-speed, and the layout entirely conventional for the period, with the sleeve gear concentric with the mainshaft and running in ball-race bearings. Interestingly on the 7R, the bearings were rollers.

The layshaft was underneath and rotated in bushes. Gear selection was by moving one gear on each shaft, and the selectors were controlled by a drum cam operated directly by a change mechanism housed under the gearbox outer cover. Under this also went the kick-starter quadrant and a new form of clutch lift mechanism, although the old type was also offered to those customers (not AMC) who preferred it. The new design employed three ball bearings held between two steel pressings with ramp recesses to take them; one pressing held in the end housing, whilst the other turned by the clutch cable so the balls ran up the ramps and operated the pushrod.

Prototype swinging arm AJS scrambler being tested by a youthful Tom Mortimer, circa early 1950s.

The clutch itself had four or five friction plates, depending upon use, whilst an adjuster screwed into the outer (pressure plate). Access to this was via a small inspection cover added to the primary chaincase for the 1952 machines, held in place by three screws. A cable adjuster screwed into the gearbox outer end cover, and access for hooking the cable to the lift mechanism was by removal of a screwed cap.

From then until the end of 1953, virtually no development took place on the scrambles (and trials) models, except those changes introduced across-the-range on single-cylinder models (*see* Chapter 4).

Changes in 1954, 1955 and 1956

All AJS (and Matchless) models, excluding the 7R road racer, received a full-width alloy front hub for 1954, featuring straight spokes. The off-roaders, including the scramblers, were also given internal gearbox changes, improved gearbox-to-crankcase seal, a different oil-filler cap, and an aluminium fuel tank. The sprung-frame roadster singles, and the scrambles models now featured an enlarged timing-side mainshaft, lighter flywheels and a modified oil tank.

There was little change for 1955, except for the full-width alloy rear hub, and on the scrambles bikes only, an Amal TT carburettor.

When the 1956 AJS scramblers were announced, the 347cc 16CS retailed for £218 8s, and the 498cc 18CS retailed for £235 4s. Lighting could be supplied for an additional £9 18s.

Modified Engines for 1957

For the 1957 season the AJS scrambler engines were modified for increased power. Both engine capacities featured modified inlet ports and larger inlet valves. The choke size of the Amal carburettor (the new Monobloc had replaced the TT instrument) on the unit had been increased by ⅟₁₆in (1.5mm) to 1⅛in (28mm). On the five-hundred engine the carburettor bore was increased to 1³⁄₁₆in (29mm).

A production AJS 18CS Scrambler; circa 1957. Features include full-width alloy hubs, Teledraulic forks Girling rear shocks, Lucas racing magneto, and alloy head and barrel.

In addition there were revised bore and stroke dimensions for both AJS dirt racers. This saw a change from 347 to 348cc and 498 to 497cc; thus the smaller unit became 72 × 85.5mm (formerly 69 × 93mm), whilst the five-hundred became 86 × 85.5mm (formerly 82.5 × 93mm). The trials and roadster singles engines' size/bore and stroke dimensions remained unchanged.

Like the roadsters, the dirt bikes received the AMC-developed gearbox (and clutch) to replace the previously Burman components for the 1957 model year. Yet another switch was from AMC's infamous 'Jampot' rear shocks, to Girling units.

Page from the 1957 AJS brochure showing the latest 18CS saying: 'The 500cc Scrambler machine that is unsurpassed for performance, ease of handling and reliability under rugged cross country conditions.'

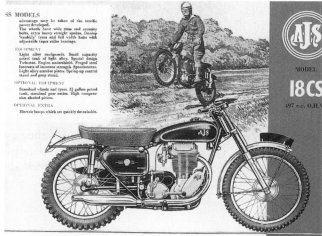

American brothers, John and Joe Disimones, with their twin-cylinder scrambler in the late 1950s – and the many trophies they had won. The twins were built in CS guises in 500, 600 (shown) and 650cc with the AMC power unit. Later, a 750cc Norton engine was used.

More Developments for 1958

Although coil ignition with an alternator had been adopted for the 1958 single-cylinder street models, the competition bikes (both scrambles and trials) remained loyal to the magneto. Meanwhile, the AMC gearbox introduced a few months earlier, had been modified to provide a lighter gear change action. The scramblers were given a new seat and wider mudguards, whilst the oil tank was set more inwards; there were also quickly detachable lights, similar to the trials model.

In response to demand for its scramblers in the Stateside market, AJS introduced twin-cylinder versions for the 1958 season, powered by 498cc (66 × 72.8mm) Model 20 and the new 592cc (72 × 72.8mm) Model 30 ohv parallel-twin engines. These new models featured the single-cylinder's scrambler frame, full-width brake hubs, 2gal (9ltr) fuel tank, siamezed

The 1957 18CS	
Engine	Air-cooled, ohv single with vertical cylinder; alloy head and barrel; vertically split aluminium crankcases; fully enclosed valve gear; coil valve springs; built-up crankshaft; roller-bearing big-end; gear-driven cams; integral pushrod tunnels in barrel
Bore	86mm
Stroke	85.5mm
Displacement	497cc
Compression ratio	8.7:1
Lubrication	Dry sump, two-start oil pump
Ignition	Magneto, Lucas
Carburettor	Amal Monobloc 389 1⁵⁄₁₆in
Primary drive	Chain
Final drive	Chain
Gearbox	4-speed, foot-change, AMC
Frame	All-steel construction, full cradle with single front down-tube
Front suspension	AMC Teledraulic oil-damped forks
Rear suspension	Swinging-arm with twin Girling shock absorbers
Front brake	7in, SLS drum, aluminium full-width
Rear brake	7in, SLS drum, aluminium full-width
Tyres	3.00 × 21 front; 4.00 × 19 rear
Wheelbase	55.2in (1,402mm)
Ground clearance	6.5in (165mm)
Seat height	32.5in (825mm)
Fuel tank capacity	2gal (9ltr)
Dry weight	324lb (147kg)
Maximum power	33bhp @ 6,200rpm
Top speed	80mph (129km/h)

exhaust pipes, speedometer on fork crown, old-style headlamp shell, scrambler handlebars, knobbly tyres (3.00 × 21 front and 4.00 × 19 rear), competition (alloy) mudguards and QD lights. Prices as at 12 September 1957 (including British purchase tax) were as follows:

348cc Model 16CS £250 14s 11d
497cc Model 18CS £271 19s 1d
498cc Model 20CS £288 15s 11d
592cc Model 30CS £299 8s 0d

Bill Nilsson's 1957 World Championship Machine

In the autumn of 1956, then aged twenty-four, Bill Nilsson was viewed by many as Sweden's best motocross rider. For the previous two seasons he had raced a BSA Gold Star with considerable success. Then he did what seemed a strange thing – he purchased Olle Nygren's 1954 three-fifty 7R road racer! And set about converting it for the dirt. A plumber by trade, Nilsson did most of the work at home. First requirement was to enlarge the engine displacement from 348cc to as near practicable to the permitted 500cc. The 74mm cylinder liner was bored out as far as it was felt safe, which came to 80mm, whilst the stroke (increased from 81 to 96mm) was achieved by manufacturing a new pair of crankshaft flywheels. This set of changes pushed the capacity up to a fraction under 483cc. A special flat-top German Marle forged 3-ring piston was made, which in conjunction with the increase in bore size, gave a squish effect in the combustion chamber.

Although Nilsson switched from the road racing GP instead to one of Amals 10TT carburetors, he stuck to the standard 7R carb size – and valve sizes. Combined with the engine's now long-stroke dimensions, the result was excellent low-down torque. A large capacity air filter kept dirt and dust out of the engine, whilst a special one-off exhaust saw the header pipe fit snugly behind the offside front downtube, close round the timing chest, inside the footrest and under the gearbox. The Motor Cycle called it 'a real gem of ingenuity'. This exhaust system was produced from no less than nine short lengths of piping; the only flanged piece (from the original 7R system) was that connected to the cylinder head.

The length of this piping came through experimentation – probably the longest in terms of the time it took in producing the whole bike – together with the innumerable trial assemblies to obtain the correct clearances between valves, piston, cylinder head, conrod and crank flywheels.

One item from the original 7R racer which was immediately ditched was the Burman close ratio gearbox. In its place was substituted a BSA Gold Star scrambles 'box with the mainshaft modified to accept the Burman clutch. Another change was the fitment of an AMC-type oil-bath primary chaincase, suitably modified.

The frame was another area where modification was required, after it was found motocross riding bent the front down-tubes of the original 7R set-up. This was twice strengthened by welding in gussets to the steering head and adjoining tube-work. Further stiffening was required in the diameter of the vertical

The 1957 500cc World Motocross Champion, Bill Nilsson, with his AJS 7R-based machine.

Moto Cross des Nations: Sweden's Billy Nilsson (7). The other rider (9) is Dutchman Broer Dirks.

seat tube. In addition, to provide a lower seat height the top tube at the rear was bent downwards.

At the front a dual purpose was achieved by lengthening the front fork stanchions – the wheel deflection was increased, as was static ground clearance. Rubber gaiters were fitted to protect the stanchions from flying stones and the like. Ground clearance was further enhanced by the fitment of a 21in steel rim in place of the original road racers 19in aluminium component. The original 7R oil tank was retained, but the fuel tank was replaced by a Gold Star aluminium assembly.

The result was a motorcycle good enough to beat the world – winning in the process the 1957 500cc title (the first to wear the 'World' title). Nilsson then went on to claim the runner-up spot in 1958 and 1959. The Swede's success, I'm sure, gave AMC the idea for the G50 road racer . . .

Factory trials star Gordon Jackson and his five-hundred AJS 18CS during the Sidcup & District MCC Scramble, Canada Height, 15 June 1958.

A New 250 Scrambler

Then for the 1959 season, AJS (and Matchless) launched a new 250-class scrambler, the Model 14CS (G2CS). This was developed from the newly released Model 14 roadster (*see* Chapter 11).

Featuring a 248.5cc (69.85 × 64.85mm) power unit, the design gave every impression of being unit construction, but actually the gearbox was a separate assembly. The AMC engineers had introduced several changes into the scrambler version, to make it suitable for its new dirt bike racing role. For instance, the compression ratio had been raised to 10.5:1, with modified crankshaft flywheels and a higher lift camshaft. An improved grade of steel had been specified for some of the gearbox internals.

The only notable change to the main frame was the employment of heavier-gauge tubing for the front down-tube section. The same rear subframe tubes as the roadster were fitted, but to alloy 19in wheels to replace the stock 17in. The horizontal tubes were canted upward, whilst the diagonal tubes were welded to them further forward. Extended Girling shock absorbers were fitted to suit the altered triangulation. The more robust front fork was based on the Teledraulic assembly specified for the 350 trials bike. Mudguards were of lightweight polished alloy, with tyre sizes of 3.00 × 19 front, 3.50 × 19 rear. Other details of the 14CS Scrambler were its open exhaust, knobbly tyres, offset hubs, smaller seat, energy transfer ignition and one-off handlebars.

As for the larger-engined dirt racers, these continued into 1959 unchanged. Nevertheless later in that year the Model 16CS three-fifty single and the Model 20 CS five-hundred twin were axed following poor sales the previous season.

Like the latest street bikes (except the 250/350 lightweights), the surviving scrambler models, the 500 single and 650 twin (the latter having replaced the 600), gained a new frame for the 1960 season. This featured duplex front down-tubes, taken back to pass beneath the engine and gearbox. A single 1¾in (45mm) diameter, 14-gauge top tube (larger than the roadsters) combined with a vertical seat tube to complete the main frame. The rear subframe was bolted to lugs just below the rear of the gearbox and the front of the saddle. Previously found only on the 250 roadster, the 3-point fuel tank mounting was a feature of the new frame, there being two mountings at the front and a single one at the rear.

As with the roadster single-cylinder 500, the Model 18CS scrambler cylinder head had been revamped, with the combustion chamber shape now hemispherical and featuring a flat-top piston with small recesses for the valves. As on the 500 scrambler, the oil tank had been relocated to the nearside (left) of the seat tube to enable a 1⅜in (35mm) Amal GP carburettor to be fitted to the new head. The oil tank's previous home was now occupied by a comprehensive air filter.

Both the 18CS and 31CS scramblers were usually shipped 'ex factory' in a stripped, ready-to-race mode. However, if customers so wished these could be equipped at the Plumstead works with an AC generator in addition to the magneto. The battery was then fitted on the offside (right) of the seat tube beneath the air filter.

The 14CS two-fifty had been given a larger inlet valve for 1960, whilst the gears had again been uprated. Also in light of experiences gained the previous year, the gearbox internal ratios had been altered and included a higher first gear. The new internal ratios were 3.24; 2.44; 1.56 and 1:1.

Axing the Last Twin

When the 1961 AJS model range was announced at the end of August 1960, the last of the twin-cylinder scramblers, the 31CS six-fifty, had been axed.

Ian Horsell 498cc AJS-engined BSA-framed special with AMC forks and hubs. North v South Scramble, Pirbright; 5 June 1960.

An AJS competitor taking part in the 1961 100-mile Scramble at Pirbright, Surrey.

Also for 1961 AMC introduced additional engine modifications to the 14CS two-fifty scrambler, these being made in the light of experiences gained. Inlet valve size went up from 1¹⁄₁₆in (27mm) to 1⅛in (28mm), whilst the combustion chamber altered in shape because the increase in power thus achieved required a more robust crankpin (increased in diameter from ¾in (19mm) to ⅞in (22mm)) and also a beefed-up connecting-rod.

There was a change from energy transfer ignition to battery/coil. This was done because the former system needed extreme accuracy when checking the ignition timing, something which was often difficult to achieve whilst working in the field. A Varley dry-cell battery was employed to avoid the risk of spilling should the machine fall on its side – as often happened in the heat of battle.

Little change was seen on the five-hundred 18CS, except for a modified oil pump introduced that year for all the heavyweight singles. The 18CS was given an inlet valve-guide circlip; again, a modification shared with the roadsters.

For the next couple of years there was not much change to the two remaining scramblers, the 14CS two-fifty and 18CS five-hundred. Then in late 1962 the smaller model was discontinued. The 18CS, now called the Southerner, was priced at £293 11s 7d (including UK taxes).

The 1962 AJS Southerner was better known under its original 18CS coding.

A Norton Oil Pump

It was not until the autumn of 1963 that the next revision was carried out to the 18CS model, following testing with the factory team bikes ridden by the likes of Dave Curtis, Vic Eastwood and Chris Horsfield (riding Matchless versions).

So for the 1964, the 18CS scrambler gained a Norton oil pump (as did the roadster singles), but very little else. In fact, by then, not only was AMC in deep financial trouble, but the emphasis was very much on Matchless as the scrambles model, whereas AJS was promoted in the trials field. Strangely, AMC policy

The 1961 14CS	
Engine	Air-cooled, ohv single with vertical cylinder; alloy head; cast-iron barrel; vertically split aluminium crankcases; fully enclosed valve gear; hairpin valve springs; built-up crankshaft; single gear-driven camshaft; cross-over enclosed pushrods; roller-bearing big-end
Bore	69.85mm
Stroke	64.85mm
Displacement	248.5cc
Compression ratio	10:1
Lubrication	Dry sump, plunger worm pump
Ignition	Coil; 1959–60, energy transfer
Carburettor	Amal 376 Monobloc 1¹⁄₁₆in
Primary drive	Duplex chain
Final drive	Chain
Gearbox	4-speed, foot-change, AMC, adjustable type, with improved materials and different ratios from roadsters
Frame	All-steel construction, brazed and bolted; single main and front tubes; pressed steel under-channel in heavier gauge materials and modified subframe
Front suspension	AMC Teledraulic; two-way oil-damped forks
Rear suspension	Two-piece swinging arm, with oil-damped, adjustable, extra-long Girling shock absorbers
Front brake	7in, SLS drum
Rear brake	7in, SLS drum
Tyres	3.00 × 19 front; 3.50 × 19 rear
Wheelbase	54in (1,372mm)
Ground clearance	7.2in (183mm)
Seat height	32in (813mm)
Fuel tank capacity	2.75gal (12.5ltr)
Dry weight	321lb (146kg)
Maximum power	22bhp @ 7,500rpm
Top speed	75mph (121km/h)

Besides road racing, sprinting and motocross, the AJS 7R even found its way into grass track racing as this picture proves.

meant that AJS machines were campaigned in the ISDT during the 1960s, in what were in effect Matchless G80CS/G85CS models after the AJS 18CS was axed from production in August 1965.

As is recorded elsewhere AJS and AMC were now only months away from financial collapse the following year. However, the AJS scrambler was to be reborn, albeit in a completely new form and with a 2-stroke rather than a 4-stroke engine. So for the AJS 18CS dirt bike racer, 1965 really was the end of an era.

AJS Motocross Successes				
British Championships 500cc			**British 500cc Grand Prix**	
1951	Geoff Ward	1st	1953 Geoff Ward	3rd
1952	Reg Pilling	2nd	1955 Geoff Ward	6th
1953	Geoff Ward	1st	1957 Bill Nilsson	5th
1954	Geoff Ward	1st		
European Championships 500cc			**British Championships 250cc**	
1953	Geoff Ward	6th	1967 Fred Mayes	2nd
			1968 Malcolm Davis	1st
World Championships 500cc			1969 Malcolm Davis	2nd
1957	Bill Nilsson	1st	1970 Malcolm Davis	1st
			Andy Robertson	2nd

★All 250cc results gained with 2-stroke machines; *see* Chapter 14.

13   Two-Stroke Racing

The story of the AJS Starmaker road racer began back at the end of 1962, just when production of the classic overhead cam 7R single was coming to an end. And the Starmaker was to begin its life as an engine, not a complete motorcycle, built by Villiers Engineering in Wolverhampton which was, of course, where the old AJ Stevens company had begun operations at the beginning of the twentieth century!

The Road Racer Appears

Sired by the single-cylinder Villiers Starmaker scrambles engine, the road racing version made its public debut at the London Earls Court Show in early November 1962, as the prime mover to the new Cotton Telstar over-the-counter racing machine. A works prototype which had competed in the Isle of Man Southern 100 races that summer had proved that the idea worked.

When the Starmaker racing engine entered production in February 1963, it was fitted with a pair of Amal Monobloc carburettors working on the primary-secondary system. And in fact a handful of Cotton Telstars (and at least one DMW Hornet) were thus equipped. This early development work on Bernard Hooper's design boosted maximum power from 25bhp at 6,500rpm to 28bhp at 7,500rpm.

Improved breathing through a new cylinder and head in 1964 lifted the output to a claimed 30bhp at 7,500rpm. A redesigned exhaust system also played a vital role in this increase.

An early problem centred around big-end failure, caused through over-revving, and this problem was not helped by the standard Starmaker 4-speed-only gearbox.

All thoughts of an AJS involvement were then in the future, as the closest Villiers got to AJS at that time was an involvement with the parent AMC group in supplying engines for AMC's James and Francis-Barnett roadster models.

The 'Inchley Special'

Although the 4-speeder was to remain for paying customers (due to cost considerations said Villiers), works-supported riders (such as the Cotton duo of Derek Minter and Bill Ivy) soon found they needed more ratios to extract maximum power. With this in mind, Villiers provided a 6-speed 'box. Designed by John Favill in February 1964, this was also used on the factory development racer which engineer Peter Inchley created the same year. And it was the 'Inchley Special', as it was to become known, which ultimately became the AJS Starmaker racer.

Inchley's bike employed a Spanish Bultaco TSS rolling chassis, with the frame suitably modified to take the Wolverhampton-built Starmaker engine and Flavill's special 6-speed transmission. Technically the Starmaker engine was a piston-port single cylinder 2-stroke of 247cc (68 × 68mm) using aluminium alloy for the crankcases, cylinder head, chaincases and gearbox shell. An austenitic-iron liner was spun-cast, integral with the light-alloy cylinder

The original Villiers/Bultaco special of 1964. Basically a Bultaco TSS chassis with a Villiers 247cc Starmaker engine and John Favill-designed 6-speed gearbox.

muff. A 12:1 compression piston featured a large diameter gudgeon pin to assist heat transfer away from the crown, and narrow anti-flutter rings were fitted.

The crankshaft was carried on two roller bearings and needle-race assembly. Connected to the timing-side shaft by a nylon coupling, a subsidiary 'mainshaft' carried the contact-breaker cam. This outrigger shaft was unaffected by whip and there was consequently no vibration in the make-and-break of the contact points. Dry weight of the 1964 Inchley Villiers Special was a low 203lb (92kg).

Peter Inchley's engine tuning was subtle but effective. The inlet port was larger than the stock Starmaker, so were the transfer ports, with the exhaust port being an exceptionally wide bridged affair, almost being modelled on

a twin tunnel, with a narrow supporting middle wall. Even with these modifications, externally it was difficult to see any difference between the Inchley engine and the standard production model. This state of affairs was helped by the fact that both shared the same Amal 1½in GP carburettor and there remained the conventional 3-port loop-scavenge layout.

Racing Successes in 1966

The Inchley bike sprang to fame in 1966, when the Isle of Man TT was put back from its normal June date to late August, due to the infamous seamen's strike of that year.

With AMC's future in the hands of the Official Receiver at that very time and Villiers

Peter Inchley at Brands Hatch with the Villiers Special, 8 April 1966; Peter was really the man who made it all happen – both as rider and technician.

*Peter Inchley, Villiers Special, Mallory Park, 30 April 1967.
The forerunner of the AJS 2-stroke racing project.*

already under the control of the Manganese Bronze Holding Company, chaired by Dennis Poore, the 1966 TT could be said to be the AJS marque's unofficial return to racing. A few weeks later Dennis Poore had acquired AMC itself, with a new company being founded in October that year, known as Norton-Villiers (the Triumph section was added later).

And what a return it was, because Inchley, entered as a 'Villiers Starmaker Special' came home an amazing third in the Lightweight (250cc) TT behind the works 6-cylinder Hondas of Mike Hailwood and Stuart Graham. *Motor Cycle News* commenting in the 31 August issue said:

> the surprise of the day was provided by Peter Inchley, who brought his Starmaker-engined Villiers Special into third place at a speed of 91.43mph [147.2km/h]. It is the first time since 1950 that a British machine has finished in the first three.

But perhaps the most interesting aspect was that Inchley's machine at 118.4mph (191.6km/h)

was only the thirteenth fastest through MCN's electronic speed trap, compared with Bill Ivy's Yamaha at 149.4mph (240.5km/h). Other speeds recorded included Stuart Graham's Honda six at 142.9mph (230.1km/h), Heinz Rossner's MZ twin at 136.9mph (220.4km/h), Tommy Robb's TSS Bultaco achieved 120.8mph (194.5km/h) and Alberto Pagani's Italian Aermacchi pushrod single-cylinder Ala d'Oro 120mph (193.2km/h).

Peter Inchley, in effect part designer, part tuner and part rider, was by then an acknowledged 2-stroke specialist. He had been born in Smethwick (an area of Birmingham), and had joined BSA in 1960 and, in the same year, began racing his friend, Stan Cooper's, Ariel Arrow. Inchley later transferred to Ariel (itself then owned by BSA), where he was concerned with much of the development work on the Arrow series, which included outings on the works supported machines in the annual Thruxton 500 mile endurance race. His next move was to EMC (Ehrlich Motor Company), where he worked with the Austrian-born Dr Joe Ehrlich (known to many as the Professor) on 2-strokes. Ehrlich was funded by the de Havilland aviation concern. Inchley's best placing for EMC was a fourth place in the Spanish GP at Montjuich Park, Barcelona, May 1963. He began his association with Villiers in late 1963.

At the time of the 1966 TT, Inchley's Villiers engine was credited with 35bhp at 8,500rpm, and was noticeably quicker than the standard Starmaker unit supplied for fitment into customers Cotton and DMW racers. Villiers claimed around 30bhp for the standard unit, so maybe Inchley's engine actually gave more than the 35bhp figures, probably between 37–38bhp, as it had around 10mph (16km/h) over the production Cotton Telstar and DMW Hornet.

With the Norton-Villiers merger in place for the 1967 season, new owner Dennis Poore got well behind Inchley's racing project – and gave it a new name – AJS.

Not only was there a name change, but Poore authorized the replacement of the Bultaco cycle parts with a new set of clothes thanks to Ken Sprayson of Reynolds Tubing. This frame was of the backbone variety, constructed from 2½in × 18 gauge tubing. Dual loops of ¾in diameter tubing ran from the steering head to act as front down-members, then passed beneath the engine to terminate on mountings for the pair of Girling rear shocks.

The 'new' AJS Starmaker proved even quicker round the tortuous 37.73 mile (60.71km) Mountain circuit in the 1967 TT, Inchley averaging 92.89mph (149.55km/h) before being forced to retire when holding fifth position. His retirement was caused not by any fault of the bike or himself, but was due to human error by the oil company in charge of the refuelling process. When Peter Inchley and his AJS two-fifty came in to refuel, instead of petroil mixture being placed in the tank, only neat fuel was given. Not surprisingly the engine soon cried enough, the result being a total seizure.

An interesting new feature of the bike for the 1967 TT was a new tank and seat design, with an additional 1¼gal (5.68ltr) fuel tank being located behind the engine, where an oil tank would have been found on the 7R. The engine itself remained virtually unchanged, with its close-finned cylinder, 6-speed gearbox and duplex chain-driven diaphragm clutch. However, the machine now sported an entirely new exhaust system with greatly reduced tail-pipe diameter.

A Commercial Failure

The TT 'incident' did not stop NV (Norton Villiers) announcing in a fanfare of publicity that replicas of Inchley's 1967 machine would be offered for sale at £418.

However, this was to prove a poor commercial decision, as the new AJS was never to be sold in more than a handful of machines. Why? Well, you didn't have far to look to get the answer: Yamaha's twin cylinder TD1C. Cotton had in any case already halted production of its Telstar in 1966, as had DMW with their Hornet – and Royal Enfield with its GP5. Only Greeves had managed to soldier on until the spring of 1967, which is when poor sales results saw the Silverstone axed from production too.

So why, one has to ask, did Norton-Villiers attempt to sell what by then was an outdated concept? One reason is probably that Inchley's superb showing in the 1966 and 1967 TTs had raised public and press expectations – and it was after all an all-British bike with the famous AJS name.

And in the final analysis, a motocross version of the Starmaker, the AJS Y4, did prove a big success, both from a racing point of view and in the showroom. Its story is recounted in Chapter 14. And guess who had a major hand in this new success story on the dirt; why, a certain Peter Inchley, of course!

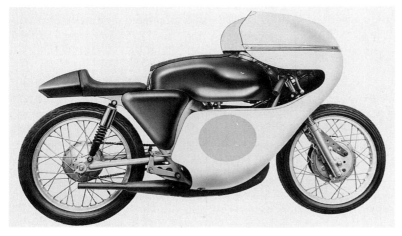

1967 Norton Villiers (NV) AJS 250cc road racer.

One of the AJS racers on display at a classic bike show during the early 1980s.

Starmaker-powered AJS two-fifty road racer in its definitive guise.

Dennis Poore

Dennis Poore was the man who attempted, with mixed success, to re-establish the major players of the British motorcycle industry when it collapsed at the end of the 1960s and the beginning of the 1970s. He ended up owning many of the great names at various times including Norton, Villiers, BSA, Triumph, Matchless and AJS.

This situation came about in his position as Chairman of Manganese Bronze, which acquired the assets of AMC from the Official Receiver in 1966.

Norton Villiers supremo Dennis Poore (left) during the John Player Norton days of the early 1970s.

Manganese Bronze also went on to take over Villiers and the remains of the BSA group. The latter acquisition was made with encouragement from the controlling Conservative Party. Unfortunately this was a decision he was to soon to regret as Labour came to power shortly afterwards and Tony Benn (as Industry Minister) tried his best to make life as difficult as possible. This included backing striking Triumph workers who eventually formed a co-operative which was to result in BSA's demise and problems for what by then was known as NVT (Norton Villiers Triumph).

However, this was very much in the future in the mid-1960s when Poore first became involved in the industry by purchasing AMC. This involved taking over the manufacturing rights of existing designs from Norton, Matchless, AJS, Francis Barnett and James. It soon became apparent that the business was to be centred around Norton and the design and production of a brand new big twin, the Commando. The Matchless name was retained for a few Norton-engined Matchless models, plus the 500 motocross model. As for the Francis Barnett and James commuter models, they were promptly axed from Manganese Bronze plans. But what to do about AJS? Well, as discussed in this chapter and the next, this was very much centred around a series of competition models (road racing, motocross and trials) powered by 2-stroke engines, based on existing Villiers designs – Manganese by then controlling the Wolverhampton-based engine manufacturer.

Dennis Poore *continued*

Poore realized a complete reorganization of his motorcycle portfolio was needed. The original AMC facilities in Plumstead, south-east London were, in Poore's opinion, totally unsuitable for his needs so a decision was taken to move to a new factory at Andover in Hampshire. This decision took some time to come to fruition, not least that planning permission and construction had to be undertaken, which was not obtained until 1968. The new facilities eventually came on stream during 1969.

Poore's Background

Dennis Poore had been a successful competitor during the early post-war period in car racing, having won the RAC Hill Climb title with a 3.8ltr supercharged Alfa Romeo. He had also competed with MG and Veritas machinery (the latter being closely related to the German BMW 328). But probably his greatest claim to fame in automobile circles had been as an official works driver of David Brown's Aston Martin team and the Connaught Grand Prix squad.

With Peter Walker as co-driver, Dennis Poore won the prestigious Nine Hours endurance race for Aston Martin in 1955. Previously in 1953 he had taken an excellent fourth position at the British Grand Prix, held that year at Silverstone, for Connaught. An even higher finish would undoubtedly have been achieved but for an unfortunate mix-up whilst making a pit stop, when Poore was mistakenly given the wrong refreshment. He should have been given lemonade, but what he got was a mixture of methanol and benzole. Not the best way to encourage a driver to go faster!

So in many ways Dennis Poore was the ideal man for the job of rescuing the British bike industry. And had he not been kicked around by the politicians, that is what he no doubt would have achieved. As it was, he was only partly successful. The Norton Commando was a big sales success, and the much smaller AJS 2-stroke competition bikes' operation had five good years with the Y4/5 Stormer motocrossers. However, the BSA/Triumph situation was what led NVT, as it was ultimately to be known, into trouble. What a pity then, with the benefit of hindsight, that Dennis Poore and Manganese Bronze did not simply concentrate on the remnants of AMC, rather than also taking on the BSA Group.

14 Two-Stroke Dirt Bikes

Although the AJS 250 road racer was not a commercial success, its dirt bike brother, the Y4 (Stormer) motocrosser certainly was. Both were developed by the same man, Peter Inchley.

The Works Effort

The Y4 story began in late 1967, when a prototype machine was constructed and test ridden in an actual racing event by the former CZ rider, Andy Roberton. Roberton was soon joined by the Gloucester-based rider/dealer Malcolm Davis, the latter making his AJS debut at Canada Heights in November 1967 in the opening round of the BBC Grandstand Trophy. By the end of the televised championship, Davis' points tally was only exceeded by World Motocross Champion, Jeff Smith.

The winter BBC series was to be only the beginning, with Malcolm Davis winning the 1968 British Motocross title. Bearing in mind that there was strong opposition from the likes of Bultaco, CZ, Greeves and Husqvarna, this was a mighty performance. At season's end Davis had 45 points, whilst his nearest challenger was Bultaco importer Derek Rickman, nine points adrift on 36. So in truth AJS had a comfortable points cushion.

Dennis Poore and his management team at AJS's owners NV (Norton Villiers) were highly delighted with the new Y4's performance. And who wouldn't have been for a machine in its first full year of competition?

The result was promotion for Davis and Andy Roberton to the World Championships for the 1969 season. Peter Inchley carried out more work on the design and also on the riders, who were sent to Wales on a special commando training course organized for AJS by the famed SAS (Special Air Service). Unfortunately all this effort was largely to be of no avail as the British team was plagued by a series of problems in the championship series itself. For example in the Spanish Grand Prix, Malcolm Davis set up the fastest lap and was leading by some ten seconds when his engine was affected by the ingress of water, causing his retirement. To cap a miserable day precisely the same thing happened in the second leg.

Other problems encountered that year included a cracked spark plug, chain jumping the sprockets, broken throttle cable and fuel blockage. Malcolm Davis quit the team after a disagreement with management and his replacement, Jimmy Aird, fractured two bones in his right hand at the West German Grand Prix. Adding insult to injury, his team-mate Andy Roberton broke two ribs at Farleigh Castle. With its riders sidelined, the AJS championship hopes took a dive. A great pity, after all the hope and expectation earlier that year.

The Production Y4

If the Y4's 1969 world championship hopes did not materialize, the same could not be said for its over-the-counter production brother, as this was to prove a real success story – and a money spinner for owners NV.

Factory-supplied photograph of the AJS Stormer, available in 250, 368 and finally 410cc engine sizes.

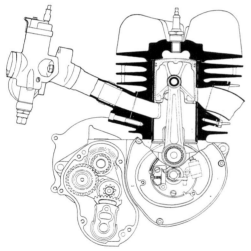

Side-section drawing of the AJS Y4 247cc (68 × 68mm) piston-port 2-stroke engine showing details such as piston, con-rod, porting and gearbox.

The 1969 production AJS Y4 Scrambler, the 247cc engine giving almost 30bhp.

The heart of the Y4 was its single cylinder, 2-stroke engine development from the original Villiers-made Starmaker racing unit. Running on a compression ratio of 12.3:1, it was constructed from aluminium alloy. This included the cylinder head, barrel and crankcase. The cylinder was equipped with a spun-cast iron liner. Each Y4 engine had its piston, connecting rod and crankshaft flywheels individually balanced. As before with the Starmaker, the engine displaced

247cc and featured square bore and stroke dimensions of 68 × 68mm. At the time of its launch the recommended petroil mixture was at a ratio of 20 parts premium grade petrol to 1 part castor-based lubricating oil.

Although power output could have been as high as 32bhp, chief development engineer Peter Inchley was of the opinion that a lower figure of 27bhp (at 6,400rpm) would provide a better balance of performance and reliability. Of course, as already discussed, the customer Y4 development programme benefited from the participation of works models ridden from late 1967 onwards by the likes of Roberton, Davis and others. So unlike some manufacturers, AJS could rightly claim that their model had been 'proved in competition'.

The 1969 Y4 Stormer	
Engine	Air-cooled piston-port 2-stroke single, gravity die-cast light alloy piston with H 622 cast-iron rings; light alloy cylinder head and alloy barrel with cast-iron liner
Bore	68mm
Stroke	68mm
Displacement	247cc
Compression ratio	12.3:1
Lubrication	Petroil mixture, 20:1 ratio
Ignition	Energy transfer, with coil and AC generator
Carburettor	Amal Concentric Mark 1 932 32mm
Primary drive	Duplex chain, foot-change
Final drive	Chain
Gearbox	4-speed
Frame	Duplex full cradle, bronze-welded; Reynolds 531 tubing
Front suspension	Teledraulic oil-damped forks, with 6¼in travel
Rear suspension	Swinging arm in steel tubing with sealed-for-life polyurethane bushes; twin Girling shock absorbers
Front brake	5in, SLS conical alloy hub
Rear brake	5in, SLS conical alloy hub
Tyres	3.00 × 21 front; 3.50 or 4.00 × 18 rear
Wheelbase	55.5in (1,410mm)
Ground clearance	9in (229mm)
Seat height	31in (788mm)
Fuel tank capacity	2gal (9ltr)
Dry weight	218lb (98.9kg)
Maximum power	27bhp @ 6,400rpm
Top speed	78mph (126km/h)

Besides the engine unit, other notable features of the Y4 included ultra-lightweight conical brake hubs (featuring a sealing system to prevent ingress of dirt or water), leading axle teledraulic front forks, a hi-level exhaust system, Girling rear shocks, a folding kickstarter, aluminium mudguards, a comprehensive air cleaner, racing number backgrounds, hi-tensile wheel rims (21in front, 18in rear), an Amal 932 Concentric Mark 1 32mm carburettor, spring-loaded footrests, an all-metal diaphragm-type clutch, 4-speed close ratio gearbox and fibreglass 2gal (9ltr) fuel tank.

The full cradle, duplex frame was, as one journalist called it, 'a masterpiece of lightweight construction', being manufactured from Reynolds S31 tubing and bronze-welded. This helped retain the dry weight of the Y4 to a shade over 200lb (91kg) – a very impressive figure indeed. Not only did the Y4 sell well in Great Britain, but also in several export markets, notably North America and continental Europe. Mike Jackson joined AJS in 1969 as the European Sales Manager, after five and a half years with dirt bike specialists, Greeves. It was Jackson, together with Fluff Brown and Bob Trigg, who were instrumental in getting sales off the ground. After a year of being a nuisance to his NV bosses, Mike was posted to the USA to become General Sales Manager of Norton-Villiers Corporation, and there he continued to ride the Y Series (by now commonly referred to as the Stormer) in Stateside desert races, flying the British Union Jack and thus helping increase sales still further.

Larger Engines

By 1970 the engine unit had lost much of its Villiers Starmaker ancestry and had become widely known as the AJS Stormer; this was now to be joined by the new Y5 assembly, which had a larger bore and 83mm diameter piston to bring displacement up to 368cc.

By the end of 1971 the Stormer had been stretched to 410cc, using the same piston as the '370', but with the stroke increased from 68 to 74mm. This latest version embodied lessons learned over the previous season of race testing by riders who included development consultant Vic Eastwood and the Shell Under-21 British Champion Roger Harvey (now a leading figure with Honda UK).

A total of eighteen modifications had been made to the 410 over the 370 it replaced. The latest 250 benefited in a similar manner. The extensive track testing programme had revealed

The 1970 Y5 Stormer

Engine	Air-cooled piston–port two-stroke single, gravity die-cast light alloy piston with H622 cast-iron rings; light alloy cylinder head and alloy barrel with cast-iron liner	Frame	Duplex full cradle, bronze-welded; Reynolds 531 tubing
		Front suspension	Teledraulic oil-damped forks with 6¼in travel
		Rear suspension	Swinging arm in steel tubing with sealed-for-life polyurethane bushes; twin Girling shock absorbers
Bore	83mm		
Stroke	68mm		
Displacement	368cc	Front brake	5in, SLS conical hub
Compression ratio	10.5:1	Rear brake	5in, SLS conical hub
Lubrication	Petroil mixture, 20:1 ratio	Tyres	2.75 × 21 front; 4.00 × 18 rear
Ignition	Energy transfer, with coil and AC generator	Wheelbase	55.5in (1,410mm)
		Ground clearance	9in (229mm)
Carburettor	Amal Concentric Mark 2 1034 34mm	Seat height	31in (787mm)
		Fuel tank capacity	2gal (9ltr)
Primary drive	Duplex chain	Dry weight	218lb (98.9kg)
Final drive	Chain	Maximum power	28bhp @ 7,000rpm
Gearbox	4-speed, foot-change	Top speed	N/A

Y Series/Stormer Development History

1966 Cotton and Villiers/Metisse scramblers used to develop Starmaker engine into Y4.

1967 Pre-production Y4 raced and tested by Andy Roberton and Chris Horsfield. 247cc (68 × 68mm) single cylinder piston–port two-stroke engine, Amal 932 carburettor; 25bhp. Black duplex frame, Y4 development engine, green fuel tank, chrome exhaust, Ceriani front forks, Motoloy aluminium brake hubs. First experimental 370 engine tested in prototype frame.

1968 First production Y4 250 models built; 27bhp. Orange GRP fuel tank, steel welded frame, chrome wheel rims, Mark 1 Stormer cylinder (Mark 2 Starmaker type), no muffler. British 250 MX Championship; 1st Malcolm Davis.

1969 Production moves from Wolverhampton to Andover. First exports to the USA. Improvements to frame.

1970 Larger finned Mark 2 Stormer cylinders. '370' Y5 introduced 368cc (83 × 68mm): Amal 1034 carburettor, 32bhp. Yellow GRP fuel tank; rear shocks positioned further up swinging arm.

British 250 MX Championship 1st Malcolm Davis, 2nd Andy Roberton.

British 500 MX Championship 5th Andy Roberton.

Swedish 250 MX Championship 3rd Bengt Arne-Bonn.

1971 New 10-fin cylinder. Y series tag dropped in favour of Stormer name. '410' Y51 introduced 400cc (83 × 74mm). Yellow GRP fuel tank. All models have Akront alloy wheel rims, stronger chain guide, improved fork damping, stronger seat base.

New models include: Special Edition 250 called Championship 250 and Special Edition 410 called 410 GP. Both machines feature dyno-tested engines, Reynolds 531 tubing and bronze-welded frames, aluminium fuel tanks, skimmed hubs, Magura levers and hi-tensile handlebars.

1972 The following improvements introduced: forged pistons, folding kickstart levers, Tommaselli control levers. Deeper clutch groove, strengthened con-rod, alloy handlebar clamps, 10-bolt sprocket fixing, bayonet-type filler cap.

1973 370 dropped from range. All frames now made from Reynolds 531 tubing and bronze welded. The 410 given aluminium fuel tank, stronger exhaust, improved forged piston, modified porting, new cylinder head.

The 250 has a yellow GRP tank (alloy optional) and now fitted with 410-type cam-barrel, 410 clutch pressure plate.

1974 Fluff Brown takes over business (September) and moves tooling, production and parts operation to Goodworth Clatford. 'FB' models produced from Goodworth Clatford premises through to early 1980s.

1990s A quantity of 40 motocrosses and 10 road racers built using development of Stormer engine and sold under Cotton brand name.

several defects which were addressed. The
clutch circlip was prone to pop out whilst
under load, so this was given a deeper groove.
A steel inlet manifold replaced the original aluminium item, which was prone to cracking.
The engine was given a forged instead of cast
piston and a heavier forged connecting rod, and
the transmission was given an improved cam
barrel. In addition a silencer was provided for
both the 250 and 410 models as standard equipment; even though AJS offered no guarantees
that it would pass the ACU decibel test.

Vic Eastwood and Graham Evans joined
forces to build a full five-hundred AJS
motocrosser, but this attempt, which used a
410 engine as a basis, vibrated so badly that it
had to be rubber mounted! Using Norton
Commando isolastic mountings and a new
frame, the '500' was eventually tamed, but
although producing 47bhp, the prototype unit
was still a fearsome beast to control. A redesign
was carried out in an attempt to cure both
vibes and power delivery and, with a Norton
gearbox added, the revised engine's power
output dropped to 'only' 39bhp. However, it
was much easier to control, with power now
coming in right from tickover and continuing
on to its nearly 8,000rpm maximum.

To cope with the massive amount of torque
generated by the full five-hundred, the duplex
primary chain of the 410 would have needed
to have been replaced by a triplex type. But in
turn this would have made the chaincases too
wide for comfort. The solution came by the
fitment of an inverted tooth primary chain;

The 1973 410 Stormer

Engine	Air-cooled piston-port two-stroke single, gravity die-cast light alloy piston with H622 cast-iron rings; light alloy cylinder head and alloy barrel with cast-iron liner
Bore	83mm
Stroke	74mm
Displacement	400cc
Compression ratio	10.75:1
Lubrication	Petroil mixture, 20:1 ratio
Ignition	Energy transfer, with coil and AC generator
Carburettor	Amal Concentric Mk 2 1034 34mm
Primary drive	Duplex chain
Final drive	Chain
Gearbox	4-speed, foot-change
Frame	Duplex full cradle, bronze-welded; Reynolds 531 tubing
Front suspension	Teledraulic oil-damped forks, with 6¼in travel
Rear suspension	Swinging arm in steel tubing with sealed-for-life polyurethane bushes; twin Girling shock absorbers
Front brake	5in, SLS conical hub
Rear brake	5in, SLS conical hub
Tyres	2.75 × 21 front; 4.00 × 18 rear
Wheelbase	55.5in (1,410mm)
Ground clearance	9.5in (229mm)
Seat height	30in (762mm)
Fuel tank capacity	2.25gal (10.2ltr)
Dry weight	229lb (104kg)
Maximum power	37bhp @ 6,000rpm
Top speed	80mph (129km/h)

Hi-Tac

Prior to the 1974 closure, Peter Inchley had already
left and set up shop with Frank Higley to manufacture high performance 2-stroke components. This
new company, known as Hi-Tac, specialized in
liquid-cooled conversions for air-cooled Japanese
racing engines. The most popular were for the
Suzuki T500 and Yamaha TD/TR2 series. But then
in 1977 Peter Inchley became involved with the Vil-
liers/AJS Starmaker once again, helping Hejira build

a batch of three racers to contest the new single-
cylinder class. Despite the use of Brian Gittens (formerly one of Mick Walker's Ducati team riders),
Hejira's own monoshock chassis, 6-speed gearboxes
and Inchley's undoubted expertise in 2-stroke technology and tuning, the Hejira team bikes were not
quick enough to catch Vic Camp's Suzukis or the
best of the Ducatis which ruled the roost during that
era.

AJS Stormer-powered grass-track racer from the early 1980s.

gear drive was also considered. However, in the end the bigger engine was never to reach production status, due to problems at Norton Villiers at the same time.

Luckily the Stormer itself, in 250 and 410 guises somehow managed to survive the troubles suffered by the parent Norvil and went on to several British championship titles during the early 1970s. Production was relocated to Andover in Hampshire, close to other parts of what became known as NVT (Norton Villiers

British Manufacturers to have used Villiers engines from 1945	
Aberdale	ABJ
AJS	AJW
Ambassador	BAC
Bond	Bown
Butler	Cheetah
Commander	Corgi
Cotton	Cyc-Auto
Dayton	DMW
Dot	Elstar
Excelsior	Firefly
FLM	Francis-Barnett
Greeves	HJH
James	Mercury
New Hudson	Norman
OEC	Panther
Radco	Rainbow
Raynal	Sapphire
Scorpion	Sprite
Sun	Tandon

The Villiers Company

By far the most famous of all British-made 2-stroke engines is of course the Villiers. The company began operations in Villiers Street (hence the name!) in Wolverhampton during 1913, later moving to a much larger site in Marston Road, where by 1960 Villiers' facilities occupied an area of no less than 17½ acres

One of the company's great strengths was that, unlike many others, it carried out nearly all its own manufacturing, having its own pattern shop, foundry, forging drop hammers, coil winding and a huge number of machine shops to cover every conceivable method of the manufacturing process. Thus raw materials came in one end of the Villiers plant and complete engine assemblies came out the other end. This 'in-house' approach also helped maintain quality control as problems could be traced much easier than if various suppliers had been involved.

The Wolverhampton company's first engine, built in 1913, was a 269cc single cylinder with square bore and stroke dimensions of 70 × 70mm. It was, of course, a 2-stroke, as this was what the Villiers company specialized in during its entire existence. The piston, like the cylinder, was of cast iron, and was of the deflector type. Ignition was by a chain-driven magneto at the front of the crankcase, with lubrication being taken care of by a simple drip-feed into the crankcase from a hand pump with sight feed located in the fuel tank. There followed a vast array of power units of varying capacities, including 98, 150, 172, 197, 246 and even 349cc. Post-war came the F series, the D series, the E series, the '3' series competition engines, the T twins, and of course the Starmaker.

A full list of (post-war) manufacturers is given in a separate box, but suffice to say that much of Britain's motorcycle industry was Villiers powered during the 1940s, 1950s and 1960s. There were also several concerns who carried out their own development of the Villiers original design; these included Alpha, Greeves, Parkinson, Vale-Onslow and Marcelle.

Villiers, like the majority of the British motorcycle industry, began to hit problems from the mid-1960s onwards. In Villiers' case it failed at the end of that decade and was merged with the remains of the AMC and BSA groups to form NVT (Norton Villiers Triumph).

Triumph). However, as a result of the infamous workers' blockage of the Meridan Triumph factory, AJS ran into trouble from which it could not recover. Thus production of the Stormer finished in 1974, with the remaining stock and manufacturing rights being purchased by Fluff Brown, to form FB-AJS of Andover Ltd.

The Trials Bike

Far less remembered today than the Y4 and Y5 Stormer motocrossers is the 37A-T trials model which used a Villiers 37A engine. This was manufactured first in 1965 and stemmed from the 31A introduced in 1958 (other engines in the series were the 32A, 33A, 34A and 36A). All these power units shared the same 66 × 72mm bore and stroke dimensions.

Unlike the motocrosser, the trials AJS used a single down-tube frame, wide ratio gearbox and Metal Profile front forks. The engine produced 12.4bhp at 5,000rpm and ran on a compression ratio of 7.9:1. The frame was built for AJS by Cotton Motorcycles Ltd.

1969 AJS 37A-T trials bike used a Villiers 37A (hence name) engine with cast-iron cylinder and alloy head.

Compared with the motocrosser, far fewer of the 37A-T trials models were built and sold; in fact it was only produced for a single season, 1969, whereas the motocrossers were built from 1969 until 1974.

1969 37A-T Specifications	
Engine	246cc (66 × 72mm) piston-port 2-stroke single. Cast-iron cylinder, alloy head
Carburation	Single Villiers S25 carb, with renewable paper element air filter
Electrics	Flywheel magneto ignition
Lubrication	Petroil mixture; ratio 20:1
Transmission	4-speed, constant mesh wide ratio gearbox. Ratios: 3.6, 2.4, 1.56 and 1.00:1; 29:1 bottom gear (58 tooth sprocket). Primary chain drive with wet multi-plate clutch
Frame	All welded, steel, cold-drawn tubing with tapered top tube
Suspension	Metal Profile telescopic front forks with progressive oil damping. Swinging arm in steel tubing with sealed-for-life nylon bushes; twin Girling shock absorbers with multi-adjustment
Wheels	WM1 front and WM3 rear high tensile chrome steel rims; Dunlop trials tyres, 3.00 × 21 front and 3.50 × 18 rear. Full width 6in light-alloy British Hub Co wheel hubs, with cush drive in rear assembly
Tank	Fibreglass petrol tank, fuel capacity 1.75gal (8ltr). Quick release filler cap
Dimensions	Wheelbase 51½in (1,308mm) Ground clearance 9½in (241mm) Seat height 30in (762mm) Dry weight 212lb (96.1kg)
Maximum power	12.4bhp @ 5,000rpm
Maximum torque	16lb/ft @ 3,200rpm
Maximum speed	62mph (99.8km/h)

Fluff Brown

For the last three decades Fluff Brown has played a vital role in keeping the AJS name alive. It was also Fluff (christened David) who, together with Peter Inchley, had been responsible for the development of the AJS Stormer back in the late 1960s when the AJS brand was marketed by NVT (Norton Villiers Triumph). And it was Fluff who, in September 1974, purchased the remaining AJS business, moving all the spares and tooling for the Stormer series to its present base at Goodworth Clatford (a small village south of Andover, Hampshire).

Born on 24 July 1930 at Chard, Somerset, Fluff Brown first became interested in motorcycles as a teenager. Riding an ancient 4-stroke Ariel, which Fluff described as 'handling like a camel', he still managed to win the South Western Championship. Later Fluff moved on to more modern machinery, including the likes of Gold Star BSAs, Dots, Greeves and Cottons. The latter was the big career move as Fluff served seven years with the Gloucester-based firm, before being, as he describes it, 'poached by

Norton Villiers' where he did another seven years on the AJS 2-stroke family of machines, as a development engineer.

As explained in the main text, the Stormer line was designed by a formidable team with each stage of the design process being tested on the track and then subsequent modifications being retrospectively carried out. Of course, there was no such thing as CAD (Computer Aided Design)! It was a work-intensive task and as Fluff Brown describes it: 'a long process of joy and pain, elation and disappointment. But most of all, a gratifying feeling of doing a job one loved.'

From 1968 until production ceased at the NVT-owned factory in Andover, the Villiers Starmaker-based Y Series/Stormer series of motocrossers built a strong following and had considerable success in national championships – British 250cc MX 1st 1968 and 1970; British 500cc MX 1970 and Swedish 250cc MX 1970. All this meant that when production ceased in 1974, Fluff Brown's decision to purchase all remaining spares and tooling made sound

Line up of Fluff Brown AJS models at the company's Andover headquarters in the late 1970s. Fluff had taken over from Norton-Villiers in the middle of that decade.

One of the Fluff Brown AJS enduro models pictured at the Cheffins auction at the Imperial War Museum, Duxford, Cambridgeshire, June 2004.

financial sense. Also his intimate knowledge of the product and enthusiasm meant that not only did dealers continue to have a ready supply of spares, but the 'FB' firm also continued limited production of the Stormer model until the early 1980s, from its Goodworth Clatford base.

By the 1990s, with son Nick as co-director, some sixty complete machines had been built using either the AJS or Cotton brand names (patents for both having been obtained on the 9 August 1991 and the 28 April 1995 respectively). The frames for these machines – which comprised some forty Stormer-engined motocrossers, ten unit five-hundred Triumph twin-engined motocrossers and ten road racers (the latter based on the Cotton Telstar, but with telescopic front forks and Italian Grimeca front brake) – were crafted by Nick Brown himself.

As Nick admitted recently, 'This was very time consuming and although personally enjoyable [he described it as 'a labour of love'] it is unlikely to be repeated' as his time is now needed in other sectors of the business.

The Fluff Brown operation today, besides Starmaker and Stormer spares, includes acting as UK distributors for Chinese Coyote kiddies bikes, importers of Italian Grimeca hubs, distributors for Monkey-Bike tuning goodies and selling their own range of Speedline products (including handlebars and the like).

However, even though the current Fluff Brown enterprise does not rely exclusively on the AJS name for its living, it does retain the AJS trademark and operates under AJS Motorcycles Ltd, and is thus an integral piece of the famous old company's history.

Index

190